GAMES

FOR MASTERING FEAR

How to Play the Game of Life
with a Calm Confidence

L. Michael Hall, Ph.D.
Bobby G. Bodenhamer, D.Min.

©2001

All Rights Reserved
The materials for this book were derived from the Training Manual, *Mastering All Your Fears*, designed by Bobby G. Bodenhamer and L. Michael Hall. It was reformatted here using the *Frame Games format*, a user-friendly version of Meta-States.

Authors:

L. Michael Hall, Ph.D.
P.O. Box 9231
Grand Jct. CO. 81501
(970) 523-7877
Fax: (970) 523-5790

Bobby G. Bodenhamer, D.Min.
1516 Cecelia Dr.
Gastonia, NC 28054
(704) 864-3585
Fax: (704) 8641545

Michael@neurosemantics.com

Bob@neurosemantics.com

Institute of Neuro-Semantics Web Sites:

www.neurosemantics.com
www.neurosemantics.org
www.learninstitute.com

GAMES FOR MASTERING FEAR

PREFACE

This is a book about developing your *emotional intelligence* about *mastering fears*. To achieve this, we have used the NLP and Neuro-Semantics models. To this extent, this book is about *state of the art techniques* (patterns, processes, "games") for developing an intelligent, courageous, and informed ways for handling fearful objects, events, people, and ideas.

This book is also about learning the art of accessing the best kind of mind-body states so that your fears can be appropriate, useful, and empowering. Then you can use them to enrich your life and eliminate all those that only put you into a spin.

What will you learn in this book?

What new insights will you discover?

What new skills will you develop?

You will learn that *emotions are just that—emotions*. They are not absolute messages from Heaven about what to do. They only tell you the difference between how you have mapped the way things should go and your experience of the way things actually go. You will discover that *you are more than your emotions*. They make up a valuable part of you, but you are more them what you feel. Feelings can misguide you.

You will learn about how to *Quality Control your brain*. After you detect an emotion, check out its accuracy and validity, then you still need to explore it in terms of its "ecology."

- Does it really serve you?
- Does it enhance your life?
- Will it empower you as a person?

If not, then you will discover how to turn down, minimize, reduce, or even eliminate unuseful, unproductive, and dehumanizing emotions. You will discover how to take control of the internal cinematic Feature Movies you play in your mind. And there's a lot more. You'll learn processes for using your own mind and emotions for becoming more resourceful, courageous, focused, and congruent with your own values and visions. You'll discover the sneaky and subtle way that "talk" (how you language things) can make life a living hell or a glorious paradise.

You discover the structure of how to make life full of meaning and how to develop a great relationship to ideas.

How Do We Know this Approach Works

Does this model work? Has it worked in our lives? Does it work in the lives of those with whom we have worked?

The history behind *Games for Mastering Fear* began fifteen years ago when Dr. Bob and I first learned NLP. That's when we first discovered some of the "magical" techniques in this book for vanquishing fear. My own discovery that life-long fears and phobias could be resolved in a few minutes took me into the field of NLP while still disbelieving.

When I was first introduced to the so-called "Phobia Cure," I didn't believe it. Though a cognitive-behavioral psychologist, I really did not see how the process would work in the way described. When I first ever "ran the pattern" with a client, a delightful lady suffering from a phobia, I told her that I had recently come upon a new process and that I didn't know if it would work, but if she was game, I'd like to give it a try. She was game. A few minutes later I asked her to get the phobia back, she could not. In that moment I was more shocked and surprised than she!

That continued for the next half a dozen times that I used the pattern. Each time I was sure that it would not work, not this time. Yet each time it did work. The individuals consistently experienced a transformation before my very eyes and would be unable to get the phobia back. Though I was still unconvinced, I was also totally captivated by the process. I had to know, "How does this work?" "What explains this incredible transformation?"

Those were the questions that originally led me to study NLP, to read everything in the field, and to be certified in NLP as a trainer. Bob had a similar story. He tells about how the field of NLP similarly entranced him and drew him forward to learn about the "magic" within the human mind and nervous system that could produce these kinds of results. His fascination even led him to change careers and to head off on an entirely different path, all the while seeking repeated demonstration that it works and that the transformations last.

Some years later, I discovered yet another model about the way the human mind and body creates its "realities." It happened one day when I was researching *resilient people* who had the magic-like ability to *bounce back* from any trouble or trauma without getting traumatized in the first place. I called that model, *Meta-States*. Bob and I eventually initiated the creation of the field that's now known as *Neuro-Semantics* (see www.neurosemantics.com).

Later, with Bob's constant encouragement, I reformulated *Meta-States* (1995/2000) into *Frame Games* (2000). This refers to how we play the *Games* of life (what we say, feel, and do) with ourselves and others and how we do so according to our understandings of the Rules of the Game (the Frames). This has led to various application trainings and books, *Games Business Experts Play* (2001), *Games Slim People Play* (2001), and now this third one in the series of *frame game* books.

We tested the original materials on *mastering fear* using NLP and NS specifically through Bob's presentation of this material at Gastonia College in North Carolina. He presented this material to adults under the course title, "Mastering All Your Fears." Then I took it and formatted it into the Frame Games structure. That's the story in a nutshell.

Who Should Read This Book?

We have written this book for anyone who struggles with fears, phobias, anxieties, or other negative emotions which keep one feeling worried, apprehensive, intimidated ... afraid of life, afraid of yourself, afraid of your emotions. We have written it so that you get to continue the story as you discover and experience the "magic" yourself. That's our hope. We hope for you that you will refuse the old Games and enter into new Games of Vitality and Courage and Confidence that will make all of your life an exciting adventure.

Do you need to know NLP or Neuro-Semantics to use this book to eliminate fears? No you don't. Even though that would help immensely, it is not necessary.

Now on to the Games... to refusing the Old Games that have undermined your success, happiness, and resourcefulness, and onto the New Games that will make your life more magical and blessed!

In Appreciation

Several people have helped to bring this manuscript into this present form. We thank them here for their insights and improvements. They have made the work clearer: Jim Polizzi, Debi Stevenson, and Cheryl Buffa. We are indebted to their passion for this work and their generosity.

Chapter 1

GAMES
FOR MASTERING FEAR

- Do you run scared in life?
- Does fear, anxiety, apprehension, or dread fill or even dominate your everyday life?
- Do you have a few basic fears that hold you back from some of your most cherished goals?
- Does it seem that you take far too much counsel of your fears?
- Would you like to turn the Game around so that you master the fears rather than your fears mastering you?

Suppose you could *shift the Games you play* so that you operate with a calm, courageous, and resourceful attitude as you deal with things that would otherwise create fear, or even terror. Would you like that? Would that be valuable enough to captivate your interest?

There are people who move through life living in states of fear—apprehensive, full of worry, hyper-alert, timid, etc. They live in dread and terror. In this they are playing *Fear Games.* Perhaps they are playing,

"They're out to get me!"
"But what if I make a fool of myself?"
"Suppose I lose my investment?"
"Something bad could happen if you did that..."

Regardless of the specific *Fear Game,* these are the Games that undermine resourcefulness and that make life hard to bear. Do you live your life in states of fear? Are you tired of living that way?

There are also people who move through the world playing some very different Games. They play *Mastery Games*. When it comes to fears, stresses, challenges, etc., they play Games that enable them to take risks knowledgeably and to stand up for their values and visions. As they play and develop their skills, they play a Game of Life with a calm and confident courage. While they occasionally feel fear, it's not a very common state. That's what this book is about.

Games for Mastering Fears

We wrote this book for anyone who wants to *master* his or her *fears*. If you want to learn how to effectively *master your fears* and to do so in a healthy, balanced, and ecological way, this book is for you. In this work we do *not* offer *fear mastery* by way of banishing the fears and making them go away. Rejecting and denying fears may work temporarily. But it will *not* work in the long run. If you've been struggling with fears for years, you undoubtedly know that all too well. It is the most "intuitive" thing to do... *and* it is the worse thing you can do. In the long run, forbidding, banishing, and tabooing fear (and other negative emotions) creates internal "dragon states" and sets up a Game whereby you turn your psychological energies against yourself.

> [That's what we mean by "Dragons" and that's the theme of the book, *Dragon Slaying,* 2000.]

Here we offer a different approach to *mastering fears*. In fact, when you first hear about it, you may strongly feel that it is so counter-intuitive. Yet it works. And it is the only thing that works. By the time you finish reading this book, you'll understand why and any other approach will seem silly and trivial.

What is this different approach?

It is to welcome your fears into your mind with acceptance, with a calm confidence, and with an appreciation of your neuro-linguistic "powers." When you do that, then you'll learn the *secrets* for truly mastering your mind and your emotional states. Then you will not only master your fears, but every emotion and develop a higher level sense of personal confidence in life.

How does that sound?

So this book is for anyone who wants to develop *personal mastery* in handling risks, dangers, threats, and stresses. That means that this book will not be for everyone. Not everyone is ready for it. For some, the old Games may be stressful and distressful, but at least they are familiar. This book is for those who have had enough of the Old Games and who truly want and are willing to play a different Game. It's for those who have submitted to fear and played the Fear-Dominated Games enough. It is for those who have had enough of running scared, acting timid, being intimidated, playing it safe as a lifestyle, and being tormented by negative emotions.

This book is designed for those who *recognize* that they have given far too much meaning and importance to fear and who have taken too much counsel from their fears. It's for those who already know that the *Fear Games* don't make life much of a party. They know that playing such Games induces them into states of fear, dread, apprehension, worry, fearfulness, timidity, stress, etc.

Have you had enough?

Are you *willing to do whatever it takes* to master your fears?

That's who this book is for. It's not for you if you want to merely audit the book, do some light reading, or dip your toe into these waters.

But, if you have had enough and you're ready to make life-changing transformations so that you can move from fear to courage, from fear to faith, from fear to self-confidence, from fear to optimism, etc., this book is for you. So, get ready. It will change your life. You will come out the other end a transformed person.

The model and patterns in this work will wonderfully transform your life. We have used these principles and processes for many years and with many people. We know this stuff works. We see them working at every training we do whether the training is aimed for business people, sales people, those interested in personal development, becoming fit and slim, becoming financially independent, etc. We see it working on a daily basis in our personal consultations.

That's why we know it will work. Or rather, we know that *it will work for you if you work the patterns*. That's why *merely reading* will not suffice. Merely reading a book or attending training will not activate the life-changing mechanisms within you. To make it work, *you have to work it*. We can show you the path to the mastery of all your fears, we can and will point you to the door, but *you* have to walk through.

And that will take an act of courage on your part.

Are you ready?

Are you willing to become ready?

Are you willing to become willing to become ready?

Are you willing to do the "thought Experiments," to play the Games, and to trust the process?

Are you willing to suspend your doubts until you understand and experience the patterns for taking charge of running your own brain?

Are you willing to give it a chance as you follow something wonderful?

Are you willing to test and question after you've given the Games a chance?

The Structural Analysis Games

As you read this book, you will discover that we have taken *a structural approach* to mastering fears. Rather than the hard approach of "gutting it out," "facing the fear" "toughing it out," or "facing down the emotion," we look at *how* we play the Fear Games to discover how to change them structurally. The first approach makes change an ordeal, painful, and dreadful. None of that here. We know a far better way.

Instead of playing the *Change is an Ordeal Game,* we have used the cutting edge models of cognitive psychology known as Neuro-Linguistic Programming (NLP) and Neuro-Semantics (NS) to give you the *structure* of things. Here you will learn the structure of fear and panic as well as the structure of transformation. You don't have to force yourself through the pain again, you can use some very precise instruments and fine-tune the magic and wonder of your mind-body system.

Change is not about pain (unless you want to play *that* Game, the "Change is Painful" Game). Change happens easily and naturally when you know the Rules (or structure) of the Game, the rules by which you play the Games. When you know that, you will know how to change the very *frameworks of your mind-body system.* When you change the actual fear-creating frames, then you end the old Games of Fear and begin the new Games of Faith, Courage, Passion, Vitality, and Boldness.

"Will it hurt?"

Only to the extent that positively changing your life for vitality, energy, purposefulness, good relationships, greater personal mastery, effectiveness, and the like hurts. How much do you think *that* will hurt?

Actually this approach makes the transformation process easy and gentle. It makes it desirable and fun. In fact, you will probably *not even notice* when the change occurs. Really! You won't notice until you wake up and discover that the old fear isn't there any more, that it has changed, and that you're acting and feeling confident in a bold and courageous way. You will find yourself playing a new Game without even noticing the shift.

NLP and Neuro-Semantics typically work this way. That's why we often use the adjectives *"magic"* and *"magical"* to describe these structural models. It's the same kind of "magic" that happens when you put in a new piece of software into your computer. Suddenly everything is different. The screen looks different, the keys do different things, the whole "computer world" that you're operating in is different. It's like magic.

Or, so it seems. Yet above and beyond that sense of magic, there is *structure*. On the surface, it seems that magicians do impossible things. But that's the illusion. Above and behind the magic is a form and structure that enables the magician to do what seems so magical. Given that structure, the changes, the transformations, and the new world all make perfect sense. The transformation follows naturally from the *frameworks* built into the software. As goes the Frame, so goes the Game.

Human personality works in a similar way. When you know the *programs* (of frames) that a person uses mentally, the Games the person plays make perfect sense. You can't play a new Game until you have new frames, frames that set up the new game, that establish the new rules of the new Game.

As you will soon discover, *the way you "work" right now,* the way your mind-and-emotions and your body work to create the experience (and game) of "fear" throughout your entire body works, and works perfectly. You may not like the results you get, but you run that program regularly, consistently, and dependably, do you not? Don't you run it systematically and even without thinking? That's the Game. There is nothing wrong with you at all! You may be playing some old, toxic, and unenhancing games– Games derived from your frames which you're running really well! We could say that the computer works well, it's the software that needs updating.

The way you have learned to think about dangers, threats, stress, unpleasant things, and fear itself may no longer serve you very well. It may make your life a living hell! But, you've got to admit, it works and it works regularly, methodically, and dependably. If only you could run some different content through your neuro-linguistic processes!

This describes the heart of NLP and Neuro-Semantics—running new Games in our brain and neurology that enhances our lives. These models give you the power to *choose your Game.* What Game do you want to run? What Games do you want to play in your mind-body system? You can opt for "fear" if you want. Or, you can opt for faith, boldness, courage, confidence, calmness, etc. The choice is yours. Isn't it nice to have *that* choice?

With this book you are about to embark on an exciting journey into a whole new set of *Frame Games.* We have prepared a program whereby you can learn to play all kinds of wonderful Games: Confidence, Faith, Calmness, Personal Empowerment, Taking Charge of your own Brain and Running It according to your highest Values and Visions, etc. If you're interested in those kinds of Frame Games, this book is for you.

This work comes directly out of the NLP and NS models. It most directly comes from *Frame Games* (2000), a new expression of the Meta-States model (*Meta-States*, 1995/2000). About the text that follows, we have included numerous inductions for new states (or Games). When you come across three dots ... (ellipses) those dots mean -- Pause ... Think ... Experience. So slow down and use the reading to change your Game.

Also, you will need a notebook as you read.

So, get a blank book that you can use for your own *Frame Game Notebook.* Entitle it, *"Mastering Fear Game Plan."* Then, from time to time we will ask you to stop and write. It's a neuro-muscular technique to activate your programs, to flush out old frames, and to install new ones. Now, as a way to begin the process of flushing out the old Games and anticipating the installing of the new Games, take a few minutes and write in your notebook answering each of the following questions.

- As you consider mastering all fears in your life, *how* will this affect your self-image and self-definition?
- *Who will you become* as you master the old fears by playing games of faith, hope, and vision?
- What will be the three most critical "fears" that you want to completely master?
- How will mastering those fears affect your life? Your professional life and your personal and private life?
- How will that be valuable to you?
- When you think about the "you" for whom the old fears are no longer a problem, what are the most exciting and significant facets of that new you?
- Who will be most affected in your life by this mastering of these fears?
- When you fully step into the place where you have mastered the fears, what frame of mind will you be in?
- What will you, as the Game Master, look like, sound like, and feel like?
- What evidence or proof will you have when you have reached your goal of mastering your fears?

OVERVIEW:
Games For Mastering Fear

As this is a book about *Games*, it's about the Games for mastering fear, the Games that enable us to live with courage, boldness, heart, and power.

We can learn to play the Games that replicate the success of those who are experts at handling fear. To do that we will explore how the experts think about the triggers of fear, how they frame (or perceive) such objects, how they refuse to be seduced and recruited for inappropriate fear Games, and how we can replicate such frames of mind. Then we too can become more productive and efficient in the Games of Life. In this book we will set new frames of mind and refuse the old frames and the old games that undermine personal and professional success.

Here is a description of the Four Parts of the book. While we have written them in a particular order, you do *not* necessarily need to follow that order. The *Fear Mastery Games* really begin in Chapter 9, *Games for Producing New and Better Movies.* If you have a strong and powerful Movie going on that keeps creating intense states of fear, panic, semantic reactiveness (reacting in an unthinking way to ideas and meanings), and/or negativity, consider starting there with the first Game, *The Stepping In and Out Game.* While it is best to have someone who knows this pattern run it with you, you can on your own read it, become acquainted with it, and then use it. Don't let its simplicity put you off.

Part I focuses on *Figuring Out the Fear Frame Games.* We will take a wide-eyed look at fear as a "Game"–what makes it work, how the Games are structured, the payoffs, etc. We will look at the foundation of the Fear Games, the Fight/Flight/Freeze pattern, etc. This provides the basic orientation to this book.

Part II presents the *Frame Games Model.* This will give you a structured way to think about the things we feel, say, do, and experience. It will give you a structured way to think about the Frames in your Brain that set up the Games you play. You could very well read this section first to get the basic orientation of this work. This section combines theoretical and practical facets of the *Frame Games* model and informs you about how to shift to thinking in terms of *frames* and *games*. This sets the stage for everything else: how to detect and identify the Games, how to appreciate the driving power of our mental frames and not get seduced by thinking that they are real. It is a brief summary of the book, *Frame Games*.

Part III describes the *Foundational Resource Games.* There are certain foundational Games that are essential for Fear Mastery. This section presents a few of them: the Relaxation Game, Stress Management Game, Leverage Games, Quality Control Game, Meta-YES-ing and Meta-NO-ing Game, It's Just an Emotion Game, It's Just a Map Game, etc.

Part IV introduces the actual Games for *Fear Mastery.*   From Games for Producing Better Movies, to Games for making Fear Games Redundant, to the use of Language in encoding Fear Games and to the Games for mastering the fears that create semantic reactions (what we will call "meta-fears"), this section gives you lots of New Games to begin playing that will abolish inappropriate fears and will transform useful fears into positive energies. It will introduce you to all the tools you'll need for personal mastery.

A Template for the Games

While we have provided a thorough model for thinking about Games in Chapter 8 and have two worksheets there for more extensive Frame Analysis, we actually use the following template as a simple way to think about the Games in the following chapters. It follows from what we mean when we talk about a set of actions and interactions as a "game."

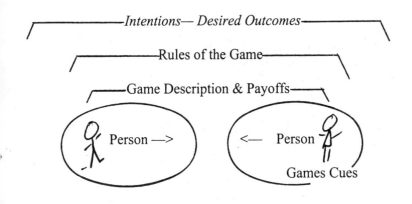

- *The Name* and *the Description* of the Game: What is the Game? How does it work? Does the game enhance or limit you?
- *The Rules* of the Game: How is the Game set up and structured? Who plays the Game, when, etc.?

- *The Cues* of the Game: What are the questions that elicit the Game, the terms that reveal the Game? What triggers recruit us to playing the Game?
- *The Payoff* of the Game: What are the benefits, values, and outcomes of the Game?

Toxic or Empowering?

It doesn't matter what we call a Game. We've invented lots of insightful as well as silly titles in the following pages and we invite you to do the same with the Games you play. What matters is whether *they work for you or against you.* You need to know both. Those who master their fears do. It's not enough to know the positive, wonderful Games that you want to play in life and say "Yes!" to. Frequently, we can't say a thunderous "Yes!" to what we want until we've said an equally impactful "Hell, No!" to the Games that undermine and sabotage our best efforts and that keep recruiting us to the Fear Games.

For this reason we will be contrasting *Bad Game/ Good Game* as we move through the following pages. Your clarity regarding which Games are toxic and which are enriching gives you the personal power to *cut* (de-*cision*) a clear path toward your desired outcomes.   It will also empower you to stand strong and firm when the toxic games put on a seductive show and try to recruit you for them.

Becoming an Expert Game Player

Here's the overall game plan of this book.

First, we learn to *detect* Games. By naming the Games we put the spotlight of awareness on them. This allows us to flush out the sick and morbid games that have terrible payoffs and empowers us to refuse them. Game detection means becoming mindful, aware, conscious. It's the wake up call. It's like the wake up call that Neo received in the movie, *The Matrix*. Until he took the red pill and woke up to the Matrix that he had been sleepwalking in, he didn't even know what Game he had been playing.

Second, we *access the personal power* it takes to play the Games. It takes energy, power, and vitality to become conscious, to look the Games in the face and to decide which ones to give thumbs up and which ones to give thumbs down.

Third, we access the higher frames of our mind to turn on even greater sources of power and insight. This introduces the human dynamic of *frames* into the picture and underscores the cognitive-behavioral nature of our lives. As we think and believe, so we play the Games that we do. Games are governed and directed by frames. This provides us the central leverage point regarding how to transform things quickly. It doesn't take years of analysis. It takes the change of a frame. We use two raw and primordial powers to do that—our powers to confirm and to disconfirm, to say "Yes" and "No." By these powers we exercise executive control regarding which games we'll play and which we will no longer tolerate.

Fourth, we will *temper this power* least it goes to our heads. We will qualify our frames with the kinds of frames that will texture our Games so that we play the Fear Mastery Games with the kind of values, visions, and beliefs that truly keep us balanced, healthy, and sane.

Fifth, we will learn a *structural template* so that we can quickly or extensively analyze Games. Frame analysis will enable us to become more strategic and thoughtful in our approach. It will enable us to not be blind-sided by facets of our Games that we didn't see.

Sixth, we will explore *the Mastery Games that courageous people play*. This is Part IV where we have many recommended Games (patterns) that you can use to begin transforming and mastering fears. These are the games that allow you to take charge of your world, your responses, and your ability to make a difference. Here you'll get to decide which Games to say "No" to and which ones to validate with a "Yes! Let's Play!"

Seventh, in the area of fear, as in most other complex domains of life, there will be Games for different kinds of fears, different situations, different levels of fears. There will be Games for positioning yourself to stand up to fear and to refuse to take counsel of fears that are inappropriate, unuseful, and/or limiting. There will be Games for leveraging yourself against fears so that even when fear is appropriate you can keep your head, think at your best, and do so with an inner calm. There will be Games for handling things with mastery when situations get tough. There will be Games for transforming the very quality of your internal movies so that you stop scaring the hell out of yourself.   There will be Games for making the old Fear Games redundant. There will be Games for mastering Meta-Fears and Games for mastering Semantic Reactions.

Ready to Play?

   If you're ready to have at it, then I'd recommend you read the book in its entirety to get a sense of the overall game plan. Then return a second time with a Game Plan Notebook and the ability to play the Implementation Game. Then you can pick and choose the games for mastering fears that you want to make *yours*.

ALL OF LIFE
IS A GAME
PLAYED
WITHIN FRAMES
WITHIN
FRAMES OF FRAMES

The Frames Establish the Game's

- **SET-UP**
- **RULES**
- **PAYOFFS**
- **POINTS**
- **PLAYERS**
- **AGENDA**

The Game is the way we act, feel, relate, behave and the skills we demonstrate. We cannot not play a Game. It's just a matter of which Game we plan and how resourceful we find it.

PART I:

FIGURING OUT

THE FEAR GAMES

AND THEIR STRUCTURE

**Exposing the Fear Games
That Undermine
Success, Vitality, Health, and Effectiveness
And That Prevent
The Games of Personal
Confidence and Courage**

Chapter 2

INTRODUCING
THE FEAR GAMES

There is Structure in the Games we Play.
A Game is what it is
According to how the Game Plan sets it up.

Imagine mastering all of your fears so that you move through life with a sense of energy, vitality, confidence, purpose, and courage. Wouldn't that be great? What would you need to pull that off? To do that, you will need to learn some new Games, to learn to play a different kind of Game. You will need to learn how to play the Games of calm, confidence, courage, strength, and focus. That's the purpose of this book and the Games you'll find in it. Yet before we get there, we first have to make another stop. First we have to expose *The Fear Games.*

Why in the world would we do that?

We have a reason for this. Actually, we have a great reason for doing this. Because *if* you know those Games, how you play them, and the triggers that recruit you to play those Games of Fear, we can use that mindfulness as an ally in refining some of them and outright refusing the rest of them.

After all, the power of the Fear Games lies in how they sneak up on us and sucker us into playing. They depend upon deception, misinformation, and false hopes. That's why they typically deceive us. They pull us into them in ways outside of our awareness. They promise to make our lives better, to give us peace of mind, to make conflicts and distresses go away, but all of that's a lie. They only make the conflicts and distress worse.

That's why we need to develop *a mindful awareness* about the cues, hooks, and triggers of those Games. When we do, we will find it much more difficult to go there. We won't get sucked in so easily. When we learn how to play some of the games for Refusing Fear Games, then we can utter a strong *"Hell, No!"* to some of the old Horror Games that may have a particular hold on our neuro-pathways and hence, emotions. Also, mastering the Games of Fear creates the space to learn the new Games of vitality, energy, confidence, and success.

In the following chapters we will introduce you to Mastery Games that you can learn to play to expose the Fear Games, blast them to kingdom come, refine them, or transform them. These Games will allow you to become personally empowered, resourceful, courageous, bold, and centered. These are the Games you will use to learn a positive use of negative emotions, including fears, and Games for totally mastering the unnecessary and debilitating fears. They are the Games that will put you fully into the Game of Life in an exciting and powerful way.

But before we get on to those Games, we first need to expose the old Games. The Games of Fear.

- Do you play any Fear Games, any Games that terrify you, hold you back, make you want to pee your pants?
- Have you played any *Game of Fear* today? This week?
- How have you played that Game?
- What were some of the moves of fear that you engaged in?
- What ideas, emotions, circumstances have given energy to those Games?
- What payoffs have you received from playing those Games?

As you note the fears below, gauge their emotional intensity from 0 to 10 (with 0 for none, not at all, and 10 for terrifying you, you could not be more afraid).

__ Public Speaking   __ Dogs   __ Criminals

__ Authority figures	__ Cats	__ Big Cities
__ Asking for a raise	__ Mice	__ Subways
__ Confronting a friend	__ Rats	__ Foreigners
__ Rejection from a lover	__ Spiders	__ Cold Calling
__ Criticism by a colleague	__ Snakes	__ Being Insulted
__ Asking for a favor	__ Close Places	__ Being Mocked
__ Asking for a sale	__ Elevators	__ Fire
__ Speaking to a stranger	__ Being Alone	__ Heights
__ Racially different people	__ Gangs	__ Cars
__ Being laughed at	__ Being different	__ Planes
__ Risking investing money	__ Driving fast	__ Electricity
__ Learning something new	__ Mathematics	__ Computers
__ Entering relationships	__ Dating	__ Looking foolish
__ Doing something you	__ Saying the	__ Dirt
don't know how to do	wrong thing	__ Sickness
__ Getting ill	__ Suffering	__ Other

Let the Frame Games Begin

Fred was in his mid-twenties when he made his first consultation to do something about his panic attacks. He had finally had enough. Having suffered with the experiences of intense and terrifying fears coming upon him and crippling his ability to take effective action, and having pursued every avenue open to him medically, he was finally ready to see if it had anything to do with his mind. He really hated to admit that it did or could. He didn't believe in, and certainly didn't like, anything that seemed like psychobabble. But two years without getting any better was enough. Though his family physician had prescribed various medications to deal with his symptoms, he didn't like feeling drugged, and he was not really any better.

The consultation began typically as I began by exploring *how* Fred even knew to call the fears that he experienced a "panic attack." *"So, tell me, how do you know that you're having a 'panic attack?'*

> Well, that's what the doctor called them. I have these bouts of fear and then I freeze and can't do anything.

Tell me about how you experience this. What's going on in your body?

> In terms of the body sensations that I have? Well, I experience

pain in my chest right here and then I begin to feel weird, kind of euphoric, then dizzy, and disoriented. When that happens, then I feel weak, it's like a weakness comes upon me... That's when I get really afraid. I think that maybe I'm having a heart attack ... and then I just lose it.

So you get afraid of your experience of fear?

Right. ... Well, heart attacks run in our family, and sure... I get scared that I am having an aneurysm and will die. So if I'm driving, I have to pull over and then when I pull myself together, I go home.

So after the physical sensations of fear begin, you use your family's personal history as your reference point and assume that the physiological arousal is a heart attack?

Yeah. Well, I've been afraid of heart attacks for a long time. My closest uncle died of one and he was only in his thirties... and that really scared me a lot... I guess I've been afraid that I was also going to die young since then.

Is that when the experiences of fear and the panic began?

No, it didn't start then ... but I did begin thinking about seriously dying then. It didn't become a conscious fear until two years ago when I had my first bout with panic.

And what was the trigger for that?

I don't know. It just happened one day when I was at work. I was under a lot of pressure to get a project completed...

Were there any fears connected to those pressures, anything really important to you riding on them?

Oh sure. Everything. That was the first time I really had to show that I knew my stuff and that I could produce at the level that my superiors had been counting on me to produce.

And if you had not come through...?

If I had not come through that would have showed that they had made a mistake in hiring me, that I wasn't as good at computer marketing as I had led them to believe, that I had wasted my years in college in this career, that I would not amount to anything, that I would have to start over...

So a lot was riding on demonstrating your skills and competence!

That was your moment to put up or shut up! [Yes] ... *So that sounds like a lot of pressure to me...*

Yeah, I guess it was.

It sounds like it was enough to get you breathing hard and fast and your mind racing here and there and pushing yourself and possibly pushing back all of these fears so that you didn't give them any room in your mind...

Yes, come to think of it... that's precisely how it was. I remember refusing to even think about those fears ... So do you think the pressure just got the better of me and that's what started the panic? That's what I've been thinking since then, that I'm just not cut out to handle the pressures, that something is wrong with me. I hate the office politics, and I hate having to kiss up to get along with some of the people there.

I don't hear anything wrong with you. It seems that your neurology works perfectly well given the linguistics and meanings that you use. The only thing I hear wrong with things is your frames. You are using the Frames that inevitably create your Game of Fear.

I don't understand. What are you talking about?

Well, consider the frames that you have mentioned and how they "set the frame" for the way you think, feel, and act. You have fear frames about dying, having a heart attack, following in the footsteps of your uncle, losing your health, your whole career on the line, not cut out to handle pressure, something wrong with you, etc. With frames like those, who needs enemies! Those frames alone are negative and scary enough to get anyone to panic. I certainly wouldn't want them, they'd upset my body.

But they are all true. They are ...

Oh, so now you're going to immediately jump to defending them, and not even consider questioning them as the source of the panic... Okay. That's sure to give you more of a sense of empowerment.

It's not that...

Will they empower you as a person? Will defending these negative frames enhance your life?

No. Of course not.

Figure 2:1
Frames For Playing the Panic Game

"I am not cut out to handle pressures."
"Something must be wrong with me."
"Everything is on the line– career, future, etc."

Events in World

Do you even want to waste your time defending them? [No, I don't.]
Good, then don't. **That** *they seem "real," "solid," and "unquestionable" is not a function of their truth value but familiarity. That's the tricky thing about the mental furniture in our minds... live in a house long enough and after awhile you just get used to the furniture there. The things that are there ... the old assumptions, beliefs, ideas from your family, culture, and environment ... are just the content of your mental world. I just asked you the Quality Control question. And that's a question that is just as important as the Truth question.*

What was that question again?

Will these ways of thinking and believing empower you as a person? Will defending these negative frames enhance your life?

Oh. Well, no.

Are you sure? Maybe they do enrich your mind and emotions, increase your personal resourcefulness, enable you to operate at your best, and tap into all your potentials? Maybe you need to keep rehearsing old frames and keep programming yourself this way?

No! I definitely do not need to do that.

Really?

Yes, I'm sure about that.

Then, Fred, if you were not thinking that way and using those frames of mind ... how would you be thinking that would give you a greater sense of personal confidence and competence in handling fears, pressures, things that you dislike at the office, your thoughts about your body and health?

I would be thinking that it's just pressure and that I can learn to develop new skills for handling stress and that I can take care of my health and body and not make the mistakes that my uncle made with his drinking and smoking, and ...

Stop right now... Notice what you're feeling as you're saying these things?   ... How much fear is totally dominating your mind and emotions right this minute?

Well, none. Right this minute I'm feeling determined... and kind of focused...

But not afraid?

No, not afraid.

Try really hard to get the panic back.... go ahead and try... see if you can.

[Pause...] Well, no, not right now.

That's because your emotional state at any given moment is a function of your thoughts... As you think–so you are. The focus of your mind... of your intentions ... of the direction of your life, these are the things that give you the power to take charge of your emotions. If you were able to get some of the fear and panic back– do you know how you would do so?

By getting into that mind-set again!

Exactly. The frame of mind that you have spent many years learning, habituating, developing, and confirming– that's the problem. So when you change that frame... you can play a new Game.

Yes, I see that. That makes sense to me. I guess frames can be unconscious and can operate when we don't even know that they are operating?

You've got it. In fact, that's exactly what gives them so much power and control over us... They operate like the mental atmosphere in which we live and breath and have our being ... and yet we never notice... They can operate as a trance ... a Fear Trance State loaded with lots of post-hypnotic suggestions.

So I've been playing a Panic Game? Does that mean the panic is not real?

Oh no... inside your neurology it is very real. There it is a real expression of the way you have mapped things. As you map that your family is especially liable to heart attacks, as you map that everything in your life, career, college education, etc. totally depends upon a particular project – so you feel. Think threatening thoughts of danger and Presto! You get a full-blown Panic Attack. Inside it's very real.

So does that mean that my mapping and experiencing, while real at that level, may not be real externally?

Right. As a map is not the territory, and as a map can misrepresent the territory, so our internal mappings can mis-map and inaccurately portray the world.

But the feelings are so real! How can they be so real?

*You create them from your mapping. If you label something as dangerous and threatening and believe in that danger... whether it is a danger or not, it will **feel** dangerous to you and your nervous system is marvelously designed with a program for what to do, how to feel, and how to respond when your organism is threatened.*

Fight or Flee!

Exactly. You go into Caveman Mode and you're in a state where you think about only two things– fight and flight. And all your adrenal, hormones, emotions, etc. are activated to make that happen.

Is that what a Panic Attack is? ... Yes, of course, my body is acting out a total sense of threat and danger...

Great stuff if you need to run from a bear, dash into a burning house to save a baby ... great energy ... empowering sense of focus ... but not so great when you're making a speech, taking a test, meeting someone new or doing most of the things we do in this modern age.

In this brief conversation, Fred very quickly picked up on the idea of frames and games. It took him no time at all to pinpoint the central frames of mind that got him into the position where he began fearing his body, work situations, etc. As he saw that such frames had become his way of seeing things, he recognized that such frames set forth his Panic Attack Game.

As you run your brain in this way, Fred, you have to play the Fear of Death Game. You really don't have any choice at that point. Those Frames– that Game. Of course, if you choose to refuse those frames and opted for a new set of mental frames, you would be playing a different Game. It's as simple as that, it's as complex as that. So the most important question I can ask you right now is this, What is the most powerful thought you can imagine that would eliminate or banish the kinds of fears that you've been suffering with?

At first he didn't know. So I offered him a menu list of numerous ideas, *great ideas*, that he could play with until he found one that really excited him. The menu list that I offered came from the fields of Neuro-Linguistics (NLP) and Neuro-Semantics (NS).

- There is no failure, only feedback.
- People are more than their behaviors.
- When we distinguish person from behavior, we can find Positive Intentions behind all behaviors.
- You have all the resources you need within. You only need to marshal those resources into an effective strategy.
- Because every experience has a structure, we can find and exploit it to interrupt, refine, enhance, and/or replicate.
- The map is not the territory, but only a symbolic representation of it; our interpretation of our experiences.
- Every map is fallible and liable to error with things being left out, over-generalized, and altered.
- "Emotions" reflect the difference (the relationship) between Map and Territory, between our map of the world and our experience of the world.
- Frames are primary ... they establish the form and structure of our internal mapping.
- The Games we play (everyday actions, behaviors, emotions) are functions of our Frames.

- The Name of the Game is to Name the Game.

Fred liked the idea of distinguishing himself from his behavior.

I am more than my behavior! Just because I experience fear at times and have panicked does not define who I am ...but just an experience I have had. I am more than my fear... more than my emotions. Emotions are just emotions.

Do you like that? Does that feel better?

Yes, definitely.

Great, so let's use it. Bring this great thought, this empowering belief to all of the frames you earlier described and which you recognized does not enhance your life... And let this belief set the frame for all of those ...and just notice how it transforms the lower frames.

Figure 2:2
New Frame For
Outframing the Panic Game

I am more than my Behaviors & Experiences
Emotions are Just Emotions...

"I am not cut out to handle pressures."
"Something must be wrong with me."
"Everything is on the line– career, future, etc."

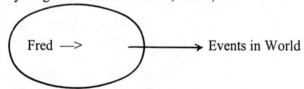

So what happens when you bring this new empowering belief to all of those old frames? ... How do you feel now?

Actually, very calm and I feel hopeful that I can do something about this problem. And I feel confident that I will not be defeated by the fear.

Congratulations! Sounds like you are on your way.

And so he was. Fred went on to set many other empowering frames in his mind and to integrate them into his body so that he really knew that the old fears were "just thoughts, just ideas, just maps and just frames." As he experimented in challenging the old frames and replacing them with more appropriate ways to map things, he discovered that his thoughts only have as much "reality" as he endowed them with.

Fred also discovered the extent to which we can actually *choose* our thoughts and therefore our emotional states. In fact, a year after the original consultation, that's what impressed him the most.

> At first it seemed utterly audacious to think that we can just think whatever we want to think. Almost as if it was cheating or doing something wrong. But as I began a search to find "great ideas" that would enhance my life and empower me as a person, I discovered that it actually worked! I could give my mind to a way of thinking and eventually find it as "the frame of mind I wake up with."

The Structural Secret

- Would you like to know a central secret to fear mastery?
- Would you like to be let in on the inner workings of the Fear Games?

Good.

At the heart of all Fear Mastery Games is the realization that *fear has a structure.* There is rhyme and reason to how we experience "fear," how we create it in our bodies, and how we play the Fear Games. It doesn't just happen out of the blue. It doesn't just appear out of nowhere. It operates according to a dynamic structure.

That there is a *structure* inside of every subjective experience and skill comes from the cognitive Neuro-Linguistics (NLP) model. Experiences like joy, vitality, charm, motivation, depression, stress, and fear do not just happen willy-nilly. Nor is the rhyme and reason of these experiences unaccessible. They have structure and that structure can be identified. And because it can, we can replicate the experience or alter it.

Knowing this about human processes (which we're calling "Games") enables us to play the Modeling Game– a Game for replicating the structures (plans and set-ups) of Games. In this Game, we walk right up to the experience and look it right in the eye, elicit its structure, specify the strategies that make it work, and name the frames that support it. When we do that, we can then use that structural knowledge for new choices. We can choose to keep doing it, change the way we're doing it, refine it, etc. This describes the heart of the fields of NLP and Neuro-Semantics which we call *modeling*.

The great thing about being able to detect the structure of fear is that *structural knowledge puts the control mechanisms into our hands*. And that's what we want, isn't it? We want the ability to run our own brain, turn our fears, angers, joys, calmness, resilience, proactivity, etc. on and off as it will serve us best. When we can do that, talk about mastery! Then, we'll have it. To that end, we will here talk about the structure of fear in terms of "Frame Games"—about the Games that we play as driven by our fearful Frames.

We will also be playing the *Modeling Game* in this work with fear itself. We will model the structure and form of debilitating and self-sabotaging kinds of fear, those that all too often govern our lives. We will also model the structure and form of the state of fear mastery, which we will do via the game metaphor. This will enable us to engage in *Game Analysis*, or more accurately, *Frame Game Analysis* on the Games of our lives.

Doing this will enable you to recognize the rules of the Game, how you play and structure the game, who you play the Game with, when, where, how you score in the Game, how you lose points, payoffs, etc. With that level of mindfulness about the Games you play, you will then be more able and skilled to shift gears and to opt for more empowering Games. Games by which you can master fear, step up into courage, and live life more masterfully.

A Structural Description of The Fear Game

In the Modeling Game, we learn to see the governing *structure* within an experience. In the case of fear (as with any mental-emotional state), it involves a *dynamic* structure. Our focus will be on *how* to stop playing the debilitating Fear Games and *how* to play the Fear Mastery games. As sub-sets of games, we will focus on learning *how* to play the Games of courage, confidence, calmness, self-esteem, mastery, and resourcefulness. To do that we will need to know the dynamic structure in such Games.

We will start with the Fear Games. We will describe how the Fear Games work, the behaviors they generate, and discover precisely how our brains create this experience that we call "fear."

- How does this Game work?
- What facilitates it?
- What makes it get blown out of proportion and run out of control?
- What reduces the intensity of the Game?
- What makes the Game use fear to create mastery in life?

In understanding how our brains create these Games and work its magic, we develop the mindfulness that allows us to re-train our brains. That will then allow us to de-construct our limiting fears and elicit emotional resources that are far more useful and productive, to say nothing of fun and delightful. We use these kinds of questions to explore the Games that we play in life and the Games that we don't want. As you use them, you might notice that merely asking such questions *sets new frames*.

Ready to play? Then let's play an experimental Game with your brain. This will allow us to explore and develop its neuro-linguistic and neuro-semantic mechanisms so that we can play the Games really well. The following is a basic *Brain Game*. Use it to exercise your brain and get more intimately acquainted with it.

Use the following Brain Game to discover "how" you *do* fear, how you create fear and fill your whole body with horror and panic. You do have that skill, don't you? Good. I was worried there for a moment. Because, strange though it might sound, you need that ability as well as the ability to stop doing it. Welcome then to the wild and wonderful world of NLP and NS, the domain that deals with how to learn to truly *run your own brain*.

[If this delights, excites, and creates wonder for you, then see *The User's Manual for the Brain* (1999), *Using Your Brain for a Change* (1985), and *The Sourcebook of Magic* (1998) as basic introduction books to NLP.]

The First Brain Game

Have you ever experienced the sensation of *pleasure*? You have? When did that happen? Where were you? With whom? Or were you alone? On a scale of 1 to 10, how pleasurable was that experience?

Allow your mind to go back and fully recall that *pleasant* experience. And as you do, you might notice that various things will pop into your mind: perhaps one pleasure and then another, or you may get talking to yourself about such and such. Just let all of that happen. Let whatever pops into your mind pop up... and just notice it and just go along with it until you find a time and a place in your thoughts that was really pleasant.

As you do this, think small and simple. A day on a beach bathing in the sun. Playing with a puppy dog in the backyard. Enjoying a sunset. Watching a movie. Hearing a baby laugh.

If you find it difficult to find a good instance in your memories, then just allow yourself to creatively imagine what such a pleasant experience might be like. Also, if you need to close your eyes, do so. It usually helps in this process.

As you get the pleasant experience in mind ... just be with it for awhile... seeing what you saw, hearing what you heard, feeling what you felt. Welcome it and re-experience it fully. Mmmmmmm. Do you like that? Yessss!

Now in a moment I would like you to do something very special in your mind, I'd like you to step out of this pleasant experience just enough to start noticing some of its structural features. Then you can step right back in and enjoy it with a new appreciation. Okay?

First, notice the visual features and aspects of this experience. What do you see? What images, colors, and sights come to mind? Typically we do not see on the inside as well as we do on the outside, and sometimes our visual images dart to and fro so quickly that it may not even seem like we're visualizing. If you're experiencing that, it's okay. Because minds move very quickly: seeing beaches, white sand, green grass, babies cooing, hot tubs, and other things. Just enjoy the pleasant experience and what it *feels* like. And allow yourself to *listen* to whatever pleasant sounds, or words and/or music, and enjoy that kind of internal pleasant experience.

As you notice the size of your picture of this experience, imagine that the images become much larger, double in size... and when that picture doubles, double it again ... And notice what happens to your experience, to your feelings.

Now let the picture shrink and become smaller and smaller and yet smaller. Let it become so small that you can hardly see it ... perhaps like a mere dot. And as you stay with that awareness for a moment ... again notice what happens to your feelings. Interesting, right? Let the picture suddenly explode into full view again and grow bigger like Alice in Wonderland... then smaller again. Now, let your picture of that pleasant experience go back to the way that you first found it, or in a way that you find most pleasing. You can also imagine moving the picture closer to you, and closer yet, and noticing what it does to your feelings again. ... Move the picture farther away. Now imagine that you take the color of your pictures and make them brighter ... then let them fade out to become a black-and-white picture ... then become fuzzy, then become crystal clear ... Now watch your images and see them as in three-dimensional form and then becoming flat in a two-dimensional way. Now play around with the sound track of this pleasant experience... imagining that you have a dial that allows you to play with all of the sound qualities.

Debriefing The Brain Game

It may be surprising to realize that the Brain Game that you have just played will build into you all of the skills you'll need to completely change your feelings as you change your internal representations. *"Running Your Own Brain" Game* lies at the heart of NLP.

Inasmuch as NLP and Neuro-Semantics works primarily with mental *processes* rather than with *content*, this brain game invites you to change how you feel about an experience by changing the quality and structure of your internal movies. We leave the content the same and simply change the frame— the form and coding of the internal movie. When we make changes at the *process* level about objects that typically trigger fear, we are able to see, hear, feel, and talk about things while remaining calm and resourceful.

Consider the de-structuring of fear:

- What would happen to the guy who made all of his *fearful pictures* big, bright and up close? Wouldn't that turn him into an expert at experiencing fear, anxiety, misery, unresourcefulness and maybe even phobic?

- What would happen to the gal who made all her calm *experiences* small, dim, and far away? Wouldn't she also become an expert at reducing the power of her mastery skills?

On the other hand—

- What would happen to the guy who coded all of his resourceful experiences of calmness, mindfulness, resilience, being centered, confidence etc. as big, bright, and up close? Will it not create a more positive outlook on life?

- What would happen if the gal made all of her fearful *experiences* small, dim and far away? Wouldn't that reduce the influence of those negative images?

More personally, *how* have you coded your internal movie about those objects you dislike, feel threatened by, that confuse or overwhelm you? Do you have them coded as up close and personal or as far away and at a distance? How big and bright are they? If they are up close and big, and maybe bright, notice what happens inside when you push them away and off into the distance so that they become small and dim in your mind? As you try it, feel free to experiment with any of these audio-visual components as you would a television set or a cam-corder.

As you play the Brain Game, make your brain sing with music and hum with precision as you turn things up and down, move them in and out, and become the editor of your own mind. The governing principle for this Game is the neuro-linguistic principle reflected in the old proverb, "For as man thinks in his heart, so he is . . ."

Playing the Brain Game lets you learn how to use the natural processes that govern how we *process information* in our minds. Doing this puts us in charge of the mental codings that control the messages to the body which create our emotions.

The Brain TV Game

Managing the movies of our mind is actually pretty simple. Since we use internal representations to create our internal movies, all we have to do is to take control of the TV knobs. In that way, you can turn up and down, on and off, the image and sound knobs.

Classic NLP calls the knobs that control the qualities of our movies, "sub-modalities." They thought that the modes of awareness (the see-hear-feel movie) had "sub" elements like close or far, dim or bright, etc. It was a labeling mistake. These qualities are not really *"sub"* to the movie at all, actually they are the *frames* of the movie. That is, whether a picture is close or far, clear or fuzzy, two or three dimensional, etc. describes *how we frame or structure* the movie. These distinctions operate at the level of structure, not content.

Because this shows up linguistically, we can tune our ears to hear these structuring elements. Just listen to the way people talk.

"I feel pretty dull today."
"I hear you loud and clear."
"Something smells fishy about his proposal."
"I have a bright future."

These seemingly flowery metaphorical expressions enable us to recognize the knobs a person uses to create the internal movies. The terms allow us to recognize the speaker's mental map-making. We can actually hear the internal framing. These metaphors describe how the speaker frames his or her internal movie.

Brain Games

NLP and Neuro-Semantics recognizes that there is no difference in the processes our brains use to code and format memories, imaginations, and current data. Because we *represent and frame* our understandings via our neuro-pathways and networks, we use the very same hardware and processes as we create our internal maps of images that we use when we recall, images that we project into the future, and images from this present moment.

To recognize that the brain uses the same neuro-pathways to encode both something coming in as data from a current experience and in remembering, read and experience this.

> Imagine going to your refrigerator and opening the door. Feel the vegetable bin that you pull on and the lemon that you take out. Close the vegetable door and the refrigerator door and go over to the cabinet. As you now get a cutting board and your knife, take the knife. As you cut the lemon in half, feel the juice squirt on your hand. Lick it. Now cut one of the halves into halves again. With the lemon cut into two quarters and a half, take one of the quarter slices and as you squeeze it into your mouth, feel and taste the lemon juice as it oozes out of the corners of your mouth.

If you played the Game well, your mouth should be watering. Entering into a description with our mind fully engaged enables us to neurologically experience the slice of a lemon in our hand and mouth. While our brain can tell the difference between remembered images, current images, and imagined images, because it uses the same neurology, neuro-pathways, etc. to process such information, it can elicit similar responses.

> If you didn't *get into that description* and experience the neurological effect of a watering mouth, then perhaps you can hear a teacher scraping her fingernails on a blackboard and screeching them.

The Fear Mapping Game

How can *just a thought* set the whole body in motion with fear? How is it possible that *imagined* thoughts can fill our bodies with fear and that our muscles, glands and other body parts can experience the state of fear?

We will explore that when we consider the neurology of the Fight/Flight stress response Game. That will set the stage for understanding the foundational primary state that transforms fear in the mind to fear somatized in the body. It will identify the Game of neurologically mapping fear into embodied experience. There we will look at how the brain and nervous system are structured to do this. But we won't stop there. We also map fear into the higher regions of the mind as we map frames about dangers, threats, and stress.

Alfred Korzybski best explained how these Mapping Games work. In his classic work, *Science and Sanity* (1933/ 1994) he described the *neuro-linguistic* connection between mind and body. He described the connection and relationship between *language* (linguistics) and *neurology.* From an engineering point of view, he offered this foundational statement about the engineering of the mind-body-organism-in-the-world. *"The map is not the territory."*

This statement explains how we create Fear Games in the first place. At various levels, we map them into existence. They are the results of our framing and structuring of events. *We experience fear because we have created maps* that signal danger, threat, or overload. In the next chapter, we'll describe the very real human possibility of becoming fearless. But we will *not* recommend it. We need fear. But we only need a dab—a dab will do us. We don't need buckets full of it. We only need to map enough fear to add caution and thoughtfulness as we navigate through life.

When we look at a road map, we do *not* see actual roads, trees, or rivers. Instead we look at pictorial symbols that "stand for" such things in the territory. When we have a symbolic map that gives us an accurate model of the territory, we are generally able to get around better. A map doesn't even have to be accurate to achieve that, it can use highly distorted caricatures. It's the relationships and patterns of the map that make it useful. When we go to a restaurant and receive a menu, we order from the menu. We don't eat the menu. The menu is a "symbol" of the meal. "The menu is not the meal."

Neurologically, we do not deal with external "reality" directly. We only deal with it indirectly as it is mediated via our nervous system. Recognizing this allows us to play *the Map/ Territory Game* and to improve our ability to get around and to do things. Yet we have to be careful with our mapping. The maps we build and use in our minds ... eventually get into our muscles. After awhile they become our felt reality. As a semantic class of life (a species who live on and by "meanings"), we can map non-existing experiences, realities, beliefs, ideas, etc. *and install them in our body.* When we do, we experience *semantic reactions.* This means that our reactions are not created or caused by the stimulus, but by our meanings ("semantics") about the trigger. Our views, interpretations, opinions, etc. set us up to react semantically.

Just as *a "map"* does not consist of *the "territory"* it represents, the words we use do not comprise the event they represent. *Territory*, as the external reality, is what exists "out there" beyond our skins. *Map* describes our mind-body understandings. These are two levels of phenomena.

What goes on *inside* our head concerning an event does not comprise the event; it only comprises our *perception of* that event. Understanding this enables us to transcend our maps so that we can change and refine them as needed.

We map because in our experiences of external events, we need to *make sense* of them. We map what they are, what they do, how they work, why we can or should relate to them, etc. This mapping or framing sets up the Games that we play. Every Game you play, every Game I play, springs from some mapping. When we step aside from the mapping and play *the Mapping* or *the Framing Game*—we're truly on the way to mastery.

The neurological fact is that what we have *inside* is only and always just a *representation.* I see an apple. I make an internal picture of it. The rods and cones of my eyes give me the internal sense of "color." My other senses enrich this picture. But regardless of how rich, varied, or complete, my picture of it is only a "map" of it. This holds for snakes, high places, audiences, and every other thought or idea that scares you. It's just a map.

We know that when two people see an accident from a similar position (never the "same") they will report it in different ways. Why is that? Primarily there are differences in their perceptions, in their histories, in their frames, in their neuro-linguistic processing of information. Each represents the accident using his or her own senses and neurology. Such maps are not the territory they report on. Here's another secret about our Frame Games. *We construct all of our Games.* They are self-made. Even the ones we inherit and absorb from our family and culture, we have to internalize and make our own.

If we have a mentally healthy mind, we create symbols out of words and images which approximate the territory we seek to represent and deal with.   This differs from a mentally unhealthy mind.   A mind becomes unhealthy, and less likely to master things in the world, when it maps things in ways that severly distort, generalize, or delete things. The Games that a person then plays are Games that win very little that is useful.

If 20 years ago, you had a frightful experience in a lake and nearly drowned, the question for you today is this,

- How have you mapped that experience?
- How have you framed it in your mind?
- What have you done with that experience in terms of representing it, thinking about it?
- What conclusions have you drawn?
- What decisions?
- What identifications have you made? Etc.

How you have taken that experience and framed it will explain the Games you play today. If you frame it as, "Water is dangerous! You can drown and die! Stay away from water by all means. I'm just not the kind of person to survive a drowning twice." Then there's a strong likelihood that you have commissioned your fears to play various Fear Games.

If so, then you don't even have to be in water or near water to react phobically. You can do so even with *the thought* of being near water. What a skill! What a Game!

Now the new thought that will develop your own mastery is this: *"Your map of that old experience is not today's reality."* Your internal representations are only, at best, a map. And in this case, a map about a past experience. It has very little, and perhaps nothing, to do with today's experience. You are not in water. Yet to the extent that you use it as your *frame of reference*, you will play that Fear Game. That's why the "It's Only a Map" Game will begin to initiate a whole new way of operating.

Or consider John, the executive, who panics when he must stand up before a management team to give a presentation. That's his Game, the "I Have to Panic Before Other Professionals When Giving a Speech" Game. He learned it long ago and continues to refresh his frames in order to keep the Game alive. Thirty years ago when John attended public high school, he was once required to present a book review in front of an entire class. When the day came, John felt absolutely terrified about standing up before the class. He thought about being laughed at, teased, and mocked. He feared that he would make a mistake. Then, with all of that in mind, when he stood up, he froze. And sure enough, his classmates laughed.

That did it. From that day to this, even *the thought* of getting up before a group would send him into a panic. This became his Game. Even though John went on to graduate from University and move up to an executive level in his company, he still plays the "It's Terrible to be Embarrassed" Game in his head... and so in his body. Mentally, though an executive, he operates from the map he created as a petrified high school student. By constantly playing the old Game, it worked to reinforce the self-fulfilling prophecies of the old Game. In a way, his ongoing practice of that Game made him more and more effective at playing it!

He has a map for how to be afraid when even thinking about making a speech and that's the map he defers to whenever that situation arises. So while "The map is not the territory," the map does operate as our model for how to think, feel, and act. It establishes the Games.

Summary

- There is rhyme and reason to the experiences (the Games) that we play all day. Our Fear Games make sense, they operate according to *the internal structuring or framing* that we have set up. Find that frame, refine it, and the Games change.

- When we learn the basic Brain Games, we're empowered to not only run our own brain, but to take control over the Games we play. That's the foundation of Mastery. If we don't, then the Games play us and we become their victims. The choice is yours.

- What have you learned? Get your *Mastering Fears Game Plan* workbook out and review chapter two, mining it for all of the discoveries you've made so far. From those discoveries, write out the positive changes that you are going to make as your new Game Plan for playing at the Game of life.

DOES THE MATRIX HAVE YOU OR DO YOU HAVE THE MATRIX?

- To the extent that you know your Frames and choose your Games, you are the Master of your Matrix.

- To the degree that the Games just seem to play you and you can't stop them, the Matrix has you.

- If the Matrix of your Frames *has* you, then *Wake Up, Neo!*

- Where there's a Game, there are Governing Frames that describe, define, format, and control the Game. Count on it.

- Now, let the adventure begin!

Chapter 3

THE GAMES OF FEAR

Games For Scaring the Hell out of You

Frameworks for the Games of Fear

A s we move beyond the dimension of time and space and into the dimension of mind and thought, of emotion and layers of emotion, of memories and imaginations, into meaning and purpose—we move into the realm where we play *Mind Games*. This allows us to take charge of the frames we set which structures the Games, establishes the rules of the Games, how to play, when to begin, when to end, etc.

Now that you know the secret, that a dynamic structure governs our Frame Games, and that our Fear Games have a structure, we can expose that framework. We can now detect the structure, identify its form, and replicate the structure if we so choose. If we know the formula, then we can *not* only take fears away, eliminate phobias, and transform the emotional energy into something more useful, but we can *give* phobias. And as you will soon discover, there are some people who need some phobias.

How do people scare themselves?

How do we put ourselves in states of terror, dread, worry, etc. that robs us of so many of the pleasures of living?

How do we create attitudes of fearfulness and timidity that then sabotage our best efforts at work and in relationships?

Just how do we scare the hell out of ourselves and then play it safe to our detriment?

The Home Movie Horror Show

Actually how we scare the hell out of ourselves is very simple. All we have to do is play some old movies of fearful things in our heads, and then step into those movies. Typically this is sufficient to go into the freak-out state. We experience some trigger of thought, memory, or emotion, and suddenly the reel of an old fearful event starts playing in our mind. If we're conscious of it, it's like daytime dreaming... seeing what we saw all over again, hearing the sounds that bothered us again, and feeling as if we're inside the movie going through it again. Have you ever done that one?

Admit it. We all have.

Yet most of the time we do not do this consciously. The trigger goes off outside our awareness, and so does the movie. The only thing we're aware of is the physiological discomfort, distress, tension, and "bad" feelings. We say, "I have an intuition about this." That inner-knowing (in-tuiting) comes from the movie that plays outside of awareness. Suddenly, we're not feeling good. Maybe we even feel nauseous. If it continues, we may get brief glimpses of the movie, but we only sense "thoughts" that we don't like, so we push them away even further.

Yet as the movie occurs, it plays us. It puts us into a more and more fearful, dreadful, worrisome state. We begin to feel anxious. Yet there's no object in sight that explains these feelings. We only sense that "free floating fear" of anxiety that "squeezes" and "chokes" us (for so is the original meaning of "anxiety"). This gives us the sense that something is wrong with the world or with us, but we don't know what. We frequently might call this by a whole list of words: existential angst, anxiety, over-sensitivity, lack of self-confidence, unspecified phobia, etc.

But what's really going on is some suppressed or repressed old memory of some fearful event, happening, or object. And what makes it worse is that we are not aware of it. In fact, we keep sabotaging awareness. As we keep "trying to make it go away," we make it worse, give it more energy, and condemn it to the nether regions of our mind-body system.

That's why *just talking about it* very often is enough to resolve it. Paradoxical, huh? When we "try to make it go away" by rejecting it, fearing it, hating it, etc., it grows in power. When we welcome it in, look it in the face, it goes away. Yet that's what happens when we talk with a good friend or a counselor who will *just listen* and try to understand our feelings, situation, and thoughts. The mere fact of talking it out brings it out of the darkness and into the light. Typically, what seemed so fearful, so dreadful, so hateful, so repugnant that we "couldn't even think about it," when we are enabled to talk about it, it suddenly doesn't seem all that big of a deal.

What's happened? Why is this process so counter-intuitive?

What made it worse was *the way we thought about the fear.* It is not the fear itself that did the damage, it is our dislike, hatred, rejection, and judgment of the fear. The fear is one thing. Negative rejecting emotions *about* our experience of fear is another. The first occurs as a primary level experience. Suppose we are fearful of being laughed at. A common fear. Who likes that? Jim Carrey maybe. But most of us do not like being laughed at. We hate it. Ah, now we have jumped up a level in our mind, and we're framing the experience of being laughed at as "disagreeable" "and unacceptable."

These interpretative meanings (as our semantics) creates a new set of dynamics. Ever seen someone embarrassed and they just took it in stride and maybe even enjoyed it? Hard to rattle them, right? We laugh at them, "Hey, that embarrassed you, right!?" And they say, "Yeah."

But watch someone feeling embarrassed who *hates* that experience. You can really rattle that person! You can get to them. You can push their buttons. They're easy. Their rejection, hatred, fear of, and dislike of the state ... amplifies the state, making them all the more reactive.

The higher state of their mind *about* ("meta") the experience sets the frame so that they play a new Game, the *"I Hate Being Embarrassed" Game.* The rule is, "Don't embarrass me." The setup is, "I can't stand being embarrassed." "If you embarrass me, I have to feel even worse, even more embarrassed, hyper-embarrassed."

The other person plays a very different Game. *The "Being Embarrassed is Just Part of Being Human" Game.* The rule is, "Embarrassment is no big deal." The setup is, "Embarrassment comes and goes to us all. So what?"

If that strikes you as counter-intuitive, then welcome to one of the key secrets of the meta-levels of the mind. That's where what we call "paradox" occurs. [Meta-levels of the mind, as you shall shortly discover, are our higher states, our meta-states.] This also establishes one of the key Games for mastering fears (or any other negative emotion).   If we "paradoxically prescribe" or welcome the very behavior that we have hitherto feared, rejected, judged, disliked, etc., it *reduces* the primary experience. Yes, I know it's the last thing you want to do. But trust me on this one. Welcome the embarrassment.

Give it a try.

Think about some fear that gets you and this time, instead of disliking it, welcome it in fully knowing that the feeling of fear is just that, a feeling, and that it carries a message inside it. Enjoy watching yourself in a fear state. See how silly and ridiculous you can see that "you" in that fear state. Make it a doosey.

How did that go?

Now welcome in some fearful movie that you regularly play that still creates emotional distress for you. But this time, before you run the movie, freeze frame the first scene and put it up on the screen of your mind as a black-and-white snapshot. Now just sit back in the tenth row of the theater of your mind and look at that old black-and-white snapshot of that fear movie.

Normally, you play it while you are *inside* the movie, but this time you get to be *a spectator* to the movie, you get to eat popcorn while you watch this movie. In fact, forget the theater, go back to the projection booth in your mind and watch it from back there where you have lots of editing equipment for the film. Turn on some circus music and let the old reel rip. Play it through from this point of view to the end and right on past the scary parts and play it out until you find some scene where you were having lots of fun. Then, stop it at the fun scene.

How did that go?

We create *fear* by playing fearful movies in our mind in a certain way. Mostly we have to be *in the movie* and we have to *hate* being in it. Then we see scary things, we hear shriller movie sounds, the sounds of the bathroom scene in Psycho, we say terrifying things to ourselves, and do all of this from *inside* the movie so that our body (neurology, glands, neuro-chemistry, muscles) get right into the act.

We create non-fear by playing the fearful movies as if we are *outside* the movie and just watching with comfort, ease, relaxation, and control. Two games. It's your choice as to which Game to play.

The Stephen King Horror Home Movie Show

That's the basic structure of first level fear. But, hell, we can do better than that, can't we? We can make the movies in our minds a hundred times more scary than what we experienced in real life. We can make the horror scenes five times bigger ... we can make people's faces, hands, and bodies loom large over us, can't we? We can make the sounds spookier. We can add eerie sounds, Hitchcock types of sounds, we can add distorted and grotesque images— Stephen King type images. We can add dark corners, shaded faces, slanted staring eyes of an alien, horrendous smells, blood-curdeling screams. Hey, we can do all kinds of movie magic to our internal images that would do Hollywood Horror movies proud.

We can use non-specific words that actually have no meaning in the world. We can keep muttering in a dreadful tone, "It's so awful. Awful! Awfullll!" "It's the most terrible thing that could ever happen, I can't believe it. Why me? I'd be better off dead."

See, scaring the hell out of ourselves is easy. Aren't you pretty skilled at it? Well, now you know *the structure of Fear Games* which now gives you the ability to cut it out. Wouldn't that be nice, to just cut it out and leave the edited film on the floor ... something for the janitor to throw out?

Neuro-linguistically we can cut some things out by *doing other things.* As we have given you a brand new way to run your own brain, you can welcome fearful images into your mind knowing that you're in control, it's your brain. You can run the audio-visual controls in your internal cinema and change the cinematic features of the movie *in any way* you so choose. This gives you a couple of Fear Mastery Games to play:

> The "It's My Brain and I Can Run It Anyway I Choose to Run It" Game.

The "I Welcome and Accept all Fearful Images" Game.

"Watch Out! Disasters Are Ahead!" Game

Here's another Fear Game that many Fear Experts play. Above and beyond the scary movies they run of previous things that have scared them, they mortgage their future on many possible and impossible fears. They imagine all of the most terrible things that *could* happen, create a movie of it, and then *step inside to experience it*. It's a great way to freak yourself out (if that's what you want). It doesn't make for courage. It doesn't increase personal confidence, but it does activate the body and fill the nervous system with fright.

What disaster could happen in your life? Death by cancer, death by consuming disease, death by Alzheimers, death by slow torture, imprisoned and raped daily by ugly thugs, lose everything in bankruptcy, get disapproval from friends and loved ones, being laughed out, having snakes touch our skin as in the Indiana Jones movie, standing precariously on a cliff, etc.

If you have a great imagination, all you have to do is think about all of the horrible and terrible things that *could* happen, turn those frightful possibilities into internal movies, step into them, and *believe in them*. If you are afraid that the plane you have booked will crash, imagine it, use every sight and sound from the airline crashes you've seen in the movies, step into it, feel it fully ... then forget that you're just imagining it, and believe your upset feelings that it *will* happen. Believe that it's a true intuition of the future. Then publically testify to this so that your word, your integrity, your person is on the line about it. If that doesn't give you a good case of the creeps about flying, I don't know what will.

Or better yet, feed yourself a steady diet of TV news, police shows, and unsolved crimes and make a movie out of everything you see and hear and make it a movie of *your life*. That should enable you to become a master fear monger.

When I talked to Joseph, he had this Game really down pat. At only 22, he could anticipate scores of fearful events in his future and fill himself with anxiety.

> "What if I make a fool of myself at the examinations coming up?"

"If I don't make an 'A,' it will ruin everything."

"Then I won't get to go to the Graduate School that I'm planning to go... and that will be terrible, that will not allow me to get the job that I want or to marry the girl that I want..."

When I heard this, I tried to interrupt him. "Hang on there!" But off he went, predicting dire consequence upon dire consequence. He had his life programmed out, step by step, wanted what he wanted, and allowed no room for detours or any contingency. His mind was rigid to a fault! It "had to be" the way he wanted it. And if it were not?

"I couldn't stand it if it didn't work out that way. Then all of my plans were for naught. Then I'll be so far behind that I'll spend all of the rest of my life catching up..."

"My, my," I said, "So life is a race and someone has blown a whistle and if you don't get into Graduate School by 23, you're a failure?"

"Yes, of course."

"Joseph, did someone actually tell you that non-sense or did you invent that on your own?"

"Well, I guess I invented it. But it's the truth."

"Well, indeed it truly makes you miserable, undermines your effectiveness, fills your body with anxiety, and makes it much less possible that you'll succeed. It truly does that. Is that the truth you want to welcome into your mind-body system?"

The Imagining Worst Possible Scenario Fear Game

When we get into this state or frame of mind of being extremely careful and alert, our minds get into the habit (and a nasty one at that) of always going to "the Worst Possible Scenario." This way of thinking then becomes our internal strategy for how to perceive the world. It's our default state. And with a state like that, we can then scare ourselves regularly and systematically, even without actual external dangers.

Of course, this describes a great formula for misery and negativity. Imagine what your internal world would be like if you sent your mind to the Worst Possible Scenario whenever anything is mentioned. Now there's a Fear Game that I wouldn't recommend.

How do people learn such games? Many learn to go to "worst possible scenarios" by having to endure a childhood that constantly exposed them to danger, threats, and distressful events. Eventually, that frame of mind became habitual. Others have learned that way of thinking by regularly exposing themselves to horror movies or even the evening news. In doing that, they may have actually trained their brains to immediately go to what is gory, sensationally horrible, dangerous, and terrible, etc. And, as you will soon discover about the secret of frame games, as we frame, so we play the Games.

When fear becomes our perceptual filter, then we can play the Game of seeing fear everywhere. Like a pair of colored glasses, fear becomes much more than an emotion. It becomes *a mind-set* (or frame). Like red glasses which filter all incoming images in red hues, so the fear filter sees every act, challenge, and change as dangerous, threatening and scary. If this is continually held before the mind it becomes the self-organizing attractor that then governs all of your Games. For anybody who finds him or herself fearful about many or most things, fear has been made one of the key frames.

From this predisposition to look for, attend, and believe in danger and threat, the Fear Game itself becomes a self-fulfilling prophecy. In this Game, the participants find validation and support for the Fear Game in just about everything. It's inescapable.

Learning the Game Of Fear

How do we learn to play this Game?

Typically we *learn* this Game through various experiences. From those experiences we draw conclusions, develop beliefs about things, and so construct the mental "programs" that then govern our responses. In this way we learn to fear all kinds of things: heights, crossing streets, openly expressing emotions, harsh tonalities, furrowed brows, pointing fingers, loud screaming voices, etc.

That some people fear these things while others do not highlights the different learning histories and the different meanings given to such things. This highlights the role that teaching and modeling has in our lives. In this way we can pass on our fears to our children and recruit them for the same Fear Games that we play.

What kind of experiences best lead to *fear?* Painful experiences. They are tremendous teachers. The pain shouts:

"Avoid this!"   "Take care with this!"   "Do this and you will suffer."

Understanding how fears are learned explains why the more actual danger exists in one's early childhood environment, the more likely a person is to become fear-oriented, "careful," "on alert," and "negative" (given to thinking about Worst Possible Scenarios). It explains how the mental and emotional state of fear can become a deeply embedded program within.   "It's Dangerous! It's Dangerous!"

Dangers come in many different shapes, sizes, and kinds.   There are

- *Physical dangers*,
- *Emotional dangers* (as when communications are harsh, rejecting, critical, conditional and insulting),
- *Spiritual dangers* (representing God as a threatening Being who zaps people with eternal fire, life as deterministic, etc.),
- *Mental dangers* (framing the world as capricious and arbitrary, as full of bogey men, and yourself as inadequate for dealing with it),
- *Interpersonal dangers* (criticism, rejection, betrayal, etc.).

Though the people who play Passive Games move *away from* threat and try to make peace, there are different kinds and styles of passivity. Some people play the Passive Game because their neurology is wired very sensitively so that stimuli (i.e., sight, sound, feeling) can overwhelm them. This can be both their gift and their temptation. They may have a more sensitively wired nervous system with a lower pain threshold than most.   My guess is that someone's innate wiring would have to be very high to allow him or her to go into some of the more violent sports like boxing or hockey.   What seems like "getting off on pain" may simply be his or her high threshold for tolerating what to the rest of us would be extreme pain.

Others find their passivity fueled by belief systems which makes them "care givers."   They feel compassion and mercy for anybody and everybody.   When overdone they develop the ability to put out emotional suction-cups and suck in all kinds of bad feelings!   Others developed the habit of passivity to survive their early home environment. Some have a basic "go at" response to stress and threat, but have been traumatized out of that response.

Do aggressive people feel fear? Certainly they do. Yet they typically will experience fear in a different way. Usually their fear gets processed as anger. When afraid, they attack. This presents a problem for them in being aware of their fears. Many who aggress when insecure act out their fears by bullying, bulldozing, arguing, confronting, coming on too strong, or using any of their other aggressive responses.

Moving from the Old Games to the New Games

We can transform our fears as we learn new Games. How we will do this will involve noticing our feelings of threat or danger, paying special attention to our physiology and exploring the meanings we give to such alarm signals.

The feelings may invite and recruit you to play a given Game, but they do not *force* us. The invitation to a Game is not the same as *the Game itself.* That is determined by the meanings which we give to the signals. As we learn how to *step back* from the emotion and feeling itself, we can stay objective enough to choose an appropriate response. In this way we can powerfully manage fear and anger responses.

Conversely, if we ignore the emotion, stuff it, or immediately act it out—none of these responses effectively deals with it. Such improper handling of fear only makes it grow into phobias, which can then dominate personality, immobilize the body, throttle one's rationality, stifle initiative and overrule values.

The Meta-Fear Game— Fearing Your Fear

Fear is just an emotion. It is just a signal in the mind-body system that sends a message. It may be accurate, it may not be. It may be useful, it may not. The message value of the emotional signal depends on many things, many variables. So as an emotion, we first learn to respect it, hear it, explore it, and all of that means *welcoming* it as a signal and no more. When we treat our emotions as *just emotions*, and not the Final Truth, we reduce their power, control and influence over us. This describes a crucial step to mastery.

But some people don't play the Game of Life that way. While fear is not our enemy, some people don't know that. They treat the emotion of fear itself as a "bad" thing and so come to hate it. Yet neither fear, nor any negative emotion, is an enemy to us. How about that? There's nothing to fear, dread, hate, feel ashamed about in *fear*, or in any "negative" emotion. "Negative" emotions help us if we accept them as emotions, welcome them for their *signal value,* and intelligently explore them.

Fear of our fear—now that's something truly to fear because *fearing our fear* can set up frames at the higher levels of our mind whereby our own states and emotions become our enemies. Then we get into such paradoxical dilemmas as *fearing* our anger, *fearing* our ability to bond and connect, *fearing* intimacy, sexuality, caring, commitment, decisiveness, assertiveness, conflict, negative emotions, loss, growing older, being playful, making mistakes, being criticized, looking like a fool, etc.

> [We call these *meta*-fears. "Meta" is Greek for something *above* and *beyond* something else and so *about* it.]

When we set up higher levels of fears like this, we set up our emotions as our enemies and create a dynamic structuring (framing) that puts ourselves at odds with ourselves. We turn our psychological energies *against* ourselves. This creates toxic and destructive Dragon States that have nowhere to go except to create illness, dis-ease, and dys-function.

When we fear some event or situation "out there," our emotion references to *the world.* This gives us pause to consider how to navigate through a situation that if mishandled could work to endanger or threaten us.

But when we *fear* our thoughts, our feelings, our states, our beliefs, etc., our emotional state of fear now is in reference to *ourselves,* and more specifically to our states, ideas, experiences, etc. This creates and sets a very different kind of frame, one that essentially turns our energies on ourselves. It says,

> "I don't trust myself... my thoughts, my emotions, my experiences."

> "I don't accept or want to think, feel, or know this or that."

When you build *that kind of a mental map*, you essentially turn your psychic (mental, emotional, personal, spiritual, physical) energies *against yourself.* Now that's some Game!

"Let's turn our psychic energies against ourselves!"

"Let's become terror stricken or disgusted at our experience of fear."

"Let's judge our feelings instead of just accepting them for their signal value."

Whatever *frame of reference and/or frame of mind* you develop and bring to your emotional experience of "fear" (or any emotion for that matter, positive or negative) determines *"the Games"* that you will play.

Whatever *Game* you play in life around fear comes from, and reflects on, the *Mental Frames* that you've accepted, bought into, or been sold. Together, frame and game makes up the *Frame Games* that you play.

The "I'm Just a Fearful Person" Frame Game

The "You've Got to be Careful; the Whole World's a Dangerous Place" Game

The "I Know I Shouldn't be Afraid, but I Can't Help It!" Frame Game

The "It's just an Emotion to Learn From" Frame Game

The "Fear is my Friend" Frame Game

In the coming chapters we will focus first on primary fears and then we'll shift to dealing with the meta-level Games of the meta-fears. That's when we move to our highest semantic states that govern the very quality of our lives.

Summary

- To play the Fear Games, use your internal powers of representation to encode fear, step into those Horror Movies of Terror and be there until your whole neurology feels like running out screaming!

- There's structure to these Games, dynamic structures involving specific processes of framing. The frames run them, inform them, govern them. The frames tell you what to fear, how to fear, when to play the Game, how freaked out to become, etc.

- Just knowing the Fear Games, i.e., knowing how they

work and what cranks them up gives you the mindfulness to stop doing them or to play them in entirely new and different ways. This enables us to start to transform the games.

- In your *Mastering Fears Game Plan* book, identify your unique production of Internal Movies by which you have terrified yourself. As you now recognize the cinematic magic that activates your fears and anxieties– what new Game Plan will you design for yourself?

A GAME IS THE GAME IT IS BECAUSE OF THE FRAMES THAT GOVERN IT.

- If we want to change the Game that we're playing, we only need to change the Frames.

- This makes Frame Detection the first step.

- What Games are you Playing?

- Do they really enhance your life or empower you as a person?

Chapter 4

THE FIGHT/FLIGHT GAME

The Neurological Foundation of Our Fear Games

I f you have ever scared yourself about something non-dangerous, like talking to someone to ask for a raise, or a date, or to propose a joint venture in business, or to address a group of a hundred or a thousand, then you know what it's like when you transform *thoughts* into *neurology.*

Isn't that amazing? Turning thoughts into neurology is almost *magical.* It means that you have taken the ideas and imaginations that dance in your head and you have transformed them into neuro-chemistry, gland productions, and muscle tensions. Excellent!

You know how to *somatize.* That is, you can turn *mind* stuff into *body* (or "soma") stuff. That's great. You have all of the necessary neurological equipment to use the neuro-linguistic and neuro-semantic processes for totally transforming your life for becoming a master of your states and your fear states.

Now while it's true that we *learn* the great majority of our fears, it is also true that we are neurologically wired and predisposed to sort for dangerous or fearful things, for things that could endanger our lives. Our fearful somatic responses give us the ability to recognize dangers and threats in a millisecond without having to "think."

> "So the game is genetic!   So I might as well go home and
> forget *mastering* my fears."

Wrong! It does *not* mean that.   Not at all!

The Neurological Game (the Fight/Flight Game) that's wired into the makeup of our body does not argue against the higher skill of learning the Games of Mastery. Quite the opposite.   That we are wired for *flight from danger and threat* is only half the truth.   The other half is that we are also wired for *fight against danger and threat.*   We have neural wiring for both flight (fear) and fight (anger).   Both sides of that statement are only partial truths.   There's yet another and even more important truth.

We are also wired, neurologically, to *think about and recognize* dangers and threats so that we can invent even more effective ways to cope and master such.   That is, above and beyond raw fight/flight, beyond unthinking passivity and aggression, *mindful assertiveness* enables us to *choose* the appropriate response in any given situation. The Fight/Flight or General Arousal Syndrome built into our nervous system is only the foundation that we build on with regard to how we respond to threats. It only provides the two most fundamental responses to danger. With *consciousness*, with *mind*, we can temper and texture our responses so that we play more complex games, always *choosing* the best Game for any particular danger or threat.

The Automatic Fear Response

Imagine walking out of a building with a close friend and getting lost in talk as you catch up on things and imagine planning a fun day together. Now as you walk down the crowded sidewalk you step out into the street without having really looked ... and suddenly an unexpected car zooms at you just a couple car-lengths away.

Suddenly, whatever was on your mind and whatever you were conversing about is gone and in your immediate vision is this speeding car ... Suddenly a world of changes and adjustments begin occurring inside your mind-body system.   Almost simultaneous to your first awareness of the speeding car, your automatic nervous system initiates muscular and neuro-chemical changes. This creates changes in your gut, heart, and skin and activates a total body response to the zooming car. It calls upon the vestibular system that governs your sense of balance and body position in space, the colliculi that guides eye and head and neck movement with the brain-stem nuclei, and the cortices of the higher brain. Your heart and lungs are suddenly infused with energy and a *general arousal* occurs that synchronizes all of your larger muscle groups to immediately step back. Even your glands get involved.

You hear the car's brakes squeal. Your friend's hands are clamped on your clothes and also pulling at you and you both fall back toward the sidewalk.

The car passes ... to the relief of all, the driver, the onlookers, and especially you.

Now you can really feel your heart beating. Your eyes are dilated, the pores of your skin are open and sweating, blood is rushing throughout your system, your blood pressure has shot up, your stomach feels queasy and your speech seems strained and difficult. A million thoughts explode and race about in your mind, you feel relieved and scared and angry and shocked and embarrassed, and angry, and afraid...

Welcome to the world of Fight/Flight!

You like that Game? You have just experienced a proper and healthy expression of your nervous system and the state induction known as *General Arousal Syndrome.* You're normal! Congratulate your nervous system. Thank it with joy and appreciation for doing what it's designed to do. Sure you feel a little shaky now. Perhaps a lot. Perhaps you're all "shaken up." That's good. More cause for joy.

If you had to use your conscious mind to figure out the speed, velocity, disposition of the driver, weather conditions, remember the stopping distances from the driving test booklet, etc. and then consciously access states of energy, and then give commands to your motor programs to *do something*, you would have a job description for the guy at the morgue.

Consciously, we experience the Fight/Flight Game in terms of two very common emotions, Anger/Fear. These are part of the built-in Survival Program that we all come equipped with. This is good. Actually, it's more than just good, it is essential to our health and well-being. It should be preserved, valued, and celebrated. And, it is the foundation for all other fears and angers. There's nothing to be afraid of when you experience your body engaged in the Fight/Flight Game ... it's just your body doing what it does best when it received "Danger!" messages.

Exploring the Fight/Flight Games

If it is "human nature" to feel frightened when endangered, *what is this experience that we call "fear?"* Let's find out. To discover the experience, come along with us on the following "thought experiment."

Take a moment and think about something you fear. What evokes fear in you? What object, situation, or person calls this forth in you? Identify it and then recall it fully and completely ... so that you see, hear, and feel whatever it was ... see it on the screen of your mind. Be there again. Or, if you would prefer, imagine that fearful object.

Did you do that? Did you turn on the experience of fear? Good. Now let's reflect.

- As you accessed an awareness of the thing that you fear, did *even the thought* of it induce a feeling of fear inside your body?
- Is your neurology appropriately responding with lots of fear sensations? Faster breathing, the heart racing, the stomach churning, etc.
- How much were you able to "turn it on?" To what degree?
- Could you have turned it on even more? How would you have done that?

Great. If you can *think* fear and your body responds, this means that you have a very healthy and responsive *neuro-linguistic* nervous system. Congratulations. Your body (nervous system, mind, etc.) knows how to play the basic, primitive Fear Game. Good for you. This means you are normal and human and your innate Fear Program works just fine.

What exactly is this common human experience that we call fear?

If you picked a good fear (and you did, didn't you?), then you know that it has biochemical and physiological components to it. You can get your physiology into the act! Fear gets your heart and lungs going, doesn't it? Yet it's also an emotion that has an affective message regarding danger in it. Don't be afraid of this experience. It is just an experience—just an emotion.

It is also a body sensation and as a body sensation (a "kinesthetic" sensation), fear generates a state of alertness and arousal. This is part of the Game, part of the Fight/Flight response system, the General Arousal Syndrome that's built into our very neuro-biology. And yet it is more.

At the biochemical level, there's little difference between *fear and anger,* and yet there is a world of difference in the cognitions (i.e., thoughts or mental activity). This is where fear and anger differ. They differ at the higher level of the frames of the mind, the frames that we bring to our somatic experiences (or bodily experiences). *Fear* begins to differ from *anger* in the mind and then manifests itself in different actions and behaviors.

How?

In *fear,* we move away from our threat; in *anger* we move toward it. These two so-called "negative" emotions differ in the direction they move us in and in our understanding of (the meanings we give to) the threat. And they make up the basic Fight/Flight emotions. We call them "negative," but they are not really negative—they are just strong *Warning Signals* in our body (soma) that get our attention. They are there to get us to "Stop, Look, and Listen."

Figure 4:1

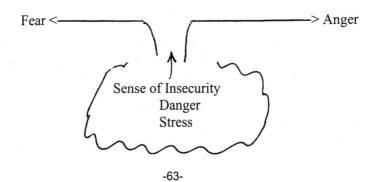

In our *experience of fear,* we feel that we want to *move away* from the threats. We may deem the threats as too big to handle or a conflict or struggle that we don't want to face. Our "emotion" (or affective cognition) of fear indicates that we have appraised the threat as more than we can encounter. This may or may not be true. When fear speaks to us it says, *"Get away!"* This may or may not be appropriate. It all depends.

In our *experience of anger,* we feel the displeasure of a threat as well as the idea that we can effectively *"take on"* that threat. The line separating fear and anger often involves a very thin one and one that fluctuates back and forth. What determines whether you go at something or move away from it depends on what you *believe about* the danger and your capacity to deal with it; it depends on your capacities and resources and your level of wanting to meet the challenge at that moment.

> Suppose you hear a growl behind you. What is your first emotional response? Fear or anger?
> Is your natural tendency to go at it or away from it?
> Suppose you turn to look for the source of the growl and see a little dog.
> What is your emotional response then?
> Suppose you see a big, two hundred pound dog. What then?
> If it is a bear?
> A mad woman?
> An angry person on a motorcycle?
> The idea of being embarrassed?
> The thought of being stared at?
> The concept of people talking about you in critical ways?

Our *going at* ("aggressing") responses and *going away from* ("passive") responses depends upon many things: our energy level, our past experiences, our understandings and beliefs, our tendencies, etc. These are but a few of the factors and dynamics of this basic Fight/Flight Response Game that we all play.

Anger and fear are alike in that both are emotional expressions of the same state of consciousness, *a sense of insecurity* that activates our motor programs to do something. But what? In the "Anger" Game, we respond by "going at" it. We growl and rush it! We become Rambo! This response comes across as a "strong" response. In the "Fear" Game, we respond by "getting away from" it. This comes across as a "weak" response (Tournier, 1963).

Where do these seemingly wired-in responses come from? They arise from the basic Fight/Flight emotional arousal system of the old brain which protects us by sorting for danger or threat. In terms of responding and communicating, this response pattern generates what we all know as the *Passive / Aggressive Continuum* in how we behave and communicate. What is not often noted (and indeed often not known) is that both fight and flight come out of the same soil. Both arise as expressions and responses of *insecurity*. You have to feel threatened, upset, disturbed, endangered, etc. for the brain and nervous system to go into this survival mode.

The fear emotions and responses (i.e., dread, terror, anxiety, apprehension, phobias, etc.) directly express our sense of insecurity. The anger emotions and responses (i.e., rage, hostility, violence, sarcasm, cynicism, etc.) typically delude a lot of people and cover up the underlying insecurity since it comes across in a "strong" way. The armored defensiveness of anger tricks or distracts us away from the angry person's insecurity. With fear, our insecurity is more obvious. But with anger, it's not so obvious. If we do not permit ourselves to be angry, we may transfer or displace our anger from one object and take it out on another, i.e., from our boss and work to driving home.

Yet both Games arise from and express the same thing, *the stress that we call insecurity.* In this sense, fear is more honest. It is more forthright and authentic since it puts us much more in touch with our insecurity. Anger is more deceptive and less authentic inasmuch as it hides our insecurity from ourselves and from others.

Which comes easiest to you, fear or anger?

Which is taboo to you?

Of these two responses, the "go at" response of anger seems "stronger." But don't let that fool you. Anger deals with things, confronts and is highly motivated to change the fear object. The "strong" approach involves expending effort and energy to encounter the threat and so often leads to success and productivity. In the process, however, it tends to masquerade fears, insecurities, and uncertainties. The schoolyard bully is a classic example of a very insecure and fearful person using an aggressive mechanism. While he looks macho, manly and tough, underneath that armor is a scared little boy.

Neurology ... not Identity

Before we continue this exploration of the Survival Fight/Flight Game, I want to underscore a critical point—one of the most empowering points you will ever read. Namely, the ability to feel fear does *not* mean that you *are* a fearful person. The ability to feel anger does *not* mean you *are* an angry person. These neurological potentials describe your fundamental *powers* and *expressions,* not your *identity.* They are part of the Survival Game, built in at the neurological level, they are not our Identity.

You, like me, and like everyone else, *can* and *do* go into states of fear and anger. You also go into states of relaxation, joy, love, confidence, empowerment, etc. *You are not your states.* You *have* and *experience* states. So don't over-identify with your states.

Why not?

Because the *identity frame* will lock you into the content of what you identify with. So use it very carefully. We'll explore this later when we get to the *Identity Game* and the *Swish Your Brain Game* (Chapter 10).

Instead of saying, "I am a fearful person," say, "Right now, I am experiencing some fear..." This will prevent you from framing it as identity, and keep it as *just an emotion,* just as a current experience, and just as a state, just as a choice about how to respond.

The Fear Avoidance Game

The *away from* coping response seems "weaker" because it moves you away from the danger, conflict, and threat. This avoidance style also has many very positive effects. Sometimes avoidance prevents something from becoming an issue altogether. Sometimes it gives others the space to rethink. Sometimes it avoids unnecessary friction or the provocation of anger.

The *away from* response is also typically motivated by the desire to make peace, create harmony, seek quick resolution, make the problem go away and not hurt feelings. When overdone this response leads to "the Nice Syndrome" where the passive person lets others walk all over him due to an exaggerated need for approval (Hall, 1987).

Yet ultimately, neither response (or Game) is better or worse than the other. They are both emotional "acting-out" responses to threat. That's all.

- How do you act out stress and insecurity?
- Do you flee or fight?
- Which is your default style?

Obviously, there are times when *going at* a threat is more effective and appropriate than *going away from* it. At other times, the passive response is more productive. The more you have choice in these response styles, the stronger your assertiveness.

This explains why, depending on the situation, fear can either motivate or de-motivate, fear can be healthy or sick. In sick, de-motivating fear there is almost always a semantic or meta-fear: fear of failure, fear of rejection, fear of loss, fear of pain, fear of looking like a fool, fear of not making it, fear of blowing it, fear of what others will think, fear of your own doubts, fear of giving up your security, fear of being vulnerable, fear of being laughed at, and fear of risk. These tormenting fears inhibit and depress as they prevent us from moving toward them. They reduce our confidence in being able to handle things. In healthy motivating fears, we use our neurological energies to get the hell out of harm's way.

"Oh, For a Healthy Dose of Fear!" Game

While some fears, like fear of loud noises and falling, seem innate and instinctual, *most fears are learned.* We learn to fear handling fire by getting burned or having a parent yell at us in a frightening tonality. Babies are not instinctively afraid of fire. They will curiously reach out to a flame to find out about it! Someone has to startle them with a loud threatening voice in order for them to attach *fear* to the flame. Or, if they get burned by the flame and it hurts, they attach *pain* and the fear of pain to the fire.

Painful consequence of behaviors teach us fear. This is how the *Fear Games* most intimately work. Attach pain, especially massive pain, to anything and you can install a flaming phobia toward anything. In this way we take the parent injunction, *"Be careful!"* and make it our highest principle. This presupposes that the world is a dangerous place and that we need to be extremely cautious in everything. If this becomes our mental program, it can run all of our behaviors. It can become our highest frame about life itself, "Be careful!" When that happens, *fear* becomes our default Game. All of life becomes the cue for having the fear program kick in. "Careful! Be careful! You might get hurt!"

This description identifies the actual nature of fear. Fear operates most fundamentally as an *early warning signal.* It *alerts* us. Our senses of sight, hearing, and sensing come to our service alerting us to dangers. This gives us the ability to quickly access danger and dangerous situations. It's as if we have antennas that put us *"on the alert"* for dangers. When that becomes overly developed, our entire mind-body goes into a hyper-alert mode. Then it seems that everything is dangerous and threatening. That can lead to the Paranoid Game.

When Fear Enhances and Enriches Life
Some people play a very different Game with fear. They abolish it entirely. They become fearless. At first that might sound good. It is not. Sure, they are without fear, but they are also without a map for caution, thoughtfulness, consequences, restraint, etc. And they pay a price for it.

When I think of the *fearless*, I think of dare-devils like Evil-Knevil. Yet their fearlessness comes with a price. They take risks that the rest of us will not, and they suffer many, many more broken bones, wrecks, disasters, etc., than the rest of us experience.

Then there are those who think in ways that we consider criminal and anti-social. What is it like for the person who thinks, feels, and behaves in anti-social ways? How does that work? What does it take to create that personality structure? Most people diagnosed as having an anti-social personality live outside the rules of society. They don't follow the rules. Why not? *They have no fear of consequences.* They have learned that there are no "real" consequences between what they do wrong and any penalties. I have worked with such individuals in the prison system and they still don't get the connection between their actions and being in jail.

They dismiss that connection. It wasn't them. It was "the system." It was someone else's fault. They did nothing wrong. There are others who are doing much worse than what I did. What I did was nothing in comparison. Jerry Isaacs (1994) has noted that they also have "learned that it's pointless to feel fear."

> "Punishment, abandonment or threats are perceived as random events, unconnected to their own actions. From their experience, they decide that there is no connection between their obedience and getting a reward and that there is, for them, little connection between disobedience and punishment." (p. 14)

They use charm, intelligence, and strategies to get what they want, feeling no need to keep their word, come through with promises, or feel any remorse. They aren't afraid of what others think, say, or do. They do not fear their own impulsive actions, violent anger, etc. Because they have gotten away with lots of infractions, they use that as their primary map for navigating relationships with others and society.

> "They lie, cheat and steal and usually get away with it. Even when caught, the punishment is minor. If the consequences happen to be large, the event is perceived by them as being out of the ordinary and that the consequences of that magnitude are not likely to be repeated. They learn to be impulsive, taking what they want when they want it because if they wait it may be taken away." (p. 14)

In the map, *"It is Pointless to Feel Fear"* such individuals master fear so completely that they lose the ability to fear. They eliminate all Fear Games, even the healthy ones. They end up with a disordering that undermines true happiness, good relationships, and effectiveness.

The solution to the Fear Games is not to become fearless, it is to become *intelligently insightful* about what to fear and what not to fear, when to fear and when not to take counsel of our fears, where to fear and where not to fear, and how to fear when that's appropriate and how not to. All of this describes a high level set of discriminations about fear and about the Games that we play with fear, as with other negative emotions.

Fear of a burning house is most appropriate. Get out of there. Yet if your child is inside and there's no rescue team around, then with mind and eyes fully open to the risks, wisely choose how to make your approach if there's any chance. Fear of ruining your reputation by going with the newest fad seems useful for using our intelligence, checking things out and not impulsively jumping on every bandwagon that comes by. And, courage to stand up to the fear of ridicule and embarrassment in order to be true to our highest values and vision may also be the most life-enhancing choice at times. It all depends. So play the *Mindful Game* of conscious awareness so that your choices are within your grasp.

The "Fear is a Healthy Emotion" Game

Emotions as *emotions* are normal, good, everyday experiences, and neutral. They're okay. They are just emotions—signals of the relationship between our frames about the world and our experience of the world.

I once worked with a guy by the name of Tracy. He had lots of tormenting fears lurking in the corners of his mind. After I set the frame that "Hey, it's just an emotion," I began asking lots of probing questions about his work and his career to find out how he was sabotaging things.

"But I don't know, what if I get one of my panic attack fears again?"

Oh that would be great. Let's hope one does. Then we can find out what it's made of and deal with it once and for all.

Eventually, one did come up. With hesitancy and apprehension and a sense of terror Tracy said,

"Ahhhhh, the fear is coming up."

"Good. Quick. Embrace it. Take your hands like this (I reached out my arms and gestured as if embracing) and welcome it in. (He did). Good. ... now listen to it. .... Does it have anything of value for you, anything that you need to hear, to learn from, to use? ... Be with that fear. .. breathe calmness into the fear ... it may just be excitement hiding and disguising in a cloak of fear..."

That did it. He said that the fear actually had no new information that he needed about anything, nothing worth listening to.

Well, sounds like its time for a good "Hell, NO!" then. That you only

need to tell that useless feeling where to go. Right?
"Right."
And that did it. His fear had actually been masquerading as an excitement that he had about launching out in a new adventure. When he realized that the somatic and body responses belonged to excitement and not fear, it changed everything.

The "Nature or Dance" Game

Any discussion about the neurology and physiology of fear inevitably brings up the questions about *how much* is genetically determined versus *how much* is learned. All too often this question becomes the "Either-Or" Game, "It's all Genetics. Biology is Destiny!" Game. "I'm just Wired for Fear!" Or, "It's all learning and environment" Game.

The truth is grayer and typically involves a matter of degree of both. Any predisposition conferred by our genetic endowment does not create a predestined life sentence. Biology only establishes biases, tendencies, and orientations. At the neurological level, we know that there are two basic behavioral profiles, the inhibited and the uninhibited. These avoidance / approach styles depend on the sensitivity or reactivity of the actual brain structures in our nervous systems.

Contemporary neuroscience shows that the almond-shaped structure in our brains called the amygdala receives information and evaluates that sensory information for potential danger. That's what it sorts for. It then signals other brain structures. If it evaluates danger, it signals the hypothalamus which controls the production of the stress hormone cortisol. If it signals the sympathetic nervous system, it mobilizes the body's responses for fight/flight (then we play that Game).

Temperamentally, we all have a neural bias and that sets a bias, a nervous bias. Yet a bias is just that, a bias, not destiny. Environment, context, and cognition also play a role. After all, the amygdala also signals the higher cortex where we engage in interpretation. Jerome Kagan (Conan, 1999) says that the

> "... relative neural activity of the left and right hemispheres of the cerebral cortex, particularly in the frontal lobes" also governs these two temperamental types of high-reactive/ inhibited and low-reactive/ uninhibited (pp. 43-45)

Where does the amygdala receive its criteria for determining what's dangerous and what is not? You've got it—from the cerebral cortex! The Game that the amygdala plays in our body is the Fight/Flight/Freeze Survival Game. That's good. But the Game set-up for knowing *what* to treat as dangerous or safe depends upon *how* we interpret, explain, and think things. That goes back to our frames. This means that we can (and do) influence our amygdala. That's why different people go into Fight/Flight reactions *about* different things... they have *learned* to do so.

The Genetic/Nurture Dance is a Game that we all play, that we cannot *not* play. Some of us start life off with a greater bias toward reactivity to danger and stress and so are more highly reactive and inhibited. Others operate from a bias toward low-reactivity and an uninhibited style. Yet as people with the low-reactivity bias can be traumatized, terrified, violated, and so learn the Fear Games well, so those with the highly reactive bias can learn to modulate their interpretations of dangers, develop states of personal confidence and competence, play the Relaxation Game, and otherwise balance their neural bias the other way.

Summary

- We have a neurological foundation for learning fear. The Fight/Flight syndrome provides us the basic General Arousal of mind-and-body when we're endangered. This gives us the ability to mold and form our fears and angers in either healthy ways or sick ways. The choice is ours.

- It's not that we want to become *fearless*. We want the ability to fear *and* the ability to learn from our fears, and to courageously face them when the fear does not identify a danger we should avoid. We only need to make sure that we have textured our fears with intelligence, faith, confidence, and courage.

- There's no escape from the experience of fear. Nor should we want an escape. We only need to make sure that our fears are healthy, appropriate, and useful. The rest we can release and exchange for courage, boldness, proactivity, mindfulness, resilience, guts, ferocity of mission, etc.

On to the Games

At this point, you might be ready just to get on to some of the first Games ... if you are, then feel free to skip Part II and Part III and go directly to the first chapter of Part IV, Chapter 9, *Games for Producing New and Better Movies*. The first two Games there will immediately assist you in fear intensity of your Fear Games.

PART II

FRAME GAMES

THE GAMES WE PLAY
FROM OUR FRAMES

Chapter 5

WHAT IN THE WORLD IS
A "FRAME GAME?"

Welcome to the Wild and Wonderful World of Games

Every day we get up and play various *Games*. Whether we get up and get ready for work, or for the weekend, or for a vacation, we get up in some *frame of mind* about getting up and about doing whatever we have to do that day. Given that frame, we then engage in playing the Games that we do.

We also do this very thing with regard to our emotions, and especially the states of fear, threat, danger, stress, etc.

- I wonder *what Games* you play?
- I wonder if you *like* the Games that you've learned to play?
- I wonder if you get the payoffs from those Games that you really want?

Through the Eyes of a "Game"

I'm sure you realize that I am not using *"Game"* in a literal or actual sense. By describing the *actions and transactions* that we engage in with ourselves and others as "Games," I'm speaking metaphorically. If we viewed our everyday actions in the world and our transactions (interactions) with others as a *"Game,"* as sets of moves and plays, what Games do we play, for what outcome or payoff, how do we score, who are we playing with or against?

The Games that we play with regard to emotions, fear, danger awareness, stress, threat, etc. are not necessarily conscious Games. *Consciousness is not required.* We can carry on (and do) without much awareness about what we're actually doing.   It's amazing, but nevertheless true. We can get into habitual ways of acting, thinking, talking, and feeling and really *not* notice the Game in play, how it affects others, or even how it affects us... at least not in the short-run. If we step back, take a breath and think about it with a larger vision of years, then we would probably "catch the Game in play."

- Isn't that true for the Games you play with fear?
- Hasn't your way of handling fear become so unconscious that you hardly even notice?
- When you do, doesn't it still just seem like normal? Like the thing to do?

To get a clear view of our Fear Games, just step back a moment from your everyday experiences with how you engage the world, interact with others, take on challenges, feel threatened, etc. Now that you've done that, I want you to do something that may seem kind of weird, but just play along with me for a moment. I invite you to view your relationship with fear through the eyes of *a Game*. This will not hurt at all. To the contrary, it offers a courageous way to deal with things, a way that will enrich your life.

Ready? Then here goes. Get out Your *Mastering Fears Game Plan* notebook (or a tape recorder) and simply respond to the following questions. There's no need to censor your responses. Just let them flow. Say or write whatever comes to mind. Since there's really no need to consciously think about your answer, respond as quickly as possible.

- *If* you viewed your way of relating to activities, people, and challenges as a Game, *what Fear Games* do you play?
- What Fear Games do others in your life play? Name some of their Games.
- If you experience lots of fear, timidity, hesitation, worry, etc., which Games contribute to that?
- Which fear Games do you find really fun and enjoyable?
- Which Fear Games bring out your best?

- Which Fear Games do you experience as really sick or stupid?

Fear *Games*

If by *"Game"* we refer to the sets of actions and interactions that occur with regard to fear, then what games have we learned best? Do we *play* the following Games:

- "It's a dangerous world; you have to always be careful!" Game?
- "I may get hurt by just about anything" Game?
- "Fear is just being aware and intelligent" Game?
- "Fear is just being realistic" Game
- "But if you were raised the way I was raised, you'd be afraid too" Game?

A *Game* not only refers to talking and acting, but can also refer to a way of thinking, a style of feeling, a pattern for communicating, along with the roles and rituals that we engage in. At the macro-level of behavior, *a Game* refers to any of the actions and behaviors that you could pick up on a video-recorder. If we asked, "How do you actually play that game?" then a video-recorder would provide the sensory referents. We would *see* the Game, we could *hear* the Game, we could *pick up the smells, movements,* etc. of the Game.

Watch someone play *The Blame Game.* Watch the index finger come out and shake furiously in the air at someone else, present or long gone. Hear the vocal chords become tight and the volume of the person's words increase in loudness. Observe the facial expressions, the breathing patterns, the jarring movements. You can actually *see and hear* the Game. "If it weren't for the way I was raised, I wouldn't be like this."

This means that *Games* give off cues and clues.

In Chess, we see a particular kind of board set out on a table and two chairs facing the table. That gives us some of the first clues about the game. If we then see someone open a small box with black and red checkers, however, we would then probably shift our thinking, "They are not going to play Chess, it's a Checkers game that they are going to play." If they then begin making the "right" kind of moves with the

Checkers on that board, we would then feel confirmed in our guess. If they used the Checkers as if Chess pieces, or in some other way that seems foreign and unfamiliar to us, we would wonder, "What in the world are they doing? They're *not* playing Checkers. I don't know what they think they're doing, but I know that they aren't playing Checkers!"

In a similar way, the Games we play in life, in business, in relationships, and with food also have cues and clues, they have rules and procedures. There is a *structure* to the way we interact, and the moves we make.

When a parent or boss begins by saying, "You didn't do this right..." and has his or her index finger pointing at you, you can pretty well bet that someone is pretty close to stepping fully into playing a round of *The Blame Game*. At least those initial cues would suggest such.

If, however, the words and actions that next occur go, "... and what I really should have told you was X, then I would have communicated more clearly..." we shift our thinking. "Maybe the boss is *not* going to play the Blame Game, but maybe he's setting up another kind of game to play with me. Perhaps, the Solution Game. Perhaps he wants to play, *'Let's collaborate on how to solve this situation.'* Or perhaps, the Mutual Responsibility Game: *'I accept and assume partial responsibility for this.'*"

Mind Games

We not only play *external games* that a video-camera could pick up in sensory based terms, we also play *internal games—head games*. We play "mind games." For this reason, *Games* also refer to our way of thinking and perceiving. That's what the confirmed pessimist plays. He or she knows how to regularly and consistently play the Game of looking at the world or any particular part of it *in terms of how things will go wrong, mess up, and make us feel bad.* If they have that Game really down pat, they will play it regularly, methodically, and persistently. When we point out their Game, they will *"Ain't it awful"* with us about pointing it out.

We can view what we *do* inside our heads as we process information, construct maps that enable us to conceptualize and construct ideas as "Games." These are *the mental games* that we play. They only differ

n that we don't actually need another person to play those Games, we
:an play them by ourselves.

That's the kind of Games we play *on our way to work.* As we get up
in the morning, get ourselves ready, and get to work or school or
vhatever, we run various *patterns of thinking, imagining, feeling,
anticipating, etc.* in our heads. We do the same every time it comes to
any challenge in life. What Games do you default to when things
become tough, when there are challenges to meet, when there are new
people to meet?

> "Oh, God, why does life have to be so hard?" (Ain't Life Hard
> Game)
> "Oh, this is great. It's a rare and unprecedented opportunity to
> discover something new!" (The Life is Wonderful Game)
> "I wish there was a way out of this!" (The Avoidance Game)
> "Just thinking about having to deal with him makes me afraid."
> (The Fear Game)

As you'll discover in *Frame Games,* we not only play conversation
games, action games, mind games, we also play games at various *levels.*
We play Games *about* our Games.

> "Let's Pretend we don't Play Games" Game Or Meta-Games
> "I Hate the Games that I Play" Game
> "I Love my Games, I wouldn't part with them for the world"
> Game
> "I Know I Shouldn't Feel this Way, but I Don't Want to
> Change." Game.
> "I Don't Understand Why I am so Afraid. Guess it's Hust
> Fate." Game.

There's a special mechanism in our minds that explains this facet of
Games. Do you know what it is? What makes it so that we do not
merely think and feel at one level of awareness, but at multiple levels?
How can we engage in a *mental game* about our mental games?

We do so because we are a symbolic class of life that can think about
our thinking, feel about our feelings. We call this "meta-cognition."
Each higher level is kind of like "the Boss of the first Thought."
Suppose we ask, "Who is the boss of that thought or emotion?" To find
the answer, we have to go upstairs, to the higher level of thought and

find the frame.

> ["Meta" means higher, a thought or emotion or state *above* another thought, emotion, or state, and *about* it.]

This means that we are the class of life that layers levels of awareness *about* our awareness. When we do that, we have moved to a higher Game, a Game about a Game.

Figure 5:1

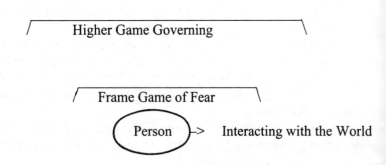

In a way, it's like *the levels within a business*. At the primary level we have people who actually create products, perform services, and engage customers. Then we have a higher level in the organization, the men and women who manage the front-line people. After that we can even move up higher and have another higher level of people who manage the managers, their supervisors, and so on until we move all the way up to the CEO who performs a very different kind of work than the front-line person.

A similar kind of "hierarchy" operates in our minds-and-bodies. We have levels governing and directing levels. As you will discover, we actually will find *the power* for change resides in those higher levels. This explains why the highest personal empowerment, competence, efficacy, and authority involves learning to access and run that level of mind. In a nutshell, that's what this book is all about.

These *levels of mind* make up *the Meta-States model*. And that is the model which provides the theoretical understandings within *Frame Games*. (See *Frame Games,* 2000).

And Then There are the Frames

"Frame" refers to the most basic process of human consciousness, namely, *frame-of-reference.* Your "frame" identifies first of all *what* you are referring to.   Without knowing that, we really can't communicate. This explains why we so frequently ask each other, especially when we're not "getting it," "What are you talking about?" To talk or think, we have some *reference* or event in mind.   These references govern the Games that we play. This is where *the levels of mind* come in. Because we can so easily use an actual reference as our *mental reference structure.*

Imagine that you do something at home or at work that legitimately creates a danger or threat. You got excited, took some action, it didn't work out in just the way you had hoped, and now you begin to fear the consequences. Suppose further that somebody (a boss, friend, loved one, etc.) comes down really hard on you with some strong words, anger, and even accusations. All of this as an event gives us a *reference.*

Seeing and hearing this, you will experience a state of fear or apprehension. Suppose you then *use* that reference emotion as your *way of thinking* about taking risks in general, or taking actions. This means that you have now jumped to a higher level.   Now the reference experience you began with, which once was an actual historical happening, has now become a *mental reference point in your brain.* Now you have shifted to using it as a template or as a frame of mind.

That's what we do with external references or "experiences." *We use our life experiences to create our maps of the world.* We take our experiences and draw conclusions from them. We make generalizations from the events about the events, about the people involved, about ourselves, etc. It's like we *mine* the events for the *meanings* that we think lie inside the event as we mine gold, silver, lead, copper from the earth. Yet this is precisely where we all go wrong, the "meaning" isn't out there. We invented it.

So, why do we do this?

To create meaning. "Meaning" does *not* exist *in* events and experiences. It cannot exist there. "Meaning" is a thing of the mind... a function of our entire nervous system and brain. We *create* meaning. We *invent* it. It only occurs in the "mind" of a meaning-maker. It emerges in the process of creating connections and mental contexts. In communicating with another, we often seek to *find* and *discover* another person's "meaning." Yet that's fairly difficult to do. To discover another's meanings we have to listen apart from our mental filters, intensive listening, reflecting back what we think we've heard, and continually correcting our impressions.

Because we internalize our experiences and use them as *reference points*, we build up a system of "meanings" and then *see the world in terms of those frames*. Eventually we develop layers of nested frames within frames. Then we take our *frame of mind,* and with lots of repetition it habituates so that our way of thinking eventually becomes our cognitive *framework*. It is this entire *framework* of nested frames that governs what and how we understand, think, perceive, reason, believe, etc. It forms and structures what we call "personality" and "neuro-semantics."

Figure 5:2

(frame filters)

/   Person   \\\\\   -> Events in World

Then, we can carry that reference system with us everywhere we go. We use it to play various Games. It becomes the Game set-up and plan for how we respond and act. Depending on the meanings that we've made, our *frames of mind* prepare us for specific games.

- "Never Take a Chance. Play it Safe" Game
- "What if they laugh at you?" Game
- "Making Mistakes is Terrible" Game, "Therefore always cover your butt."
- "Fear runs in families" Game.

- "You can't change personality anyway" Game
- I've tried to get over this fear, but that only makes it worse" Game

Frames describe the content and structure of our thoughts and so set us up with regard to the Games that we are permitted to play, know how to play, and want to play. Within the term *frame* we include all of the higher level mental structures, all those mental phenomena that we commonly call beliefs, values, understandings, paradigms, mental models, expectations, assumptions, decisions, identifications, etc.

Together we have "Frame Games"

Putting *games* and *frames* together gives us ***Frame Games***. This describes both the internal and external facets of our experiences, and so the full range of mental and behavioral Games that govern and define the life that we live. In moving through life facing people, events, and challenges at work, with our health, etc., we all play out various Frame Games. By our *frames* we establish the Games, both the good ones and the destructive ones. Our *Games* imply and flow from the governing frames.

This introduction to Frame Games now enables us to look at some of the not-so desirable *Frame Games* that go on in the arena of our fearful emotions. *Awareness* of the frames will give us insight into where the Games come from, what endows them with *meaning*, motivation, and power. Then, knowing that we will gain choices about what to do. Conversely, without awareness of the game or the frame, we easily get caught up in the Games. Then *the Frame Games play us.* Time for your *Mastering Fears* notebook again.

- What Fear Games are currently *playing* you?
- Are you consciously choosing to play those Games?
- Do those Games support you and move you in the kind of direction that you want for yourself?
- What Game or Games would you prefer to be playing?
- What cues and triggers hook you into the Games?
- What frames drive these Games?
- What do you believe about these Games?
- What historical or conceptual references do you use to

generate the frame?
- How long have you been stuck in certain frames?

Indicators of Unhealthy and Destructive Games

Having already enumerated some of the not-so fun Games that sometimes we find ourselves playing with fear, Games which reduce the quality of life and when unchecked lead to limitations and futility, here's another quick check-list of Games. Check those that you find yourself involved in that do not enhance your life, your courage, your sense of adventure, your self-confidence. Identify those that undermine your success.

Unenhancing Frame Games:

The Helpless Game	You Can't Really Change Anything. I'm a Victim of my genetics, family, upbringing, trauma experiences, etc. I'm Powerless to Change. I can't change my weight, my eating habits, my exercising habits, my fearing habits, my negative thinking, my panic attacks, etc.
Peevishness Game:	I Shouldn't have to do all this work in order to master my fears. It's unfair.
The Blame Game	My mother is to blame for my fears. If it weren't for the media, I wouldn't be so anxious.
Stress Game:	There's too much to do, I can't juggle everything. My entire future happiness is on the line with this!

"States" and Frame Games

There's a great way to detect the Games afoot in our lives, namely, through our state or attitude. The term *"state"* refers to the sum total of your mental, emotional, and behavioral experience at any given moment.

Are you in an excited state? A depressed state? Would you characterize your state as stressful, angry, pleasant, playful, or what?

In any given day, we typically experience a great many states regarding the Games that we play. Some of these are appropriate and resourceful, others are inappropriate and unresourceful. When we "cop an attitude," we typically enter into a pretty unresourceful state of mind-and-body. We're not at our best. *"State"* is a great word for this because it holistically captures both the mental (cognitive) and emotional (bodily) facets of our experience.

As a leading researcher in the field of psycho-biology, Ernest Rossi (1987) has noted our *states* create *a mind-set or attitude set.* This means that once we get into a state, *the state* itself governs our learning, memory, perception, communication, and behavior. He calls this *state-dependency.*

For example, once in an angry state, we tend to perceive the world in terms of hostility. Our learning and memory does service to the anger. So do our actions and communications. So with every intense state (joy, playfulness, relaxation, tension, etc.), once in the state, the state controls the rest of our psychological powers. This equally applies to fear states.

What does this mean in terms of the Fear Games that we play? It means that our *state,* at any given moment, sets the physical and emotional background (and frames) for the Games we play and determines the quality of our Games.

- What state would you have to experience in order to blame?
- What state would you have to access in order to seek solutions in a positive way?
- What state would support you in problem solving?
- What state would support you to feel de-motivated, fearful, or over-controlling?

Motivated States and Frame Games

When you think about mastering your fear, how much *motivation* do you feel to achieve that?

- How do your Fear Games affect your "motivation?"
- Do you wake up in the morning full of excitement and passion about your own self-management or about mastering your fears?

Ah, yes, we even play motivation Games *about* our motivation states.

Does it surprise you to realize that wanting to take action towards your goals and *not* wanting to take action both involve the same process—a process of setting a frame and then actualizing that frame. In both cases, we use our consistent focus on our goal to follow through. We move toward making something happen or we move toward making something *not* happen.

How is it that some people set a goal and then go after it and make it happen while others can't get further than two steps toward their goal?

It's all a matter of frames.

Summary

- There are Games abroad in the world, Games of fear, Games of courage, mind Games, action Games, all kinds of Games. These Games govern our everyday life.
- Behind (or above) every Game there is a Frame. Frames drive Games. To play a Game, we have to learn the rules, the structure, the payoffs, etc.
- *Frame Games* gives us a new way to think about the sets of interactions on the behavioral, communicational, and psychological levels for analyzing, understanding, and effectively working with the Games that aren't enhancing.
- As there are a lot of sick, toxic, and morbid Games that can make us unsane, so there are a lot of enhancing, empowering, and fun Games that make for an increased sense of sanity and enable us to become highly productive.
- If we want to become *experts* in handling our fears, handling our emotions, taking courage to live fully, we need to know how to stop playing the foolish and destructive Games, and how to play the ones that bring out our best.

THE NAME OF THE GAME IS TO NAME THE GAME.

- Naming the Game gives you a degree of power over the Game. Now, at least, you know what's going on.

- Naming the Game let's you now choose: "Do I really want to Play this Game?"

- Naming the Game puts you at Choice Point: Will you be Recruited to the Game, will you Refuse the Game, will you change the Rules of the Game, will you transform the Game?

- Naming the Game enables you to begin your journey to become a Game Master.

Chapter 6

FRAMES:
THE DRIVING FORCE
BEHIND THE FEAR GAMES

Where there's a Game,
There's a Frame
(Frame Game Secret)

It is inescapable that you show up everyday at work, at home, with friends, in some *frame of mind*. We're always in some *state* or *frame* of mind and body; we never leave home without our frames. These invisible mental and emotional states govern our everyday experiences as *the hidden driving or animating force* behind our lives. They also animate all of our experiences with regard to our attitudes about risk, security, safety, right and wrong, etc.. Given that, let's ask some questions to raise our *frame* awareness:

- What *frame of mind* do you show up with when it comes to facing a challenge or a danger?
- What *frame of mind* do you have about *that* frame of mind?
- How well does your mental frame serve you in terms of health, courage, productivity, etc.?
- Do you find your frame of mind empowering?

"Frame" is a pretty common term. I use *frame* as in "frame of reference and "frame of mind." In everyday life, there are some common synonyms that we also use a lot when talking about frames. We commonly talk about frames in terms of *"attitude,"* even "mood." And as we all know, *attitude is everything.*

It's All About Frames

When we're involved in a Game, all of our focus seems to zoom in on and gets lost in our actions and emotions and the actions and emotions that we receive from others. The Game is in play. The *Actions* grab our attention. This seems to be especially true of those Games that we do not like, the Fear Games. At those times, it seems to be all about the Game. It is not.

When someone is pointing a finger at you and blaming, it seems the actions of that Game is everything. So when someone is intimidating, manipulating, ordering you around, playing you off of someone else, running a scam, complaining, bellyaching, etc., *inside* of the Game, it certainly seems like the immediate talk, actions, feelings, and consequences is everything. But that's deceptive.

Inside the *Fear Games* there are all kinds of unpleasant feelings and sensations. It seems like the body and the mind is going to explode. The pressure is terrible. The object of the fear, whether it be a snake, a nasty tone of voice, a high place, the idea of risking an investment—

> "That object *makes* me afraid. I don't see any other alternative but to feel afraid. The fear comes upon me so quickly and automatically. I don't have to think about it, I just feel my heart racing and myself gasping for breath and my muscles getting tight."

At the level of the Game, all of this seems so obvious. What else is there? How can you argue with experience? With *real* actions? And yet it is deceptive. Why? Because—

A Game is only the Game
that it is because of some Frame.

"Checkers" is only the experience and set of interactions that we call "checkers" when there are two players and they are playing by the rules in their heads about how "checkers" ought to be played and for the reasons they played it. This highlights *the structure* within, behind, or above the Game. In other words, the structure of the Game, the Game's set up lies inside the Frame.

The Game of "Criticism"

Consider the Game of Criticism. Having once criticize freely, I became quite skilled at it. Whenever I saw something amiss from what I thought ought not to be, I critiqued it. I did so in order to make things better. Of course, I didn't find many who really wanted to play that Game with me. I would start in at various times and places and offer my insightful critiques and, lo, and behold, they didn't seem to want to play! Strange.

What's wrong with them? That's what I want to know.

Although, come to think of it, I didn't act much like an enthusiastic partner when people wanted to play the Game with me either. "You need to..." "You should..." "Have you ever thought of ...?" They'd initiate the Game of "Let's Criticize What You're Doing Wrong," and somehow it just didn't feel like a version of, "I Want to Help You Make Your Life Wonderful!" Game.

I have no doubt that one of my highest *frames* and one of their highest *frames* in criticism was to make things better. Yet there were some other frames involved.

For the One Trying to Play the Game:

I don't like what's going on and I'm going to let you know.

I feel upset, angry, frustrated, etc. and you're the cause.

I think you're Wrong and I'm going to set you Straight.

I wouldn't have done it that way; so you should not.

What's wrong with you, are you stupid?

For the Reluctant One Who Doesn't Want to Play that Game:

I hate being reproved, corrected, straightened out.

Who gave *You* the right to criticize me?

I'm in no mood to take this from you!

Shut up; I don't want to know about my failings or fallibilities.

Of course, with those Frames—no wonder "criticism" seldom works to make things better. No wonder both the person criticizing and the person receiving the communication do not use the Game for improving things, gaining deeper understandings, or feeling honored to be so engaged with each other. No wonder the Game of Criticism more typically ends up being a Push-Shove Game.

You ought to... No, You're Wrong, I ought not to do that! ...

Well, then you are just stupid about these matters! . ... Who are you calling Stupid? ...   I'm calling you stupid...

Understanding the Power of Frames

A *frame of reference* governs our thinking, emoting, speaking, and responding because it *sets a context* for how we view and interpret things. It establishes a conceptual context that governs the meanings we use and create in our responses.   Without a frame, a Game has no meaning, no rules, no winners or losers, no time limits or any other kind of limits. The power that governs the quality of our actions, skills, and even life lies in our *frames*. So as we say with someone who has a powerfully positive attitude or who "cops an attitude" in a negative and hurtful way, *attitude is everything.*

Frames create meaning.

As noted in the previous chapter, the crucial factor of "meaning" does not, and cannot, exist in an external event. This means that *meaning itself is not "real."* It is not "real" externally. That's why you never walk out of your house in the morning, or office at noon, and stumble over a hunk of meaning.

"Hey, who left this hunk of meaning in the driveway?"

"Meaning" is not that kind of a thing. It's not a "thing" at all. It's a way of conceptualizing things. It's a *way of thinking* that we *hold* in mind (hence the original significance of "meaning," "to hold in mind"). It's a way of punctuating or framing things. This process nature of meaning makes it slippery, plastic, and difficult to manage. Yet meaning (what we hold in mind as significant) is what gives our lives significance and power. Meaning drives and motivates. Meaning governs what we can sell and what we cannot sell. It's meaning that brings out our best and enables us to reach into the depths and heights of our hearts and minds and become *experts at managing our weight,* or fail to do so.

If meaning plays that much of a role in our lives, in the expression of our actions and behaviors, in our communications and feelings, in the quality of our lives, then let's explore what we mean by *meaning.*

- What does anything "mean?"
- What does your food or exercise mean to you?

- What does achieving a particular goal mean to you?
- What meanings really turn you on?
- What does looking foolish or taking a risk mean to you?
- What does failure mean to you?
- What doesn't mean that much to you?

In asking these "meaning" questions, we are asking about your *frame of references at many levels*, we are asking about your *frame of mind* at many levels, and we are asking about such frames as—

- Belief Frames
- Value Frames
- Destiny Frames
- Identity Frames
- Expectation Frames
- Outcome Frames
- Emotional Frames
- Theological Frames
- Philosophical Frames

It's Frames All the Way Up

"Mind" has levels. We never just think, we are a class of life that has the most amazing ability to *think about our thinking*. Technically we call this "self-reflexive consciousness." Upon thinking about what went on at work on Monday (first level thinking), we can then think about *the quality or nature of our thinking*. We can step back, so to speak, and reflect on ourselves—our thoughts, our feelings, our experiences, our history, future, ideas, etc. We call this recursive nature of thinking meta-cognition. The term *"meta"* here refers to a higher level that is *above* something else:

A thought *about* another thought:

What's the quality of my thinking?

A feeling *about* another feeling:

I'm *afraid* that my *confidence* in that task isn't strong enough.

A thought *about* a feeling:

I wonder if that is an appropriate fear or just a worry?

A feeling *about* a thought:
> I feel so stressed out when I think about the way he communicates.

A feeling about a thought about a feeling:
> I worry that my decision to eat and exercise more healthily will confirm my fears that it won't work.

As a symbolic class of life, our ability to denote a word, idea, feeling, experience, event, etc. with a word or a symbol enables us to move up the levels of awareness. This creates our ability to think conceptually, to abstract to more complex understandings of things, to create our sciences, philosophies, and higher psychological states of mind. It's a great power. It's also a terrible power when misused or abused. When we do not handle it well or when we abuse it, we create living hells of closed-ended spirals that only take us into more confusion and limitation (see *Dragon Slaying,* 2000).

Like the hierarchy of a corporate business, *the higher frames govern personality or consciousness* as a boss or CEO governs a corporation. In any living system of interactive parts, the higher levels organize, modulate, and control the processes of the entire system. The boss, CEO, board of directors, or someone at the top creates the policies, sets the rules, establishes the operational directives, etc.

Correspondingly, our higher frames govern our thinking, feeling, speaking, acting, relating, development and use of skills, etc. Our higher frames establish the existence of certain games, the rules that we play by, the limits we recognize or refuse to recognize, who can play, etc. The games we play with regard to our jobs and careers, our motivation and commitment, our relationships and self-discipline, etc. are all derived from *our frames of mind*.

The *Freaking Out About Flying* Game

Wanda's personal coach referred her. She wanted me to assist her in dealing with her "fear of flying." Her work was requiring her to fly a couple of times a month, and while she was still flying, she was increasingly feeling more nervous about it.

> "Some of my worst fears of flying are in good weather. I don't even have to be in a plane to feel afraid. I can panic at home

just thinking about flying. First I become nervous, then my
heart rate speeds up."

So you can play this 'Fear of Flying' Game even when the weather
s calm? And, you can even activate this Game while just sitting at
ome?

"Yes, I can."

If I was in the labeling business, I would say that you have
"anticipatory anxiety," but, of course, I'm in the 'de-labeling' business,
o I won't play the Labeling Game with you. I want to figure out
omething else, I want to know *what* you're doing inside your head that
allows you to play *the Fear of Flying Game.* Because when we know
hat, we will be able to change the framing of the game and create a new
and more empowering game to play. Does that sound good?

"Yes. I would like that very much. I'm sick of this feeling."

So, Wanda, since you have the exquisite power of becoming deathly
afraid of flying even when you are home, *how* in God's name are you
able to do that? That's quite a skill you have there! You can get
nervous, speed up your heart rate, and feel afraid of planes and not even
be in one. What do you have to see, hear, feel to trigger this, or how do
you know when to become afraid of flying?"

"When I'm in a plane and we hit turbulence, I get really
nervous."

Ah, so the turbulence lets you know *when* to start the game, that's the
trigger? You *have to* feel nervous about flying when you are in
turbulence?

"Well, yes. I get really nervous and my heart speeds up when
the plane hits turbulence."

When you are in a plane and you feel the turbulence of the air, then
you have to feel really nervous about things?

"Yes."

Having gathered this critical information about how and when her
game occurred and what drove it, I began playing the Game of *"When
Does it Not Occur?"* This "exception" frame allows us to look for the
boundaries of Frame Games, when does it *not* occur and what's different
about those occasions.

So what about when you are at home? *How* do you get nervous about flying when you are not in a plane? I assume that you *don't always* fear flying when you are *not* flying, that you get a few minutes of non-freaking out relief?

> (Laughing. Yes, of course. Sure, I'm not always thinking about flying and feeling nervous. It's just when I *think* about flying that I get nervous . . . It's when I think about we may hit turbulence that I get nervous. If I hear that the weather will be bad before I leave the house for the airport, I get really, really nervous."

You *have to*? At that point, you don't have a choice. You *have to* freak out! There's *never* been a time when your thinking didn't make you play this Game?

> "Well, no... there are times. It doesn't always happen. I can think about flying without panicking."

So, you don't get nervous about *flying,* not until you introduce the idea of turbulence, only then do you get into state?

> "Yes, that's right. It is about turbulence."

Have you always been afraid of turbulence? Or have you developed your fear of turbulence over the years?

> "No, I haven't always been afraid. It began about ten years ago when I was in a plane and we hit an air pocket. I had forgotten about it until just now. The plane dropped several hundred feet immediately. It horrified me!"

And are you feeling that horror now?

> "Yes... yes I am."

Great. So the Game has begun. And, as you experience that horror again, do you have a movie playing in your mind?

> "Yes."

What exactly do you see?

> "I see the inside of the cabin [motioning her hands around as if inside an airplane cabin]. I see the people and all the stuff going everywhere."

So, it's like you are in the cabin again, that you have stepped into the movie and you see the people around you and things tossing around inside the plane?

> "Yes, that's correct."

Embedded Frames for Creating and Cranking Up the Fear

We now know some of the key dynamic structures that allow Wanda to play this *"Freaking Out about Flying" Game.* She has used an old referent experience to set a representational frame for thinking about planes, flying, and turbulence. She didn't pick out the hundreds of flights that were safe, smooth, or bouncy in a good way. She picked the worst case and used it as her reference point. She didn't do this intentionally. She didn't even consciously remember the event. We don't have to.

But she did commission that event to be her referent point. It has, in fact, become her reference frame (frame of reference) so that she now thinks, perceives, and feels *according to it*— even with it outside of awareness. She commissioned it through various beliefs, values, understandings, and decisions (all higher frames *about* the experience).

- Air turbulence while in a plane is always dangerous and life-threatening!
- If there's turbulence, you could die!
- Turbulence means the plane is falling from the sky!

With frames like those, the mind-body system goes on the alert for any sign or indication of turbulence. It's the Game. If turbulence is that bad, that horrible, that terrifying, then you've got to be on hyper-alert for it. Once this becomes fully commissioned, then you can go into hyper-alert on your couch at home.

Wanda's *Flying Fear Game* was set up so that as soon as she thought of turbulence, she set the Game into play. She would immediately step back into the plane and be there again in that original Horror Movie.

Actually, this is the dynamic structure of almost all phobic reaction games. Unconsciously we step back into the fearful experience and live out the horror movie from the inside. We layer horror thoughts upon horror thoughts about our fear thoughts. We say things like, "The plane is falling! I am going to die!" You can't play the Game really well unless you say things like that inside your head. And when our brain gets these signals, it can confuse the difference between these messages as just imagined representations and those triggered by some outside stimuli. Without the map/territory distinction, then we're off and running inside the horror movies.

When Wanda thought about flying in turbulence, the game automatically zoomed her back into that old plane as it dropped from the sky. That enabled her to re-experience the emotions. No wonder she wasn't feeling very well.

I decided to let Wanda follow the absurdity of her thinking and to pry open a leverage point so that she could use some other frames to interrupt this old Game.

So the plane *is going to fall* with you in it!

> "No. I know the plane isn't going to drop, I am just thinking, 'The plane is going to drop!' 'I'm going to die!' I know those are just thoughts."

Right! You know the plane isn't really going to drop. You know that isn't happening and it isn't happening now, nor will it.

> "Well, yes, I know. At least one part of me knows that."

This separates out some of the different meta-frames that are creating and spoiling the game at the same time, and which are yet *not* freeing her from the Fear Game.

So, perhaps you are more *afraid* of your fear than you are about the plane dropping?

> (Laughing) "Yes, that's right. I guess I am."

As I quickly sketched out a diagram to illustrate how we create paranoia by *fearing* our fear, I presented the experience as a framing process. "This rough diagram sketches out a way to think about the structural dynamics that you're using to create your experiences of fear and the games that you've been playing. See if this makes sense.

You started out with your sensory movie ... reproducing in your mind that B-rated movie of the event that originally scared you. Then you juiced it up so that it is even worse now in your memory than in reality. (She smiled knowingly as I said this). Then, you went into high gear horror, as you used a screaming tonality, "The plane is falling! I'm going to die!" But did you stop there? No. Then you mapped out how to play this freaking out Game with even more terror as you layered frame upon frame, "I am going to die!" wasn't good enough. You have to fearfully dread that! "My God, I'm not ready to die! Why me?" Then, as your body, heart palpitations, sweating palms, and everything got into the act, it made it seem even more real, didn't it?

Then, over the years you've come up with even more terrifying lines. Lines that you continually run through your head, "Flying in planes is really dangerous." So while it did begin with a fear, it has evolved into fearing your fear so that you have been experiencing a paranoia about flying. What a Game!

Self-Organizing Frames or Games Validating Themselves

Now the interesting thing about our mental framing of beliefs, values, convictions, decisions, understandings, etc., is that *inside of our mind-body system, they become self-organizing systems.* The frames then operate like magnetic attractors attracting internal and external experiences that will support and validate their existence. This is just the way frames or meta-states work. In everyday language, we describe this as self-fulfilling prophecies.

If a person believes him or herself to be incompetent at a given task, not only will that person not even attempt the task, but they will look for reasons that substantiate that belief. And though he or she may find many instances of competence, such will be discounted and treated as flukes. The mental framing prevents seeing counter-examples for what they are. Playing *the "I'm so Incompetent" Game* filters them out.

When I said that to Wanda, I asked if that made sense.

"Yes, it certainly does. I believe that. So... if I am afraid of turbulence, then as I frame turbulence as bad, as a death warrant in my mind, that frame actually attracts things around me to validate itself and that's why it feels so real, right?"

Mastering Fear Frames for Transforming the Game

Right. That's exactly right. So, how many times has that frame of mind created turbulence for you when there was no turbulence around?

(Laughing), "I am afraid too many times."

In this I sought to elicit some humor and use it as a frame to lighten up about the exaggerated fears and about the silliness of engaging the whole *Fear Game* apart from any appropriate trigger. And sure enough, her laughter helped her to gain even more distance from these processes.

You said that when you turned on your movie, you were immediately

inside of the airplane?
          "Yes."
     So as you see the inside of that airplane and feel it drop, you feel what?
          "I feel tightness." [placing her hand over her stomach]
     So, you feel tightness and it is right there in your stomach?
          "Yes."
     And what do you feel underneath the tightness? ... And just feel it now for the last time ... and now just drop down through the tightness ... as if you're free falling and the bottom has dropped out and drop down through and notice... what is underneath it? [The Drop Down Through Game in Chapter 13]
          "Nothing. I don't feel anything."
     Great. And, be with that nothingness ... and what is under the nothing? Just drop down through it and out the other side.
          "Calm, I feel a calm."
     Great. You feel calm ... and you can notice the kind and quality of that calm ... and how much you enjoy it. And you can even let that calm grow and get stronger, can you not? ... And now, what is beneath the calm? What feeling supports calm?
          "Space. I just feel a sense of space. It is extremely calm."
     And being there in that calm space, what happens to the old fear of turbulence?
          "It is gone. I can't feel it."
     Wonderful. And what is that space, that extremely calm space like?
          "It's like doves ... so calm and peaceful."
     Yes, of course, we think of doves as symbols of peace. So what if, from this day forward, whenever you experience that fear or that turbulence, you can just recall sitting here and seeing the doves of peace and calm in your mind and know how calm you can feel regardless of where you are, whether at home or in a plane. And know that you don't have to play that Fear Game anymore, unless you want to, because you know that it began so innocently from an experience, and that you over-mapped it, and you set up the game, and that you don't have to anymore, do you? It happened a long time ago and is no longer happening and has not happened in years. And now you can just feel greater calm and

imagine playing the Calm and Relaxed Game as you move into your tomorrows.

After that, I asked her to put those calm feelings into her future and imagine flying and experiencing turbulence ... and playing the Calm Dove game so that she could use calmness and relaxation to enjoy her flights.

A month later Wanda sent the following e-mail.

"I have just returned from a trip to Los Angeles, my first flight since the consultation. *Thank you* so much for helping me. ... I have really discovered that *my nervousness didn't have as much to do with actual turbulence as it did with my anticipation of fear.* How amazing that I didn't need actual bad weather to make me nervous. Well, I was so calm on this trip. It was just amazing. On the return flight, I had to deal with a canceled flight, missed connections, and an announcement of severe thunderstorms. Normally, that would have been enough to put me over the edge since in the past when I've been tired and exhausted after a 16 hour day at airports, I am more susceptible to nervousness.

Anytime the flight got bumpy or they announced coming turbulence, I just played the new game that you showed me. I am still amazed that it works so well. I simply said the word "Peace... " to myself, and suddenly I was no longer on that bumpy plane, but watching the doves... Then I went from there to this beautiful valley at the base of a mountain. At the base of the mountain, I was engulfed by that great sense of nothingness that I told you about. The sound of an eagle overhead was the only sound I heard. It is the most relaxed sensation I have ever felt. I never sleep on planes, and I slept for hours both going and returning. Take offs and landings were fun! I actually enjoyed flying again. Simply amazing!

While I was in LA, I read an article in USA Today about a technique for fear of flying that used very expensive virtual reality equipment. The treatment was long and very expensive. I wanted to write the author and tell him he was looking in the wrong places. Bob, thanks so much."

That consultation took less than an hour. It doesn't always go that quickly, but I love it when it does.

Quality Controlling our Frames & Frame Games

Given this, as soon as we recognize and detect our Games and Frames, shouldn't we *Quality Control* our frames and Games? We *quality control* by checking out our frame games to make sure that they support and contribute to our goals. Shouldn't we make sure that we're playing healthy and life-enhancing games? And how do we do that?

- How healthy are the *Games* that you play with life's everyday encounters and challenges?
- Do the Games enrich your skills, relationships, development, etc.?
- Do you have any *frames of mind* that get in your way and undermine your ability to achieve?
- What *Frame Games* limit or hinder you?
- Which ones support, empower, enrich, and bring out your best?

As the Total Quality Movement raised awareness in the work place about the role and value of *quality,* so this technique gives us a *human technology* for bringing *quality* to our brain and to our Games. In business, we have learned that *quality* sells, it makes money, it creates long-term business and enduring relationships, etc. It similarly enriches our personal lives.

Quality thinking and feeling at the personal level has a whole list of similar benefits in terms of the habits we establish. When we make sure that the Games we play with ourselves and others are *Quality Games*, it supports our long term success.

Here's another great thing about all of this. When we learn how to play *Quality Games*—others will want to play with us. This creates quality relationships that not only support our health, vitality, energy, fitness, etc., but enables us to enjoy ourselves and become more of who we can become along the way. This contributes to keeping us balanced and healthy.

Frames for Changing Games

If frames operate as *the driving force* within the Games that we play, then *when we change a frame, we alter a Game.* Transforming our frames of mind (or attitudes) can involve many different transformations. We could change the rules of the Game, the name of the Game, the conditions and situations for the Game, the players, the way we score, how we value the Game, what we believe about the Game, etc. Sometimes the tiniest change in the frame alters the Game in an irrevocable way. At other times, a frame change will refine, hone, and heighten a Game— make it more sane, humane, compassionate, fun.

We call a change or alteration in a frame, *a reframe.* In the place of one reference point, we substitute another. This could involve a change of perspective, another set of criteria, or a transformation in the structure of the frame. Reframing, as a mental shift, invites us to try on a new perspective. Accordingly, reframing operates as *one driving force* that can renew, rejuvenate, and refresh the Game that we play.

Frames for Excellence

Excellence in any field involves finding and replicating the strategies of those who show the highest expertise in that area. At the surface level of things, this directs our focus to *the content of what* the expert does that defines him or her as an expert. What are the necessary skills, activities, understandings, etc.?

Yet excellence involves more. Much more. It involves *attitude.* What are the beliefs, ideas, and attitudes that support the expert in attaining, sustaining, and demonstrating such high level performances? What is the expert's attitude about the boring details that are involved in the process? What attitude does the expert take about any given facet of eating or exercising? How does the expert think or feel when failure, rejection, frustration, etc. occur?

Such questions as these enable us to look at not only the external factors that contribute to excellence, but the internal and psychological factors of success. In terms of the model here,

- What are the mental Games that experts play that set them head and shoulders above the rest of the crowd?
- What are the verbal and linguistic Games that they play

that enable them to control their states and stay fresh and creative?

- What are the behavioral Games that they play?
- How do they frame things about X or Y which enhance and support their persistence?
- How do people who live with courage, faith, confidence, determination, etc. frame things?
- How do they frame the emotion of fear? Of excitement? Anxiety?

Summary

- There is a *structure to excellence* and within that structure, the driving force for expertise in any field involves the higher frames of mind that governs the person's internal world.
- A Game is only the Game it is because of the Frame that drives it. This makes Frame Game detection critical for mastering fear.
- It's frames all the way up because we are a special class of life—a class that lives and thrives on symbols, and especially language.
- Now that you know that all of your *Fear Games* are functions of *your* frames, use your *Mastering Fears* notebook to catch every frame of mind that supports and increases your fears. What frames, beliefs, thinking patterns make you more fearful and anxious? Which reduce the fear and supports your confidence, courage, and calmness?

Chapter 7

HOW TO PLAY & MASTER FRAME GAMES

An Overview of Mastering Frame Games

You will find playing these *Frame Games* easy because you already know what a Game is and how to play Games. You've been doing it all of your life.

A *"Game"* simply refers to a set of actions and inter-actions that allow you to structure your energies so that you can achieve some desired objective. That's why we play Games. We want to accomplish something; we want to "win" at something, express our skills, show off or discover our knowledge and abilities, relate to someone in a certain way, and/or simply enjoy the process of living and expending our energies.

Further, as we play Games, we do so according to *the Rules of the particular Game*. These rules set up the structure, form, and nature of the games. The rules give us an understanding of when we play, who we play with, how we play, why we play, how we score, when to start, when to quit, exceptions, etc. Without the *rules* of the Game, we could not play. Without the rules, there would be chaos.

All of this holds true also for *Frame Games*. The Games that we play arise from, and are given form by, *our frames of mind*. This highlights the very first thing we need to do as we learn any new Game, namely, we need to clearly identify the *frames* that initiate, institute, and structure the game. When we first learned chess, monopoly, baseball, tennis, or any game, we began by asking, "Okay, how do we play?" "How do we get started?"

We typically do not learn Games by studying the formal rule books. We learn just enough rules to begin and then we play around with the game until we get the hang of it. *We learn Games best by trying them on and giving ourselves a chance to learn the ropes.* We also give ourselves a chance with the new Game by *not* expecting that we have to begin as experts or masters. We know it will take some time, lots of practice, and that we will improve our Game through experience. We also know that if we begin by just having fun with it, learning, making mistakes, using the feedback of what works and what does not that we will learn the new Game more efficiently.

Given that, as you read about some new Games here, these are my recommendations for how to begin:

1) First, get an initial impression of the Game.

Start with the name of the Game. What is it called? Often, just knowing the name of the Game is enough to get you started. This is also the value of giving Games colloquial names that are memorable. "The No-Blame, No-Shame Game," for instance, provides a nice initial impression that specifies the governing frame. Undoubtedly you have already noticed this in some of the Fear Games that we've mentioned. "It's just an Emotion" Game. "The Map is Not the Territory" Game.

2) Begin playing the Game to experiment with it.

We learn best and most thoroughly as we experiment, test, and play around with the Game. Take the *governing idea* and play around with it. Toss it back and forth with someone. Get a feel for it. Express it in numerous ways. Apply the Game to work, home, exercise, friendship, etc. Don't aim to do anything with it except just testing and playing with it.

If you took *The Courage Game* or the *Quality Control Game*, you'd think, inquire, and explore things *in terms of* these Games and the frames that make them up. Playing the Game in the spirit of the "It's Just Temporary" frame or only in certain contexts may give your mind the freedom and permission to test it out in a non-threatening way. This is analogous to playing a game of stickball on the neighborhood lot as opposed to the championship state baseball game.

3) Visit the description of the Game to begin filling in some of the details.

Have you ever read an actual Rule Book, perhaps one on baseball, chess, etc.? Boring. You have to really be into a Game to read a rule book. Rule books are full of details, game boundaries and set-ups, exemptions, etc. That's one reason that we don't start there.

There are other reasons. Most of us do *not* learn or start a new Game by reading the rule book because we do not want to overwhelm ourselves with all of the Game details. Yet another reason is that we usually discover the meaningfulness of the rules by learning them bit by bit, trying out what we know, testing it in experience, getting a feel for the initial structures, experiencing the contexts in which they make sense, and then returning for the next piece. In this, it is similar to learning to work with a computer or computer program. We start by reading a step or two, acting on those, seeing if we get them right, making sure that we are orienting ourselves to the computer or the program properly, and then adding one or two pieces at a time.

Perhaps the most important reason for this incremental approach is that it makes *the Game primary* rather than the rules. The rules and frames are there to support the game, not as a substitute for the game. A weird thing happens to a person when the rules become uppermost and the game secondary. People who come to care more about *the rules* than the game tend to become tyrants and poor losers.

4) Continually renew your focus and awareness on the objective of the game.

What is the purpose of the Game? Why do you want to play this particular Game? That which enlivens and energizes any Game is its sense of direction, outcome, and purpose.

In the *Frame Games* of our lives, many games actually operate as sub-games within yet larger Games. The purpose of one game may therefore be to enable us to play a larger Game. Knowing this can give our playing more meaning and purpose. So look for the larger Game frames within which you're playing. When you win this particular Game, what higher Game does it allow you to play?

5) Have fun as you play.

No matter where you are in the process, whether you are a novice at a new Game or a master, don't forget to have fun and to enjoy the process. This will support your learning, development, and expertise. Remember also that most of the fun is in the play itself rather than in the game prize; it's in the process. Even in the sick Games, nothing gives us more control over them than our willingness to play around with them.

6) Keep aiming for mastery by developing more skills and taking on more challenges.

In any Game there is a relationship between your skills in playing the game and the challenge which the Game offers you. When we experience high challenges, but have a low skill level, we typically feel overwhelmed. This creates anxiety and reduces our fun and delight in the Game. We then get serious, stressed, and often will feel inadequate. That's why we need to start off slow and easy.

Yet, not too slow. When we face a Game that has low challenge *and* do so with low level skills, the Game hardly seems worth learning. It feels boring. It doesn't seem to matter much one way or the other. So our interest wanes. We feel no passion for the Game. We easily dismiss such Games, "So what?"

Similarly, if we have developed high level skills for a particular game and yet face a low challenge from another player, then we also get bored. "Why bother?" The Game seems like a child's game, there's no real call to or challenge to our skills. It's too easy. And as it becomes too easy, our interest and passion wanes.

The best situation occurs when we coordinate highly developed skills with bold challenges which call forth our highest passions. Then we not only feel drawn into the Game, compelled to play at our best, but we can get lost in the Game. When that happens, something magical occurs. Psychologist Csikszentmihalyi called it the "flow" state. In Flow, the world goes away, time goes away, a sense of self goes away, and all of the higher levels of the mind vanish as we become totally present in the moment and fully experiencing the Frame Game.

The following chapters enumerate lots of "Games" —Frame Games that you can learn to play for greater management over yourself, your emotions, your fears, ideas about dangers, etc. Treat them as *Games*. Treat the *frames* as all of the rules, structures, and formatting that allows you to play the Games. As you identify the old Games that you have been playing (and their corresponding frames), and the new Games that you can play if you so choose, you move to a new position. You can now choose how and why you play the Game of life as you do.

Mastering Games Via *Frame Game Analysis*

After we learn to become a master at controlling the games that we play, we move up to an even higher Game to play. We can engage in the Game of Game Analysis. The following questions enable you to play this higher and nearly magical Game of *Game Analysis*. Thinking through the structure and form of the Game brings insight and clarity. And since clarity is our strength, it empowers us to take charge of the Games that we play and the frames that we allow to control our mind.

There is rhyme and reason to the Games we play. They do not occur as accidents or as mere happen-stance events. Unique and personal understandings govern our Games.

To transform your fear habits, grab your *Mastering Fears Game Plan* notebook so that you can use it to record the Frame Games that you catch. Then you can analyze them. The following questions will lead you to more fully describe the Game. It enables you to name the Game. That's important. It's one of the *Frame Game secrets*. Namely, *The Name of the Game is to Name the Game.*

By naming the game, we gain control over it. That's the first step. As long as *the Game plays us* and we don't know it, we don't know *how* it controls us, or the structure of the Game features— we are its patsy. As you stubbornly refuse to tolerate that kind of mental and emotional slavery, you'll be able to develop true mastery over the Games that you play.

Frame Game Analysis

Frame Game Analysis blows the whistle on the Games that go nowhere and that waste our time and energy. The analysis gives us the mindfulness so that we can make some really clear choices. Then we can powerfully say *"No!"* to the toxic old Games and *"Yes!"* to the empowering life Games.

What's the Game?

What's the Game that you're playing with fear?
With fearing your fear?
With experiencing your body in the General Arousal response?
With negative emotions?
With threat?
With embarrassment, shyness, sense of exposure, vulnerability?
With looking foolish?

Who are the Players in the Game?

Who do you play the Games with? (Just self or others?)
How many people do you invite into the Games?
Are all of the players living?

How healthy, productive, useful, enhancing, etc. is the Game?

Do you like the games you're playing?
Do they serve you well?
Do they enhance your life?
Do they empower you as a person?
Are they useful, practical, or productive?
Would you recommend them to your children?

What are the hooks that pull you into the Games?

What starts the Game? How does it begin?
How do the Games hook you?
What's within the Games that's seductive, tempting?
What's the payoff that pulls you into the Game?
What are some of the triggers that get you?
What bait does the Game depend upon to get you?

What are some of the cues that indicate the presence of a Game?

How do you know when you're involved in playing a Game?
What lets you know?

What are some of the linguistic cues? (The way that you talk)
What are some of the physical cues? (Things that you are doing)
What are some of the environmental cues?
What begins and ends the Game?
When is it over?

What are the Rules of the Game?

How is the Game set up?
How do you play?
How do you "score" points in the Game?
What comprises a "win?"
What lets you know that you are "losing?"
Who makes up the rules?
Do you like the rules?

What would you like to call this Frame Game?

Now that you have described many of the facets of the Game, what would you like to *name* this Game so as to take control of the Frame Games that you play?
What funny, silly, memorable, and colloquial name would really summarize this Frame Game?

What frames of reference support and drive this Game?

Are you using historical referents?
Imagined referents?
Conceptual referents?
Vicarious referents (something that happened to someone else)?
Healthy or unhealthy referents?
Enhancing or limiting referents?

What's the Agenda of the Game?

What's the intention or motivation that drives the Game?
What payoffs do you get from the Game?
What hidden agendas may be motivating the Game outside of your awareness?

What's the Emotional Intensity of the Game?

How much intensity does the Game generate from 0 to 10?
Are there any somatic responses that the Game produces?
Are there any other symptoms that the Game produces?

What are the Leverage Points in the Game?

What ideas, thoughts, emotions, beliefs, expectations, etc. operate as a leverage point in how the Game is set up?
If you wanted to change the Game, where's its weakest point?
What would be the easiest thing to do to mess up the Game?

What New Frame Game would you prefer to Play?

If you had a magic wand and could play a better, more empowering, more enhancing, and more productive game, what Game would it be?

How would the New Frame Game go?

How would you play it?
With whom?
At what times?
How would you set up the new Game?

What would be the Objective of the New Frame Game?

What would be its outcome or goal?
Why would you play it?
What would be the outcome for the others?

How would we establish the New Game and Install it?

If we can shift from the old to the new, how would that occur?
If we have to reject the old entirely before initiating the new, how strong of a definitive "No!" do we need to say?
What processes would help us to establish and solidify the new game?

Summary

- Life itself is a matter of *Games*—the Games we play with people, situations, and ideas. And all of our Games are driven by Frames.
- When you know how to view our actions and interactions in terms of Games, it puts you at choice with regard to what Games you'd like to play.
- We cannot *not* play Games. It's only a question of *what Games* we'll choose, and why.

Frame Games Worksheet — 1
Diagnosing a Toxic Game

1. What's the Game? Describe the "Game" being played out in terms of states and meta-states. *What's the script of the Game?* What sub-games or sub-frames are part of it all?

_____

_____

_____

2. Cues & Clues: What are some of the cues (linguistic, physical, environmental, etc.) that indicate the presence of a Game? How do you know? What cues you to it?

_____

_____

_____

3. Players: Who plays the Game? With whom? Who else has Games going on? What's the larger social system of the Game? (Use another Worksheet, one for each additional person).

_____

4. Hooks (triggers, baits): What hooks you into the Game? How does the Game hook or recruit others to play?

_____

_____

_____

5. Emotional Intensity of the Game: How intense is the Game (0 to 10)? What are some of the possible somatic responses or symptoms?

_____

6. Rules of the Game: How is the Game set up? How do you play? List Commands, Taboos that set-up the structure of the Game.

_____

7. Quality Control: Do you like this Game? Is it a sick Game? Just how sick is the Game? Are you ready to transform the Game?

8. Agenda of the Game: What's the intention, motivation, or payoff of the Game? What are some of the un-intended payoffs?

9. Name the Frame Game:

10. Style: What is your Frame of Mind? Style of thinking? Meta-Program or attitude? [See *Figuring Out People* for extensive details about Meta-Programs.]

    _ Matching / Mismatching   _ Reactive/ Thoughtful
    _ Fast/ Slow   _ Rigid / Flexible
    _ Aggressive/ Passive/Assertive _ Self / Other
    _ Options/ Procedures   _ Global / Specific

11. Leverage points: Where is the leverage point in this Game? What leverage points can you use to stop, change, or transform the Game?

12. Preferred Frame Game: What Game would you rather play? If you had a magic wand and could conjure up a new Empowering Game, what would you wish for?

Frame Games Worksheet — 2
Design Engineering a New Frame Game

1. Desired Game: Name the new Game that you would find more enhancing and empowering.

_____

2. Target: Name the person/s you want to influence (it will undoubtedly include yourself, it may even exclusively be yourself).

_____

3. Emotional Agenda/Motivation: What concerns him or her most? Values? What's really important to this person? What would hook X or recruit X into this Game? Vested interests?

_____
_____
_____

4. Larger Systems: What's the larger social system of the Game? Who else is involved?

_____
_____

5. Objective and Outcome: What do I want in this? What do I want for the other/s in this?

_____
_____

6. Description: How will the new Game be played? What frames will work best to enhance this Game? Describe. In what contexts?

_____
_____

7. Leverage points: which leverage point can you use to change or stop the old Game and initiate the new Game? What frames will best leverage this person?

_____

_____

8. Process: How can you set up these frames? How can you implement your persuasion process as you invite others in your world to play this new Game?

_____

_____

9. Check-list Stages: Will you need to interrupt, shift, loosen, and/or transform the frames? Which patterns or techniques would provide the most leverage for this?

_____

_____

10. Patterns for Installation: Which Frame Game pattern or patterns could you use to install the new Frame Games in yourself?

_____

_____

11. Frames: What frames of mind do you need in order to play the new Game?

_____

_____

_____

PART III

RESOURCE GAMES

FOR MASTERING FEAR GAMES

Chapter 8

THE RELAXATION GAME

Games The Confidently Relaxed Play

A foundational Game that will make most of the Fear Games unnecessary and wonderfully texture the Healthy Fear Games with a calm mindfulness is *the Relaxation Game*. This Game enables us to take a calm and relaxed attitude toward the events of life that don't need a full blast of the Fight/Flight Survival responses.

Given all of the stresses and pressures of everyday life, pressure that can threaten us, undermine our effectiveness, and trigger us to react, learning to play the Calmly Alert Game provides us a great resource.

- What Games do you typically play when physical, mental, or emotional stressors arise?
- What Games do you play when you face demands of the job, scheduling challenges, financial problems, difficult people, or other things that challenge your sense of safety and efficacy? What are you default Games that you use for coping?
- Do you ever default to the Stress Game?

If we play one of the Eustress (good stress) Games, we will stay resourceful in the midst of stressful events, pressures, and unpleasant people. If we play any of the *Di*stress Games, we'll freak out, react, get sick, and in other ways sabotage our best interests.

The correlation between stress and excellence is simple: to be effective and productive we have to manage our *stress reactions*. Excelling in any field necessitates avoiding the primitive stress reactions (i.e., fighting, fleeing, freezing). When we play the Stress Game, we almost never operate at our best. At such times, we lose presence of mind and so out goes clear thinking, as well as our most highly developed skills.

If stress shows up as muscle tension, tightness, soreness, inflexibility, headaches, backaches, and various other symptoms in our mind-body system, if it plays a significant role in most bodily diseases, if it significantly contributes and exasperates heart disease, ulcers, cancer, etc., then it is critical that we learn to play *the Stress Management Game,* is it not?

The Relaxation Game essentially operates by the principle that the more confidently relaxed we are as we face various events, the more likely we'll see them as challenging, but not threatening. Here we want to briefly sketch out the structure, rules, and processes for playing this Game.

> [For more on this topic, see *Instant Relaxation: How to Reduce Stress at Work, At Home, and In Your Daily Life* (1998, Lederer & Hall).]

The Stress Awareness Game

There are so many different kinds and sources of stress involved in everyday life whether it is in business and career, finances, personal relationships, succeeding in our goals, health and fitness, etc. What stresses you out? As we begin to play the Eustress Games, we need to begin by mastering awareness of stress.

- What do you find *stressful* that evokes fear, anxiety, and reactiveness in you?

Here's a checklist to begin with:

Demands	Management	Taxes
Dead-lines	Employees	Confrontation
Schedules	Red Tape	Conflict
Customers	Relationship	Bureaucracy

Technology   Company Politics   Misunderstandings
Diversity   Downsizing   Differences
Pressures   Speed of change   Lack of Rapport

The "Stress is in the Beholder's Eye" Game

Like beauty, stress lies in the eye of the beholder. Because you can not see, hear, or touch "stress," it does not refer to any brute fact in the world. We can put neither beauty nor stress on a table. They are not real in that way. Both refer to a different kind of reality, to the evaluative phenomena that occurs *in the mind*. They describe a set of actions that we label as "stressful," as stressing the limits of our mental and emotional resources.

If this is the case, then what do we mean when we use the term *stress*?

"Stress" came into our language in the late 1900s from the field of bridge engineering. Engineers used the term to refer to the amount of *pressure* on a bridge from the forces of gravity, earth movement, winds, earth shifting, weight, use, etc. They would measure the pulls and pushes of these and other forces as they talked about the amount of *stress* on a bridge and how much *stress* a bridge could take.

Dr. Hans Selye, a stress researcher, first applied the term to humans to refer to the amount of *pressures* we can take. He studied and wrote about mental, emotional, financial, sensory, etc. pressures and about the emotional states of stress, distress (destructive stress), and eustress (good stress, in fact, he coined the term "eustress").

As a mental frame about perceived "pressure" in the face of various situations, people, challenges, tasks, etc., *stress* depends on lots of things. It depends on the amount of perceived *resourcefulness* we bring to situations. The lower our sense of perceived efficacy and empowerment, the more *sense of stress* we feel. The higher our sense of personal confidence, the lower the sense of *stress*. That's the frame.

Both the Stress Game and the Relaxation Game arise from our mental frames: our expectations, desires, objectives, and resources. That's why we sometimes experience the same *situation* as "stressful" while at other times as "excitement." This highlights that *stress does not act as a thing out there,* but operates as yet another neuro-semantic reality.

The Stress Fight/ Flight/ Freeze Games

We looked at the Fight/Flight response patterns and the Survival Games they set up in Chapter 3. This now becomes useful as we look at the stress and fear Games which arise from those neurological patterns. We play Fear and Stress Games as we think and interpret things in fearful and stressful ways. We cue the stress response of Fight/Flight Games by cuing one or both of two messages:

- **Danger! Threat!**
- **Overload! Enough! Too Much!**

These messages signal the cortex, which then pass the message on to the thalamus, and activates the Fight/Flight Syndrome. As this triggers the *General Arousal Syndrome,* everything inside of us goes, "Let the Survival Games Begin! The time has come to Fight or Flee!"

Blood is withdrawn from the brain and stomach and sent to the larger muscle groups, adrenalin is released into the blood, heart and lungs beat faster, eyes dilate, skin sweats, then fats, cholesterol and sugar in the blood stream increase, the stomach secretes more acid, the immune system slows down, and thinking shifts to a more black-and-white, survivalistic mode. Then in our mind and perceptions, we sort for one thing:

- Should I Fight or Flee/ Freeze?
- Should I Attack or Run?

This sets up the two central *directions or orientations* for the Stress Games that we described earlier. We play the Stress Games of *Aggressively Going At* the threats and dangers, and *Passively Going Away From* or *Passively Freezing in our Tracks.* Most of us have a favorite game (Approach or Avoidance) with its style and direction. This typically creates two non-assertive communication styles: Passive and Aggressive.

- Which style do you typically adopt when in stress?
- Do you have a predominant one?
- Do you have a preferred style at work?
- When things become stressful in relationships, do you "Go At" the situation or "Go Away From" it?

In *The Passive Games* we move away from stressors, we take actions to make the stress and/or stressor go away, and we go into an avoidance mode. That's the Game.   To play this Game, stuff your emotions, remain constantly on the look-out for dangers, problems, things that could go wrong, be afraid, over-value "peace," tranquility, pleasantness, and resolution, and desperately care about what others think and say.

In *The Aggressive Games* we move toward stressors, we take actions on the stress and/or stressor, and we move into an approach mode. To play this Game, turn your anger outward and let others experience your wrath, constantly look-out for challenges, think more about what could go right, what you want (not what others want) and can do, long for directness, forthrightness, putting things out on the table, etc., care more about getting things done than what people think and say.

By way of contrast, in *the Assertive Game* we avoid these two extremes as we refuse to let stress feed a state of insecurity and reactiveness.   Instead, we access a practiced calmness to develop mindful understanding about our relationship to real and imagined threats and dangers as we move through the world. We play the Assertive Game, by accessing resourceful states so that we feel centered, focused, clear, valued, etc. while coping with the pressures and demands.

The literature on stress designated the passive fear-driven Game as ""the *Type B* stress response style." The literature designates the aggression-driven Game as "the *Type A* response pattern." It is a driven state, driven either by anger or passion, by what it hates and won't stand for or by its great vision. In the 1980s, *Type C* was invented to describe the assertive response style. This describes the ability to think and talk out one's internal stressors rather than act them out in fight or flight.

The Stress Management Game

After the *"Danger!"* or *"Overload!"* message is sent to the brain and cues the autonomic nervous system, the Stress Games begin. At that point, the best we can typically do is manage the stress reactions until they pass. We mostly aim to keep our reactions down so we don't kill each other. We play the *State Interruption Game* to frustrate the pattern and to not let it continue.

Generally, once we enter into the stress state, state-dependency takes over so that we are not in a good place to learn new patterns. Not at that moment.   State dependency means that all of our *communication, behavior, perception, memory, and learning* is almost completely governed by a given state at a particular time. The state (whether anger, fear, depression, joy, laughter, love) controls what we see, how we think, what we feel, our memories, behaviors, communications. As state dependency takes over, it takes some time for all of the neuro-transmitters, adrenalin, and autonomic nervous system activation to run their course. At best we can develop some good ways to *interrupt* state, *add some calmers* (count to 10, lower the voice), distract, and suggest some larger frames (you don't want to go to jail).   Other calming techniques involve: intentional deep breathing exercises, shifts in postures, focus, affirmations, visualizations, pattern interrupts, etc.

The time to learn state management skills, of course, is **not** during the stress storm. Learning navigation skills when a ship is tossing and turning in the open sea in the midst of 40 foot waves is a bit late in the Game.

The primary secret of stress management is to learn how to avoid sending the *"Danger!"* and *"Overload!"* messages when we are not facing a physical threat. This takes some doing. It means learning to run our own brains and to take charge of the higher levels of meanings that we give to things. It means exchanging our semantic *reactions* (blindly reacting to ideas) to triggers for semantic *responsiveness* (choosing when and how to respond) which are under our control. We will get to this in the last chapter. Accessing the highest levels of our mind enables us to play *The Stress Management Game* by framing, deframing (tearing frames apart), and reframing our concepts. This allows us to simply eliminate our perception of "stress" in the first place. And when stress goes, so will unnecessary experiences of fear and anger. When that happens, we simply do not get recruited to play the Stress Game in the first place. When we play the Reframing Game, we manage the meanings we give and the frames we set when we face disappointments, frustrations, set-backs, resistance, etc.

Other stress management skills involve learning how to play *the Resourceful Game* when challenged by threats, dangers, and overloads. This means learning how to access calm and confident states of mind and having them at ready access. *Instant Relaxation* (1998) uses both

NLP and Yoga exercises to develop the art of instantly accessing a calm state of mind so we can then commission it as our everyday frame of mind when we take on challenges. Doing so allows us to operate from a calm relaxation in our passion and commitment.

The Stress Management Game also involves managing our schedules and energy over time to work more efficiently. It involves learning to recognize the bodily symptoms of stress, to accept such as just the functioning of our body, to breathe more fully and deeply, to relax tight muscles, to stretch, and to use yoga exercises to train the body for calmness.

How to Play the Game of Masterful Relaxed Alertness

How can we become truly masterful in coping and handling the demands, challenges, threats, fears, etc. of everyday life at work and at home so that we don't stress out about things? How can we avoid the Fear/Anger emotions that set off insecurity and fear reactions?

Step 1: Recognize the Presence of Stress

Because we cannot control or effectively manage anything *outside-of-awareness*, we first make stress conscious. So, first grant yourself permission to notice the presence of stress and its symptoms in your life.

Begin with your body. At the primary level, *stress* shows up in the body as tightness, muscle tension, inflexibility, fatigue (feeling drained), aches and pains, ulcers, shallow breathing, tired dry eyes, etc. How are you doing?

Enter into the tension or fatigue and let it teach you. Quiet yourself and establish communication with that part of you. You might ask your stiff neck or sore back or racing heart,

"What message do you have for me?"

"If you were to speak to me, what would you say?"

"Is the tiredness physical or mental?"

Use various breathing, stretching, and moving exercises in order to "come to your body senses."

The other day a good friend of mine who definitely operates from the *Go At It mode*, arrived home and decided to walk down three houses to the group mailbox in the subdivision. On the way to get her mail, she met her neighbor who said, "Where are you marching to so fast?"

"Marching? Who's marching?" she responded.

You are ... look at yourself.

And she did. And because she did, she discovered that, sure enough, she was marching as she rushed along. Yet until it was brought to her attention, she had no awareness of it. Stress is like that. It can operate unconsciously in the background of our awareness.

Step 2: Specify Your Stress Strategy

There is order and structure to how you *stress yourself.* How do you do it? Begin with the stimuli that you use to go into the state of stress.

- What induces a stress experience in you? (i.e., schedules, people, activities, places, etc.)
- What things do you hate, can't stand, rattle your cage?
- When do you typically feel stress?
- What do you say to yourself that increases the stress?
- How do you express these thoughts in your mind?
- What tonality, volume, voice, etc. do you use?
- What are the quality of your pictures when you *stress*?

"Stress," as a precursor to fear, is an experience that has an internal dynamic structure. The magic of stress doesn't just occur without some "spell" being cast. So how do you do it? What *stress language* do you use to play this Game? Name your poison!

"I *have to* get this job done!"

"*Nobody ever* helps me."

"*Why* can't anything ever go right for me?"

"I hate it when she uses that tone of voice."

What *thinking patterns* do you use to crank up your stress? This gives us more information about the set-up of the game, how to play it, what frames make it more exaggerated and sick.

Personalizing: Interpreting events as "about me."

Awfulizing and Catastrophizing: Interpreting events in the most extreme negative ways possible.

Emotionalizing: Interpreting the presence and meaning of "emotions" as the ultimate source of information.

Minimizing or Discounting: Interpreting to make of lesser importance.

Maximizing or Exaggerating: Interpreting things to make them of greater importance.

All or Nothing Thinking: Interpreting things as if there are only polar choices and nothing in between.

Perfectionism: Interpreting things as if "It is not good enough," "It could be better."

What *physical elements* add to your stress or prevent you from operating from a calm alertness?

Shallow breathing

Hunched shoulders

Poor posture

Contracted abdomen

Lack of focus: constant eye shifting

Tightening and holding neck or jaw muscles

Knowing how the Game works in terms of its set-up and rules (i.e., its internal dynamic structure) gives you lots of ways to mess it up. You will then be able to prevent the old games from working automatically, apart from your awareness, and so playing you. Now you can play around with it so that it can begin to serve you well. To flush out the higher frames that qualify and texture your particular type and kind of stress state, ask:

What qualities characterize my stress?

What would others say about the properties of my stress?

Which of the following kinds of thinking/believing describes me?

- I must perform, achieve, produce!
- I have to be liked and approved of.
- I must be in control at all times.
- Who's ahead? How do I compare with X?
- Things must be done right.
- You can't trust others to do it right; you've got to just jump in and make it happen.
- What would happen to this place without me?
- I want things to happen *now!*

- I should not be frustrated or disappointed. It's not fair.

How can I alter my physiology so that it serves me better?
- How can I breathe in a calmer way?
- What tone of voice can I use in my self-talk?
- How can I use my posture?

Typically, you will find that these are higher frames that create the Stress Games that we play. They set us up for *pressures and needs:* the need for achievement, approval, control, competition, perfection, impatience, anger.

- Does your stress have a feeling of *anger* in it?
- Or perhaps *impatience?*
- Or perhaps you have *competitive, must-be-better than* stress?
- Do you experience stress as a make-or-break feeling?
- How much do you have your identity and self-definition wrapped up in achievement, approval, control, etc.?

When we think and believe in toxic ways, thinking that our very *being* is dependent upon what others think, the job we hold, status symbols, etc., we create *fire breathing Dragons* that can consume a lot of psychic energy.

Step 3: Practice Flying into a Calm

Can you fly into a rage? Most people can. In fact, I have never met a person who couldn't "fly into a rage" at a moment's notice. Can you fly into a fear– a fearful state of worry, dread, and anxiety? Well, if you can do either of these, then you have all the neurological equipment you need for *"flying into a calm."* Flying into a calm gives you the ability to access a state of *instant calm* in a moments notice and to play *the Confident Relaxation Game* with true skill and expertise.

Actually, you already can do it. I know you can. After all, you have a "telephone voice" don't you?

You know the scenario. You're in the living room or kitchen and having a fight with a loved one. You're saying things that you would never say to a stranger. You save those kinds of things for the people that you love most. It's your way of testing to see if they can keep on loving you if you do *this* to them! So you really get into state. You raise your voice. You feel really, really angry, upset, frustrated ... and then the phone rings.

You take a breath, and then politely answer it. "Hello..."

Your "telephone voice!" See, *you can fly into a calm!*

To develop your *"Flying into a Calm"* Game skills, you only need to practice this skill, orchestrate it so that it becomes stronger, more powerful, and so that you have ready access to it in a split second. It's already a resource, you only need to develop it further to put it at your complete disposal.

Amplify it. Think about a time when you really demonstrated the power of your telephone voice. Be there again, seeing what you saw, hearing what you heard, and totally feeling what you felt.

What enabled you to step out of the angry and yelling state to the calm and cool state where you said, "Hello!"? What ideas, beliefs, values, decisions, etc. empowered that response? Why didn't you answer the phone with your angry voice? Why didn't you yell at the person calling in?

Your answers to these questions will help you to flush out the "flying into a calm" frames of references that actually work in your life. As you make these clear, amplify them, give yourself even more reasons for doing this and then set up a trigger (or anchor) so that you can *step back into this place of mind and emotion* whenever you so choose.

- What would be a good symbol of this?
- What sound, sight, and sensation could remind you of this state?
- Let such be your anchor as you connect that symbol to that state.

Now practice stepping into it, setting that link to some trigger, breaking state, and then using the trigger to *step back* into that place where you manage your emotions.

Step 4: Texture Your Game of Flying Into a Calm

Access your best representation of a *Confidently Relaxed State* by thinking of a time when you were really relaxed in a calm and centered way. Recall it fully so that you can access this state and then connect it to a word, picture, or sensation.

After you have fully accessed, amplified, and anchored that primary resource state— step back from it and examine it:

- What is the nature and quality of your Relaxed State?
- What qualities and factors make up this state?
- What other qualities would you like to edit into this state?

Frequently, while the *relaxed state* that we access is appropriate for a sunny day on the beach, it really is not for the workplace or taking care of things at home. Typically such ideas have led us to jump to an unfounded conclusion, "Well, I cannot use calmness or relaxation there." Then we never again consider relaxation as a possible resource.

- What if you tempered and textured your relaxed state so that it had *the kind of alertness,* mindfulness, readiness, etc. that would make you even more resourceful at work?
- What if you qualified it with the kind of qualities, resources, and distinctions that would give you the kind of mastery you need at work?

This describes what we mean by framing and outframing. This also shows how a higher level state (or meta-state) differs from a primary state. In primary states of relaxation, we feel relaxed. Our muscles are limp, our breathing becomes easy, our calmness and comfort predominate our mind, everything feels at ease. It's a great state. But hardly the state we need at work when we want to produce creative products or effectively delight customers, or when we want to perform at our peak performance level. We need a special kind of relaxed state for such occasions. We need a higher level state of mind characterized by:

- Relaxed Alertness
- Calm Confidence in our skills
- Relaxed attentiveness in listening fully to a client
- The relaxed energy of readiness
- Accepting the frustrations of everyday life

What *kind* of relaxation do you need or want?

How do you want to feel calm and confident and relaxed when you play the Game?

I texture various activities and states with calmness. When I provide trainings, I want a kind of *calm* excitement that conveys both how much I care about my topic, about communicating it with clarity, and about enabling people to feel a part of the discovery process. When I run (even in a race), I need a *confident relaxation* that knows how to measure my energy output so that I can stay in for the duration without burning out. When I model the structure of someone's expertise, I want the *calm* relaxed mind that allows me to stay clear, not contaminating it with my assumptions, but simply to discover what's there. I need the relaxed mind of confidence that trusts in the process.

- What kind of a relaxed mind and emotions do you want or need in a given situation?
- Name the texturing qualities that you want for your core relaxed state.

Step 5: Practice Accessing your Relaxed Core State

In the book *Instant Relaxation* Debra speaks about accessing our "Relaxed Core Self." This refers to feeling relaxed with our sense of self, to feel relaxed with ourselves, to feel confident, assured, and centered. These kinds of mental frames of mind structure a Frame Game for us that enables us to operate from a sense of safety and security. This prevents the *"Danger!, Threat!* and *Overload!"* messages from triggering us into reactiveness. Wouldn't that be nice?

When we have this kind of centered sense of self, then we have a platform of comfort and security from which we can sally out to the adventures of life. This gives balance to our life energies. We shuttle out to a challenge, then we retreat to our relaxation zone to recuperate and rejuvenate our strength. We move out to perform as achievers, then we move back in to just *be* and enjoy ourselves as persons.

How do we do this? Simple. Here's an induction.

Imagine what it would look like, sound like, and feel like to completely and thoroughly access your own relaxed core state and make it your game. Float back in your imagination to capture bits and pieces of anything that will enrich your editing of such a self-image and begin allowing these pieces to come together to create a powerful sense of a core self; relaxed, confident, assured ... comfortable in your own skin, breathing fully and completely, taking charge of your thinking, emoting, speaking, and behaving... Just imagine what that would feel like and how that would transform your life....

... and when you have edited it to your liking, and it feels compelling, step into it and be there. And enjoy it... so that you experience it as a joyful relaxed core state. And now as you *translate it from mind to muscle*, imagine breathing with this and seeing out of the eyes of your core relaxed state. Hear the voice of this state—speaking with a calm confidence that radiates a sense of your inner power.

- Are all of your parts aligned with this?
- Does any part of you object to living this way?
- Would you like this as your way of being in the world?

Step 6: *Keep Refining and Texturing Your Relaxed Core State*

Nor does this process end with the first design engineering of this highly resourceful state. With the tools for modeling excellence, you can now maintain a creative attitude about all of the other resources that you can find and incorporate in that *relaxed core state*.

For instance, why not add a big dose of healthy humor to the mix? The ability to lighten up, to *not* take yourself so seriously, to enjoy people and experiences tremendously enriches relaxation. We can explode most fears by using the humor power of exaggeration. Exaggerate the fear until it begins to become ridiculous. Then exaggerate it some more. Eventually it becomes funny and then your humorous perspective enables you to operate in a more human and delightful way. (See *The Humor Game*, next)

Or, how about *appreciation?* What if you moved through the world with an appreciation of things, people, experiences? How would that *texture the quality of your stress*?

Magnanimity would be another resource. It would enable you to operate from a sense of a having a big-heart and thereby prevent you from becoming mentally ruffled. How would that enhance your life?

Then there is openness to reality, flexibility, forgiveness, playfulness, balance, and the list goes on and on. Dr. Suzanne Kobasa, who coauthored *The Hardy Executive: Health Under Stress*, quoted the research about the *three Cs* that prevent a person from spiraling in stress to illness. These *three Cs* are:

- *Commitment* to self, work, family and other values
- *Control:* A sense of personal *control* over one's life
- *Challenge:* The ability to see change in one's life as a positive *challenge.*

The Humor Game

If a calm relaxing mind enables us to *step aside* from the Horror Movies in our mind and at least think *about* them in a more thoughtful way as we just observe them, then the humor frame of mind enables us to go even further in gaining distance and objectivity to ourselves. Humor enables us to *lighten up.* This describes the heart of humor power. It is the gift of laughter, of seeing something as funny, silly, incongruous, playful, and ludicrous.

As a state of mind whereby we see something as "out of place in time and space without danger" (Socrates), humor enables us to lighten our perspective. What do we experience when we can't see humor in any given situation? We experience seriousness. We see things as dangerous and threatening. And that's precisely why we play the Fear Games.

When we can step back, gain perspective, see the things out of joint, and do so while calm, relaxed, confident, secure, safe, etc., we relate to the event without the danger and threat signals and the fight/flight states. Then we can play the Humor Games. We usually get there, it just takes time. Years later we look back on upsetting, fearful, and traumatic events and laugh. As we see them in terms of humor (incongruency, silliness, ridiculous features, etc.), they seem less fearful.

But why wait?

Why endure years of fear, dread, seriousness, stress, etc.? Why not zoom out into your future now to a time and place five or ten years from now and look back?

The week I wrote this piece, my daughter took her test for her driving license. We had spent 50 hours in the car together (state law) so I knew she was ready, a safe driver, well aware of the rules, etc. But one rule was that the tester could not talk during the testing. Jessica said that because this differed so much from the way she and I had been relating in the car, it scared her. "It was intimidating, Dad."

Afterwards she was still in a stressful and fearful state, questioning herself, her skills, etc. While reasoning could have worked to have reduced the fear, I decided on the Humor Game with her.

"So watching the Person doing the Driver Test who had to ride in a car with you sit in forced silence was kind of like having to hold it when you have to go pee... and that was really scary?"

> (Smiling) "Well, I didn't know what he was thinking, that's what made it intimidating. He wouldn't say anything."

(Licking my lips) *"That's great. You had him, you could have zoomed this way and that, darted in front of traffic, and he would have had to sit there enduring the terror ride of his life! Like those Cop shows on TV where they're chasing the criminals and drunks, imagine the ride you could have given him and he would have just had to hold it! No peeing in the car, right? Then talk about who's intimidating who!"*

> (Laughing) "Yeah, that would have been funny."

"And I can't even imagine how red his face would have gotten or how he'd put his knees together to not pee in the car with you swinging it around wildly and making him terrified out of his mind that he has the job he has!"

We both laughed and laughed. Jessica got into the Game and exaggerated the situation so that it became funnier and more ridiculous.

In an NLP training at the college, Bob invited someone to work with him as he demonstrated how to use NLP to work with a phobia. A lady volunteered. She said she had a phobia, an unreasonable fear of heights that she developed while on vacation. Nothing like using a vacation for developing utter terror of something! On vacation she went to the Grand Canyon and rode along a narrow ledge riding a mule.

During the demonstration of the NLP Phobia process (*The Stepping In and Out Game*), Bob had her play the mental movie forward while watching it from a projection booth. Then he invited her to step into the scene of comfort at the end and he told her that in NLP, we learn to "run our mental movies backwards." So she did. She reversed the movie of the vacation and experienced it while inside of the movie. When she did, she saw the mule going up the canyon backwards. And that started her laughing.

"So you are going ass-backwards, huh?" he said as he coached her, and with that, the class broke up. As everybody was bending over with laughter, Bob took full advantage of it as he began linking the humor with her memories of the Grand Canyon with an ass going up backwards so that the memory and the humor became completely associated.

Later Bob wrote to me about the experience,

"I originally used the term ass-backwards just to elicit some humor and lighten it up. But when we laughed, we laughed *about* something—and where can a mind go, but to a higher position to the experience? Even now, when I think about the Grand Canyon, I think about a mule and then about heights, and then I feel some silly but hilarious laughter about it as I think of that class."

Summary

- *Stress is not a "thing,"* but a response of our mind-and-emotions as well as a response of our body. It does not exist "out there," it emerges from the way we map what things mean, the expectations we bring to the situation, and our coping skills.
- While we can only partially change the world and environment in which we live, we have almost total control over how we think and emote. Herein lies the realm of magic for renewal and transformation.
- It only takes the power of framing and reframing to transform old attitudes and beliefs that create distress so that we can operate from more functional maps that endow life with lots of eustress, that is, excitement. This is a new Game.
- As you access your own personalized *Calmly Relaxed State*, and play that Game, you will find yourself becoming stress-resistant and increasingly more able to refuse the old Fear Games.

THE PROBLEM IS NEVER THE PERSON IT IS ALWAYS THE FRAME.

- *To think is to "frame"* ... first as a point of reference, then as a represented reference, then as a frame of reference. It's just the way we "think" or process information.

- We *learned* to think and frame things from our family, friends, culture, etc. And yet *who we are* is much more than our frames. We *think* yet we are more than our *thoughts*.

- Whatever Frames you have in your head that set up the Games you play are just that ... *Frames*. And they are only as "real" as you make them. You give them their "reality"

Chapter 9

GAMES FOR
GETTING LEVERAGE
OVER FEARS

Games In This Chapter:
The Quality Controlling Game
The Meta-No and Meta-Yes Game
The "Swish Your Brain" Game
It's Just an Emotion Game
The De-Masking Game
The Frame Game Game
It's just a Map Game

The Quality Control Game

Sometimes we simply need leverage on our Games. We need some way to leverage ourselves against a Game so that we can hold it accountable to our well-being, health, vitality, values, visions, etc. If we don't, the Game can keep sucking us in, seducing us, tricking us, driving us and ruining our lives. To prevent this, we need another Game, a higher Game by which we can call our everyday Games onto the executive carpet and get a straight answer.

- Is this Game really enhancing my life?
- Does it empower me as a person?
- Does it support my highest values and visions?
- Is it moving me in the direction that I want my life to go?

We call this the *Quality Control* Game. It is a very powerful Game that we often refer to and that we have written about in other works.

> "... our brains don't seem to have any innate quality
> control functions. Our brains don't seem to care what
> information we feed it. You feed it a 'thought,' an
> idea, a concept, data—and it will just 'process' it.
> Brains don't seem very smart about the quality of the
> content that we feed it, unlike the stomach. At least
> the stomach has enough sense to vomit when it gets
> garbage. The brain doesn't seem that intelligent."
> (*Dragon Slaying,* 2000)

If we feed our brain thoughts of fear and anxiety, our brain will simply oblige our instructions, play those movies and then activate that content. It doesn't seem particularly finicky about what it processes. Feed it garbage and it just does its thing. That's why we have to take charge and regularly check it out ... by checking out the quality of its processing. So, step back from the Game, from the frames of your brain and examine it.

- Is this what I want?
- Is this quality living?
- Is this quality thinking, feeling, relating, health, etc.?
- Does this game or this frame make life a party?

If these questions bring up doubts, questions, worries, etc.—great! That's the kind of feedback you want, isn't it? Sure. If you get an unquestionable "No!", that's even better. Now you are ready to quit those old Games and get on with life. We use this *Quality Controlling Game* to empower people all the time, in workshops, trainings, and private consulting.

I did it the morning I wrote this chapter. I was talking to a fellow by the name of Cody who suffered from several debilitating fears. He's a good friend and has been for years, but he has several habits that were getting the best of him. They were undermining his health, his peace of mind, his sense of self-confidence, etc. His drinking pattern was the worst culprit. Frequently I have brought it up, but today he did.

"I'm really needing to change things about my drinking."

Hey, Cody, maybe you ought to just give in to it. Maybe that's the best Game to play. Maybe it's time to forget quality living, health, balance, integrity, and personal power and just let the Game play you.

It has for years. What makes you think you can change anyway?

"I know you're just kidding, but I'm serious this time."

Oh, the "But now I'm Really Serious" Game? And you think that's going to hook me into offering you some excellent advice that you'll just waste away? Doesn't the "My Drinking Controls Me!" Game make life a party for you? Isn't it a lot of fun?

"No it isn't. It's destroying my health."

Well, maybe that's a minor thing. We all get older, our bodies are less efficient, hey, it's just the aging thing. Live with it! Doesn't your misuse of alcohol improve the quality of your life? Of your mind? Your relationships?

"I know what you're doing. ... Of course, it doesn't improve those things. It makes things worse."

Yeah, but you're just saying this. You don't have any intention in actually changing. And that's because you really aren't convinced that this Game is all that bad. You know it's an okay Game. It makes you more of who you can be. It's your strength and coping skill, it's your friend. You get lots of things from this, right?

"No I do not!"

And so the provocation went on. I never let up. We were at a coffee shop and I just kept at it until he had to go. I wanted to get leverage on the behavior and I wanted him to get leverage over it himself. He was afraid of trying again, afraid of failing, afraid of investing time and energy to no avail, etc. So I compared and contrasted those fears with the quality of the Game. "Yes, that's right. It's much better to *not* give it your all than to go down trying! Yeah, the *Wimp Game*. And that really makes life better doesn't it?"

Secondary Gain Game

As you *Quality Control* your old Fear Games, you might notice that at times there may seem to be some positive values, payoffs, points, or "secondary gains" that you've been getting from playing those Games. This isn't always so, but does occur. This only indicates that you have some higher frames at work which give you something (a gain) by playing those Games. Yet they simultaneously sabotage you. They fill you with fearfulness, limit your options, and debilitate your courage.

What would I have to give up to eliminate my fear?

What price would I pay to transform fear into courage?

What secondary benefits would I lose?

Your answers about the specific secondary gains sabotaging your ability to release the fears and move on with courage need to be satisfied in some way. To make the transformation without taking care of the secondary gains would rob you of important values. So we will want to be able to fulfill them using other processes than the current Fear Games.

Step 1: Step aside from the Fear Games

What is the Fear Game that you've been playing? How does it go? How do you play it, with whom, when, where, etc.?

Fully describe the Fear Game and how you are recruited to it. Do you have any old memories of old hurts, disappointments, frustrations, or traumas that still create fears in you and yet you know that you don't need these fears? Are you willing to play a new Game?

Step 2: Quality Control the Fear Game

Does this Game support your life, your values, your vision for yourself?

Does this Game make life a party?

Does it enhance your life or empower you as a person?

Does it give your life the quality that you want?

Step 3: Check out the Game Payoff

What do you get by playing this Fear Game?

When you get that payoff, those points, that gain, etc., what does that give you that's of value to you? (Access the payoff of the payoff repeatedly until you run out of payoffs.)

Do you need this fear for these payoffs?

Do you have any other way of keeping these benefits?

Step 4: Frame the old Game as No Longer Real or Useful

Do you know that the old Game that you've been playing is old, not happening now, not useful any longer? Do you know that? Good. Then say so. Declare to yourself that the old Games of fear are irrelevant: "This Game is no longer real or useful. I don't need it!"

What symbol can you use to cue yourself to tell yourself this truth? Perhaps, "Just old memories, nothing more." "Just old mappings, Games, that's all."

Step 5: Step up for a new game with your courageous self

Would you like to create an image of the *You without fear*, the *courageous* You?

Good. Make it so.

Now say to that image, "This New Me has all the resources to live without fear."

"This New Me can live fully in the present with an eye on the future."

Step 6: Separate the old payoffs and connect to new games

What new games can you play to keep or attain the old payoffs that you consider valuable?

How will you maintain those values and benefits?

Step 7: Commission the new Game to be your way of being in the world

Do you like this?

Does it support your highest values and visions? Does it support you being resourceful and empowered?

Are you willing to practice this new Game several times every day until it habituates as your new way of thinking and becomes your new frame of mind?

How will you play the new Game with this new frame?

The "Hell, NO!" "Heavens, YES" GAME

Once you find an old Game that doesn't serve you well, and you've taken care of the secondary gains, can you tell the old Game to get lost? Can you just say *"No!"* to it and that takes care of it?

The ability to actually say "No!" to ideas, beliefs, attitudes, emotions, habitual frames of mind, etc. is part of the power of personal mastery. Woe be unto the person who can't say *"No!"* to thoughts or ideas, who can't *negate* them and actually make them *go away and leave you alone.*

The *"No!"* Game is learned early and truly represents an important human power. We get our first opportunity to learn this game during childhood. About two-years of age, we discover that we are separate from our parents and can distinguish me and not-me. We learn to say, "no!" That enables us to individuate, to become our own person, to develop psychological boundaries, to become centered in our own ideas, beliefs, and values.

Of course, some parents who skipped Parenting #101 tend to take the "Nos!" of the two-year old person and try to beat it out of them. They misunderstand. They think its selfishness or something.

We all also revisit this boundary creating stage of our development during our teenage years. Again, we learn to distinguish self from other, self from parents, as we individualize from childhood into young adulthood. Again, we learn to say, *"No!"*

We have numerous ways to *negate* ideas and beliefs, but the most powerful and direct way is to recover this basic human power, amplify it, and then blast away at the frames and beliefs that set up Fear Games, self-sabotaging Games, etc. To that end, we have a Meta No-ing and Yes-ing Game that we have found extremely effective in changing all kinds of beliefs.

You've used this process before. This isn't anything you haven't already done. There are things that you once believed to be true that you no longer believe to be true. You came to the point, in your mind, where you said, "No, that's not true, that's not real, I don't believe that." And in saying "No," you turned a belief back into a mere thought.

This, by the way, is the difference between a thought and a belief. To have a belief, and therefore a command to the nervous system, you have to play the Affirming and Validating Game with that thought. You have to say to that thought, "Yes!" In so validating the thought, you transform it. It becomes more than just a thought. It becomes a belief— an energized thought in your mind that commands your nervous system about how to respond.

How to Play the Meta No-ing and Meta-Yes-ing Game
Step 1. *Get a good strong representation of saying "No!" to something*

Can you say "No!" to anything fully and completely?

What can you say "No!" to fully and completely?

Then do it, think of something to which ever fiber of your being can say, "No!" and experience that internal "No," that internal rejection fully. Show me what "No" looks like, sounds like, and feels like that truly fits with all of your beliefs and values.

Great, let's attach this feeling to the gesture of "No!" Give me that.

For example, Would you push a small child in front of a speeding bus to see its blood splash all over the street? Would you eat a bowl of filthy crawling worms? Would you slug a policeman during a parade just for the hell of it? Would you shove a knife up your nose? Ask anything that would elicit a strong and absolute, "No!"

Step 2. *Get a good strong representation of saying "Yes!" to something*

Can you say "Yes!" to anything fully and completely?

What can you say "Yes!" to fully and completely?

Then do it, think of something to which you can say "Yes!" to fully, something that every fiber of your being can say "Yes!" and really mean it. Again, show me what that "Yes!" looks like, sounds like, and feels like.

How strong is this "Yes!"? Is it strong enough to validate and affirm something that you want to make part of your life?

Let's attach this feeling to the gesture of "Yes!"

For example, Would you like to make a meaningful difference in the world? Do you enjoy laughing and having fun? Would you enjoy winning a ten-million dollar lottery? Do you or would you like to move through the world with a solid sense of your identity, worth, and loveability?

Step 3. Identify a limiting belief about fear, fearfulness, etc. that you no longer want to run your programs

What do you believe about fear or fearfulness or some trigger that you know is limiting and that undermines your effectiveness? For example, experiencing fear is the most awful thing in the world. I can't stand myself when I became anxious. If you feel afraid, you have to flee from the experience. Fear means you are not able to go forward.

Describe it fully.

Where did you learn this from? How? What were you seeking to achieve by believing that?

How does it undermine your health, wealth, success, empowerment, etc.?

Are you fully convinced that you don't need this old limiting belief?

Are you ready to reject it? Blast it away? Give it no power in your mind?

Step 4. Fully elicit an enhancing belief that masters the old fears

What would you prefer to think? To believe?

How can you express that belief even more effectively, powerfully, and congruently?

Do you like this belief? Would this really serve you well?

How would it empower you as a person, and enhance your life?

Step 5. Utter a Meta "No!" to the limiting belief that will Blast it Away

Remember that "No!" state and gesture? Give me that again. Even more fully. Full enough so that it can blast away your limiting beliefs about fear.

Now, utter your strong *"No!"* so that it blasts the old belief away.

Great. Again! And, again. How many more times do you need to say "No!" to that old idea before it feels like it has no place in your mind-body system?

And you can keep on saying *'No!'* to that limiting belief until you begin to feel that it no longer has any power to run your programs.

Step 6. *Utter a powerful Meta "Yes!" to the enhancing belief*
Do you remember that *"Yes!"* you accessed and the gesture of "Yes-ing!"? Give me that again.
Do you want to say *"Yes!"* to your Empowering Belief?
Really? Then do it!
Does this "Yes" validate that thought? Does it affirm it?
Will this improve your life?
Do you want to keep this new belief?
Will it affect your identity? How?

After you have learned and practiced the *No-ing* and *Yes-ing* Games, be sure to use these powers of negation and affirmation to blast away everything that stands in the way of your resourcefulness and to confirm and solidify everything that improves the quality of your life in a balanced way. There're Games you won't let people play with you, aren't there? Aren't there Games that you consider just too stupid, sick, or wrong which you won't tolerate for a moment? Can't you think of those now?

And as you do, doesn't that get up your dander and make you as mad as hell that they even try? Don't you feel enraged about that? Angry? Aren't you even now taking a strong stubborn stance against that? Great.

Now feeling all of that *"Hell, No!"* energy, use that same powerful energy to stubbornly refuse to put up with debilitating fears that destroy your life.

Wasn't that good? Didn't you like that? Did you say "Yes!"? I didn't hear you! Did you like that? Wasn't that good? Do you want to keep that for the rest of your life? Don't you like running your own brain?

The "Swish Your Brain" Game
By now you know that *brains go places.* This was one of the first scientific discoveries that people made when psychology entered into the modern era. Pavlov discovered that the brain and nervous system

associates things and that he could even use this neurological principle for therapeutic processes. To Pavlov we owe numerous ideas and processes for *conditioning* neurological patterns. Later, NLP made Pavlovian conditioning user-friendly as it invented ways to "anchor" or *link* thoughts, emotions, and states. This does *not* describe anything new in terms of what the brain already does. It only gives us the ability to consciously manage the processes.

To play *the Swish Your Brain Game* we will identify a trigger in everyday life that sets off or already anchors some fear state that doesn't enhance our life. It's an old linkage system that limits and sabotages rather than empowers and enhances. We will then build up a new trigger—*"the Me for whom that situation is no problem."* In other words, we will use an empowering Identity, Self-Image, or Self-Definition— one that naturally evokes courage, confidence, ease, humor, playfulness, etc. and tell our brain, "Go there!"

This is truly a great and fun Game to play. Next time you question yourself and wonder if you're nothing more than "a fearful person" and that's your fate, swish your brain to *the You* for whom living with courage in a given situation is "no problem."

How do you play this Game?

1) First, vividly imagine a *You* that's bolder, more confident, calm, focused, clear, etc. See *that You* as you really want to be. Make a mental imagine of yourself on the screen of your mind and see yourself moving, breathing, speaking, interacting, etc. with the kind of qualities that make the activity effective and pleasing. See *the new calmly courageous you* glowing with health and energy, feeling confident, assertive about your voice and values, feeling the power of self-control and discipline, etc. Texture the image so that it delights and pulls on you.

2) Keep editing this picture so that you see *that You* as a three-dimensional life-size image and until it becomes clear and compelling. See yourself as operating from firmness and clarity. Hear yourself speaking with a calm, modulated voice. Feel yourself breathing fully and with energy in your body. Keep amplifying this picture. Do so until it becomes so vivid that you feel compelled to step into it. You'll know you are doing this right when you begin to drool.

3) Now step into this *Future Calmly Courageous You* ... Then, from inside, turn and face your future and begin walking inside of this new courageous body. Experience the feel of strength and firmness that confidently can face the situation ... walk with the elegance and power of this state.

4) Still, within this *New You* for whom facing that formerly fearful situation and responding with appropriate confidence is "no problem," turn around and look back toward the past ... Notice how this self-image has helped to bring you to this place. As you do, notice other steps and activities that have brought you here as well.

5) Now step out of this Future Confident You, and float back ... all the way back into your present day body ... but do so only as you bring with you the knowledge of the processes that will lead to this new you ... and letting the feeling of intensely wanting to be there again in that future self pull on you...

There's the Game set-up. The payoffs for playing this Game is that you'll keep sending your brain to *the You* that will empower you as you move out everyday. Use this *Swish Your Brain Game* to keep cuing your mind-body system about this much more resourceful You who can make new things happen in your life. Practice this *Swishing* a couple times a day, until it becomes an internal resource and your mind-body swishes to it automatically.

> And now as I see my more Ideal Self ... standing there... out in front of myself ... standing there with a stance of calm and confident courage, I notice that the image grows and as it comes closer and closer, it becomes increasingly vivid and compelling. ... so that feelings grow ... and I can now see the joyous and playful breathing of that Me, that Me for whom the situation of fear would be no problem. And as I listen, I can hear a voice, a tone of voice, that sounds confident and that speaks words of courage ...
>
> And I know that when I've refreshed this compelling image, I can let it shrink down to the size of a dot ... a dot that I can take with me for the rest of my life and let explode into a 40 by 40 screen whenever I need to get a fresh taste of the courageous me .."

The "It's Just an Emotion" Game

As an emotion, *fear* is our friend. Do you remember that from Chapter 3? Actually, for that matter, *all "negative" emotions are our friends.* They are friends, first and foremost, because they are *just* emotions. That is, just "signals" from the body. Whether they are accurate or not, whether they are appropriate or not, whether they ought to be listened to or not, those are different questions.

Only when we think that an emotion is somehow more than an emotion do we *misuse* our emotions and give them a power and level of meaning they cannot handle. If we esteem an emotion or emotional experience as "a reflection of who we are," an indication of what is real, a demand about something we have to do, as a call for automatic action, etc., we then begin to play some very strange and dangerous Games about our emotions.

Emotions are inside messages (signals) to ourselves about our maps, the world, or both. Generally, fear signals us that given our values, history, understandings and current experience it thinks that there might be some possibility of danger. It says, *"Stop, Look, and Listen!"* Check it out. It says that we may need to address or change either some habitual choice or belief that is no longer working, or take a different set of actions in the world.

Yet as message signals, a great many fears say nothing that has anything to do with today, with now. They are old programs about previous dangers. That makes them *projections* from previous situations and events. This is especially true for people who have taken far too much counsel from their fears.

When we know that an emotion is an emotion, then we can check it out. We can check out if it is accurate (many emotions are not), useful, or appropriate. To play *the "Emotions are but Emotions" Game* you need to know some things about emotions.

Primarily we need to realize that an emotion is *the relationship* between our experience of the world and our model of the world. Emotions *do not tell us anything* about what is real, appropriate, right, useful, or practical. If you have the idea that "emotions are real and you need to always act on them" as your *frame,* you'll play some screwball Games around emotions. (i.e., "Emotions are my Gods" Game.)

Emotions only tell us *the relationship* between what we have in our head as our map of reality and our experience of reality.

In that sense, an emotion operates like a set of balancing scales. On one side we have our *Map* of the World, on the other side we have our *Experience* of the World.

Imagine a scale that balances these two facets of *awareness*. On the one hand you have your *internal and personal understandings* about things. You have your internal *maps* about yourself, about your skills or lack of skills, about the world, about people, about your history, your future, about all kinds of ideas, beliefs, values, etc. That's your internal "Model of the World." You developed it from your experiences, learnings, schooling, relationships, etc. It operates as your map for navigating your way through life.

On the other hand you have your *experience of the world.* This is the world which encounters and impacts you. Thus, things happen. Events occur. You receive the impact, blows, and stimuli of the world. Such stimuli immediately impact your eyes, ears, skin, nose, and mouth. Your sense receptors "bring in" from "out there" your first level *experience* of things.

For example, if our *map* of the world is, "People should be nice and kind to me at all times," and in our *experience* of the world we work for fully fallible persons who experience their own emotional ups and downs, the scale will probably frequently tip the *experience* side of the scale downward. "Experience not living up to Map!" This will create inside us negative feelings of dissatisfaction and dislike: fear, anger, disgust, sadness, tension, frustration, etc. We keep finding the world as we don't want it to be!

The days when everybody seems to see things our way, talk to us in pleasant ways, supports our dreams and values, the scale will be pretty well balanced. The message will be, "Experience living up to Map." The days when everybody seems to be going out of their way to attend to our needs, the scale of experience tips up, "Experience is giving me much more than I had Mapped!" The positive emotions now rush in: joy, happiness, pleasure, delight, wonder, appreciation, love, warmth, care, etc.

Suppose you *experience* the event of driving down a road in town.

You experience sights, sounds, sensations, and smells. If you're color blind, hyper-sensitive to sounds, sleep-deprived, drunk, etc., your *experience* of the world will differ from what you would more "normally" experience.

Why? Because our experience of the world is governed by our nervous system, our neurology, and our learning history. It's not perfect. It's quite flawed. That's why we can suffer from visual illusions and delusions, we can mis-hear, mis-see, mis-feel, etc. As "eyewitnesses" we can be deceived, deluded, and tricked in many ways.

Our learning history affects our actual "perceiving" (seeing, hearing, feeling, etc.) in that we "learn" how to experience things. Here *ideas* play a key role in our neuro-linguistic experiencing. Suppose you believe a fear-based thought like:

> "Driving is extremely dangerous; you never know about the crazy drivers out there."

Or, suppose you believe an anger-based thought like:

> "What's wrong with these people; don't they know that the ten feet in front of my car is 'mine?'"

In this way, with either of these thoughts as our "Model of the World" it is more likely that the scale will tip downward so that our "Experience of the World" does not live up to our expectations. This will set off fear or anger. By contrast, if we believe:

> "The road is the road; driving is handling a vehicle and lots of people pay lots of attention and lots of people do not. The best thing is to drive with appropriate caution, stay alert and be prepared for poor drivers. If someone 'takes' my space, it's no big deal. I'll not build my life around it. If I see someone driving in a careless or aggressive way, I'll just note that and get out of the way. I have more important things in my life than letting 'other drivers' control my mood.

What a different program! That "Model of the World" *in relationship* to my "Experience of the World" will more likely generate feelings of contentment, calm reflection, etc.

Figure 9:1
The Balancing Scale
of "Emotions"

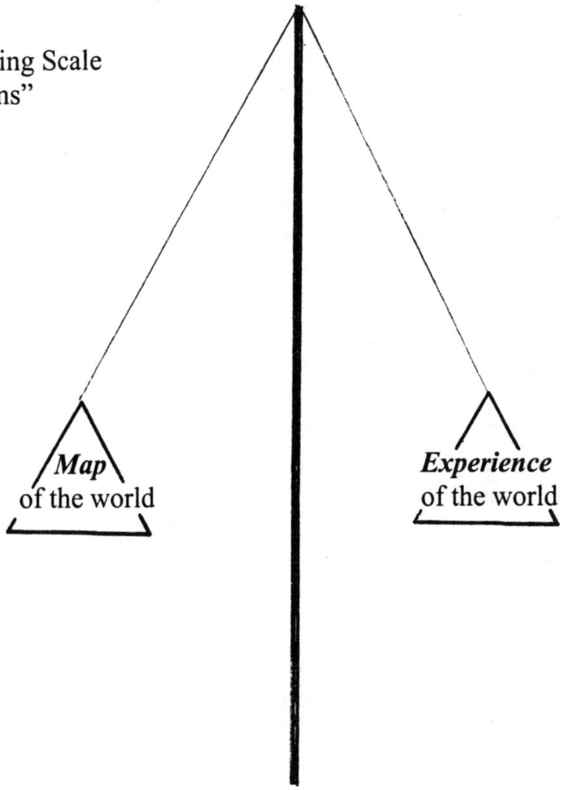

This enables us to understand what an emotion is. An "emotion" describes *the relationship* between "Model" and "Experience" of the world. As the scale tips in favor of your Model, then your mental mapping of things is being fulfilled, proved true, justified, etc. This feels *good* and so generates *positive emotions*: contentment, relaxation, joy, satisfaction, delight, feeling okay, ecstasy, etc. When the scale tips down and not in favor of our "Model of the World," our "Experience of the World" as it were, refutes our expectations, beliefs, values, understandings, etc. Our "Model of the World" feels violated, threatened, upset, etc. We feel *bad and so experience the negative emotions:* fear, dread, anger, stress, tension, frustration, upset, etc.

This explains why if we deal with an "emotion" directly, as an emotion, we misdirect our attention and efforts. All emotions make sense. As a gauge of *the relationship* between our Model and Experience of the World, emotions always provide us wonderful and accurate information.

> The driver who thinks that the space in front of his car is "his," appropriately feels anger when someone pulls in too close. Given his *frame of mind* and *frame of reference*, he has to feel angry. The driver who views the roads as extremely dangerous, needs to feel afraid. It's appropriate *given that frame of mind.*

But, change the frame, and the "emotion" changes. It's that simple; it's that profound; it's that magical.

We do not need to "face" the emotion and stare it down. That's the "hard" way to play the *Fear Mastery Games*. The easy and gentle way is to merely un-install that old program and install a new program. Then new emotions emerge.

This explains why we do not need the nonsense of "Being True to Our Emotions." Emotions *gauge relationship* between Map (our perception) and Territory (the external world). They are *not* things that we need to be "true" to. Stupid ideas in our mapping lead to stupid emotions. Being true to "stupid" ideas and/or stupid emotions is itself a stupid way to treat "information." That's what an "emotion" ultimately is, "information"—a message about the relationship between two experiences. It is an *evaluative **motion***. The **motion** you feel in your body comes from your evaluations.

To play the Healthy Fear Game, begin by welcoming your *fear* so that you can then explore both your *map* and your *experience.* Accepting our fear for what it is, a mental-emotional, neurological *signal* enables us to use it effectively. We can then backtrack the emotion to the thinking (valuing, believing, understanding, cognizing, etc.) out of which it came. And, knowing that *fearful emotions* always spring from *fearful thoughts* we know that that's what we're going to find. We have framed something in fear terms, in fear frames.

The question now becomes, is that accurate or useful? If so, then our *fear* appropriately alerts and warns us about a current or future threat. This gives us the alertness to then take effective action. If the fear thoughts are not accurate or useful, then we can change the form of the thoughts, we can challenge them, we can recognize them as just a map.

Embracing our emotions, even our "negative" emotions enables us to live more intelligently. Then we can discern between reasonable and unreasonable fears, appropriate and inappropriate fears. Reasonable and appropriate fears give us great information about how to respond more effectively as we move through the world. When we encounter bears, guns, snakes, quicksand, rapid rivers, drugs, cars, electrical wires, and a thousand other things in life, things that *could* threaten or endanger us, *fear* sets off the alarms, our Fight/Flight General Arousal system, and thereby enables us to protect ourselves. Yet even that fear must be appropriate so that we act with *awareness, appropriate caution, and intelligence.* As an emotion, fear simply refers to the somatic (bodily) energy that flows from recognizing a danger.

If fear is indeed *just* an emotion and arises as a "message" in our mind-body system letting us know about *a relationship,* then playing, *the "It's Just an Emotion" Game* enables us to make this critical distinction. You now know the Game set-up and its payoffs. It enables us to realize and recognize the relationship *between* these two crucial facts of our everyday experience:

1) Our Model of the World
2) Our Experience of the World

When a "fear" arises, check it out. What signal in your *experience* is cuing you? What does your *model* of the world say about that? Check it for accuracy, reality, usefulness, productivity, etc.

The De-Masquerading of Fear Game

The emotion that we label as "fear" often isn't fear at all, but some other emotion masquerading as fear. Fritz Perls of Gestalt Therapy used various gestalt processes to unmask the real emotion that put on a show of fear. He said that often times fear masquerades as "suppressed excitement." His key de-masking question in the Game was,

-    "What are you suppressing?"
-    "What are you squeezing off and not allowing to rise to the surface?"

So beginning with the old psychoanalytic idea of anxiety as "free floating fear," he challenged the *free floating* nature of this fear by trying to find the real object of the fear. Yet the object of the fear is not "out there" in the world. No. Rather, we're afraid of what the excitement might lead to. We're afraid of what it might *mean* for our future, identity, image before others, etc. That's why we suppress it, choke it off, and push down the excitement. We "strangle" it— which is what the original derivation of the term "anxiety" means (to choke).

When the excitement of an adventure, a chance, an opportunity, a risk, etc. arises, we push it down because we're afraid of ourselves, afraid that we can't make it, afraid of looking foolish, afraid of our sexuality, afraid of our physiology, afraid of multiple sets of meanings. So the so-called "free floating fear" transforms and starts masquerading as "anxiety."

Actually we have moved up a level in our mind and have developed a fear of an idea, a concept. Since we recognize that as a meta-state, we can play the Neuro-Semantic Game of De-Masking the Fear. We know that the person has confused levels and is perhaps looping around the levels.

To play the De-Masking Game
Step 1: Repeatedly ask the reference question
> What is this feeling *about?* You are feeling what about this trigger?
> And when you feel that, what do you feel about that?

Step 2: Separate the levels
> So when you think about approaching her (him, the boss, etc.), you think about being embarrassed, not knowing what to say, making a fool of yourself, and let's run with that, suppose you did. Imagine worse case scenario— what then? What would you then feel?
> And when you feel that, so what? Where does your mind then go?

Step 3: Invite a resourceful way to think and feel
> Now that we have sorted out what you're responding to at each level: first to "the girl" (primary level), then to "the thought of

embarrassment," then to "the thought of foolishness and blowing your chance," then to "the idea that you're inadequate," what do you think about this game?

Does it make your life a party? Does it enhance your life? Do you need this?

What resources do you need to bring to these levels of thoughts? (i.e., confidence, courage, calmness, clarity, etc.)

Play *The Frame Games* Game

Throughout this work we have been detecting and recognizing *our relationship* to fear as both an emotion and as a concept. We do this to flush out the *Frame Games*. That allows us to play *the Mindfulness Game* so that we can choose the Frame Games that we would prefer to play. Once we have identified the frames or the Games, you will be able to backtrack to the "programs" or mental software that we run in our head that sets up the frame game.

In detailing these Games, we have been using the richness and elegance of NLP and Neuro-Semantics to take charge of "running our own brains" and managing the higher levels of our mind. Since we didn't come with a *User's Manual for the Brain* on how to relate to and effectively master fear— we have been making use of these state-of-the-art models.

The good news about our Games is that whatever *relationship* we have developed in regard to fear, we *learned* it. And if we learned it, we can unlearn it. Typically, we unlearn old Games by learning much more effective Frame Games. Our way of relating to fear has developed from how we have mapped our experiences and understandings. That's why we have repeatedly said:

"It's just a map; it's not real; it's not the territory."

This is crucial. Yes, fear (as any emotion) feels "real" in our mind and body. In fact, that is precisely what we mean by our mind-body states, or as we shall call them, our "neuro-linguistic" states. Once we create the mental software in our head *about* something, it becomes our way of thinking-and-feeling about that thing. It's our map. And whatever we *map* inside our head will govern our body and emotions. So "inside," i.e., inside our neurology, it feels very "real," and it is real at that level. Yet that "reality" is only as real as we believe it to be. As meaning makers, we create that level of reality. If we want to make it more real to ourselves, we only need to believe more. If we want to make it less real to ourselves, we can disbelieve, question, doubt it, or reframe it. Ultimately, *internal "reality" is map governed.*

As this becomes clearer, this is *our ticket for taking full control over our mind-body states.* If we think or believe (a map itself!) that the outside world "makes" us think and feel as we do, we thereby give up our personal power, choice, freedom, responsibility, and personal resourcefulness. Then we will never learn how to run our own brain. If we play that Game we will never become *Bold and Courageous Fear Masters.*

Ultimately, our experience with fear is just a Game ... and it flows from, and makes sense by, the frames that we have in our head. That's the good news because it invites us to journey into the domain of truly mastering our fears.

Summary

- To master our fears we have to get leverage. Getting leverage means mostly quality controlling our current fears in terms of value, usefulness, empowerment, enhancement, etc.
- Leveraging also involves using the primal powers of confirming (Yes-ing) and negating (No-ing) to reject toxic games and lock in the empowering ones.
- We can also leverage fear games by playing the "It's Just an Emotion" Game with it, the "De-Masking" Game, and the *"It's Just a Map" Frame Game* Game.

THE ULTIMATE GAME IS THE GAME OF RUNNING YOUR OWN BRAIN

- Games *play* us unless or until we take charge of our own Frames. Others can mercilessly control and recruit us if we don't know how to run the thoughts and framing powers of our own brain.

- Yet, once we learn the secrets of personal mastery that gives us control in running our own brain– we become Frame Game Masters.

- Simple as they may seem, the personal powers which enable us to say "Yes!" and "No!" lie at the very heart of personal mastery.

- Take no Frame for granted. All frames are psycho-logically loaded ... semantically loaded. They create the heavens and hells that we experience in our minds, emotions, bodies, and relationships.

PART III

MASTERING GAMES

FOR

TRANSFORMING

FEARS

Chapter 10

GAMES FOR PRODUCING NEW & BETTER MOVIES

Games in This Chapter
The Stepping Out & In Game
The "Anchoring" Game
The >Insert> Resources Game
"Sticking Great Scenes into Terrifying Movies" Game

The Fear Mastering Games begin as we learn how to effectively run the cinematic features of our movies. That's because we create, produce, and play all of our foundational Fear Games by running scary movies in our heads. It's just the way our "thinking," imagining, anticipating, remembering, etc. works. We make movies in our heads. We then *step into* those movies and if the movies are Horror Movies, we signal our entire mind-body system to go into fear.

It is now time for us to look at the ways we code such information and how we can deal with fear in terms of our mental encoding of terrifying scenes, pictures, sounds, words, etc. Later, we will deal with meta-fears, fears at higher levels and fears that involve semantic states, but here we start with some absolutely fabulous patterns for completely eliminating debilitating and needless fears. The *Frame Games* in this chapter have been adapted from basic NLP and NS patterns that you can find in *Users Manual* (1999) and *The Sourcebook of Magic* (1998).

The *Stepping Out & Stepping In* Game

Nearly twenty-five years ago the developers of NLP stumbled upon the "Phobia Cure" pattern. Since then thousands upon tens-of-thousands have found almost instantaneous relief from frightening images that recruit them into Fear and Panic Games. Pretty amazing, eh? You can read the straight version in *Using Your Brain For A Change* (1985).

But be careful, since we develop our personality from how we map our experiences and memories, when we shift to this new Game of bold passion, we also develop a more positive identity, one of courage.

> What would it be like for you to *no longer take counsel of your fears?*

> What if you took counsel of your hopes and dreams, your reality testing skills, your intelligence and passions?

In terms of human "processing" of information, we can so design our internal movies so that we are *in* them as the chief actor, and we can design them so that we can be *out* of them, as an observer, editor, or producer on the set. When we create our movies and *step into them*, we associate into the thoughts, body sensations, and perceptions *as if we were fully there*. What a ride!

This gives us the *Stepping Into Game* or the Associating Game. Associating into memories signals all of our brain-body parts to fully re-experience the emotions that went along with the memory. The Game Plan is simple: associate into the Fearful Movie of Personal Horror and Dislike, and you get to fill your body full of fear, anxiety, and terror. You get to go to the movies and don't have to pay an entrance fee. But you will have to pay an exit fee, you will pay it in terms of loss of health and vitality in your mind, emotions, and body.

But you can't play the *Stepping Into Game* without simultaneously and inevitably playing the *Stepping Out of Game*. They go hand in hand. You step into painful memories, you step out of calm resourcefulness. You step into joy and laughter, you step out of depression and being a sourpuss. This is a two-step game: step in and step out. Content is not included; you supply that.

When you step out from a painful memory, you play the Game that psychiatrists like to call "Dissociation." They think it's bad. They have even listed it in the DSM-IV as a "personality disorder." They assume that when you step out, you have to *forever stay out of all emotions*. Foolish doctors.

Dissociating or stepping out from an ugly memory enables us to not signal, not cue, and therefore not process all of the body sensations with the corresponding emotions of the memory. We can see and hear the information while maintaining a calm, mindful, resourceful perspective. And that, in a nutshell, is the structure of the Phobia Resolution Game. It operates from the radical idea that if we access our best resources when we deal with the information we'll "think" about horrible things without confusing our thoughts with reality. We can *just think*. We can think from a state of resourcefulness–with courage, confidence, esteem, calmness, etc.

When you play the *Step Out of the Pain and Into Your Best Resources Game*, you utilize both the power of dissociation (from the threat and danger states) and the power of association (into calmness, recognition of reality, distinguishing past/ present, etc.). Using this Game of Phobia Resolution permits us to erase the negative emotional impact of memories that we no longer need. This frees our mental and emotional energy so that it doesn't have to keep working over "unfinished business." We finish with it, shake our hands of it, and get on with life.

Once you learn this *Stepping Out/In Game*, you will be able to play it all by yourself. But before you become that masterful with it, you will need someone to play with you the first dozen times. Get a coach or friend and have at it. With that in mind, I have written the following as instructions as you coach someone else through the process. To do this with yourself– just be the person and experience the processes.

How to Play the Stepping Out/In Game
To Resolve Traumas and Negative Semantic States

Step 1: Access a Solidly Resourceful State

Are you ready to play this Game? Readiness to play means that you are in a calm, relaxed, and clear-headed state. It means that you are able to engage in problem-solving, that you feel motivated and centered. To elicit this in another person, ask the following questions:

When are you at your best?

Imagine being there fully and completely right now.

What is that like? Just notice on the inside... How do you know you are in a motivated, centered, focused, mindful state?

What is your breathing like, posture, facial expression, tone of voice...

When you've elicited a most resourceful state in the person that you will coach through this Game, put your hand on the person's forearm, "And you can *feel* all of these good feelings, can't you?   Yes... so *feel* it fully. ...

We play the "Running Your Own Brain" Games from our *best states*, being as fully resourceful as possible. So we start here and "anchor" the feelings of resourcefulness by linking them to a new trigger (see the next pattern on "anchoring"). Later, if the person wants to jump back into an old "Shitty" State, we can fire off this anchor to interrupt and bring him or her back to this. Sneaky, huh? Well, not really, it is just part of the game plan.

Another part of the Game Plan for coaching resourcefulness is to totally interrupt a state if the person forgets about Mastering the Fear and tries to play the central actor in the Horror Movie again. If that happens, call a "Time-Out."

Okay, stand up! Look up there ... is that Halley's Comet?

Begin singing "Oh, What a Beautiful Morning..."

Ask him if he has his pants zipped up.

There's nothing like interrupting someone's state.   You can have them walk around, march, do martial arts, stand on their head, just about anything.

Step 2: Set some Awesome Pre-Frames for the Game

You could invite amazement at the mind's ability to learn something one time and remember it a lifetime.

You know, a phobia is a form of accelerated learning! Think about it. Someone or something scares the hell out of you, and you link it to a tone, voice, word, object, event, etc. and then you *never forget* to freak out when you think about that trigger! Amazing, don't you think? Now that's accelerated learning.

One time, pow! You've got it. And you never forget it! How amazing that you *always* remember to feel afraid or hurt when you think of that event! I can't even remember to take out the garbage. You remember to always feel phobic and to fill your body with anxiety every single time. Incredible. How do you do it?

You could create some "response potential" by seeding the idea of inevitable and inescapable change.

Now what we're going to do in just a minute is to change this old fear so that you will never have it in this way again. Is that okay with you? ... Really? When you walk out of here, you won't have it. And it might even surprise you. I want to ask you a really serious question,

- Who will you be without this fear response?
- How will this transform your everyday life?
- How will it make a difference tomorrow?'"

Step 3: Set up the Observer Movie Metaphor

We play this Mind-Game by imagining a movie screen.

I want you to imagine a movie theater, perhaps one that you really like, and just imagine sitting down in the tenth row and seeing the white movie screen. Feel and smell your bag of popcorn. Enjoy the comfortable chair as you notice the sticky floor.

Got it?

On this screen, put a black and white photograph of yourself, a still-shot of yourself just before the traumatic memory occurred. Do you see that Younger You? Do you see what he or she was wearing? The place where it happened?

Step 4: The Second Step Out

Without making it explicit, we have already framed one *step out* from the old movie. That was kind of sneaky, now we will do it more explicitly.

As you see that black and white snapshot of yourself on the screen, imagine how it feels to *float out of your body* there in the tenth row and *float back and up* to the projection booth. Float all the way back... until you can see the back of your present day self watching the snapshot on the screen.

Enjoy the feeling of putting your hands on the plexiglass separating you from the self-observing you in the tenth row watching the even Younger You on the screen knowing that we're planning for a transformation.

As you play this game, use your hands to gesture at these locations, and to pantomime the feeling of being behind a protective plexiglass. And you can feel really safe back here because this is the editing room, here you can edit your films to make them more sane and healthy.

Step 5: Run the Movie to the end

When you're ready, I want you to let the snapshot become a black-and-white movie which you'll play to the end... Let it run as you watch it from here in the projection booth through the traumatic events, just observing, just watching, feeling safe and comfortable as the movie plays out the scenes and let it play all the way to the end of the event and then a little beyond to some scene of comfort. ... Go...

And if at any time you feel a pull to step into the movie, feel the plexiglass and know that you can just watch in the safety and protection of this editing room because the movie is about a Younger You in another time and place and you are safe here today.

If at any time you need to have the movie move more quickly through scenes, do so... you are just observing the events as an onlooker... When the trauma is over... go to a scene where you're okay, things are fine. You're enjoying a hot bath or shower, a vacation, a party, reading a book, something of comfort and pleasure.

Step 6: Stop, Intermission Time

After the person has come to the scene of comfort, freeze frame that event and stop for a moment.

Good. You got through it... for the last time. In just a moment we're going to do something really weird. The explanation will come later, for now just listen to the instructions about what to do. When you have a clear sense of the game we're going to play in your head, then it will be time to do it.

In just a minute, I want you to *Step Into the Comfort Scene* at the end of the movie... be there, fully and completely, seeing, hearing, feeling, smelling, tasting through your own eyes, ears, and skin— all of the comfort and pleasure. Make it in living color. Then, when you're ready, *while inside the movie*— I want you to push the Fast ReWind Button and let it zoom to the beginning in super fast rewind so that it takes all of one or two seconds. Zoom. And you're *inside the comfort* when this happens ... so that everything goes backwards, including you... Zooming for the beginning black-and-white snapshot.

Ready? Go! ... and zooooommmm!

Step 7: Hit Me One More Time, Charlie!

Coach the person to repeat the process five to eight more times. It is very important to make sure that the person interrupts the state at the end (at the beginning snapshot), clears the screen, and begins by *stepping into the comfort scene* at the end and then quickly rewinds.

How did you like that? Open your eyes. It's over. Good.

Hey, let's do that again. *Step into the Comfort scene* again... yes, it's such a bother! But humor me. Okay, are you fully there? Ready for the Super Fast Rewind? Zooooommm.

Step 8: Test for Game Results

After 5 to 8 runs, test to see if the person *can* access the phobic state.

Okay, now let's test things. I want you to try really hard, as hard as you can to see if you can get the phobia feelings back. See if you can get the old phobia to get you to freak out as you did earlier.

No? Not as much. Well try harder.

No? Well, imagine the next time something may trigger it as it has in the past. Try to see if that will get it back.

Additional Moves when Playing
The Stepping Out/ In Game

Now that you know the basic set-up of the Game that blows phobias to smithereens, there's certain other fancy footwork moves that you can add to spice up the fun.

After *Step Four* when you've floated back and up to the projection booth, and before you play the old movie to the end and rewind from inside, you can do numerous other things as Game moves.

1) Step into a resourceful memory. Recall a time when you felt really creative, confident, courageous, powerful, etc. See what you saw at that time and step into it so fully that the brightness increases and you begin to glow there in the Projection Booth!   When into it fully, step with all of that right onto the screen and into the scene of the negative stimulus that you fear or into the traumatic memory. As you associate back into the movie resourcefully, notice how the resourceful state sets the frame for the old memory and watch closely as it transforms the old memories giving that Younger You all the resources you needed to have handled that situation.

2) Juice up your sound track. From the Projection Booth, step behind the machinery and computers and re-process your voice and all of the other sounds that make up the sound track of the old movie. Juice it up so that your voice becomes strong, powerful, firm, courageous... give it the qualities that will make the difference. Add a laugh track, circus music, Donald Ducks' voice to the scary persons. Do whatever you need to do so that the way others sound become funny, silly, ridiculous, weak, and the way you sound becomes the dominating sound.

3) Access and apply a spiritual faith. Perhaps the resource you need is a belief in God, in angels, in an intelligent universe, whatever. So, if you believe in a loving heavenly Father, then split your screen and see through the eye of your faith your Guardian Angel hovering over the earthly scene of your memory. See and hear your Angel caring and loving you. Perhaps you hear, "I am with you." "I will help you." See Jesus touch you with his healing hand.

4) Recode the old movie symbolically. For instance, you might want to make the people in your memory transparent. Or color them according to how you think-and-feel about them: black, white, golden, blue, green, etc.. Draw a line around the people to make them more cartoon-like, make one your Charlie Brown, Lucy, or Snoopy, etc.

5) Add silly and humorous things to the movie. Since laughter improves the quality of life, games, mind, etc., and gives us a sense of distance from hurt, use your humor so that you can laugh. Often we say that one day we'll look back on this and laugh. Why wait? Why not do that now? Play that Game. Zoom out into your future far enough so that you can look back and laugh.

So How Does the Stepping In & Out Game Work?

That the Game works to create new mental and emotional states and responses is plenty for most people. *That* the Game reduces the emotional impact of old traumatic events and frees us for a new life, for new responses suffices for many. If that's true for you and you don't even want to look at the neuro-semantic explanations for *why* it works, then skip this section and go to *The Anchoring Game.* If you'd like to know why, then stick around.

Neurologically, *how* we encode information governs what the levels of our brain and mind do with the information. And, if we *encode* a memory or an imagination so that it fits all of the semantic frameworks for "Real, Now, Immediate, Threatening, Dangerous, About Me," etc. (whatever the content is)– so we experience it.

This means that *the way we encode things* makes all the difference in the world in terms of our emotions, skills, abilities, perceptions, etc. It means that *the world of meaning that we live in* is created through our encoding. And that means that when we change the code, we change the experience. It is as simple as that, it is as complicated as that.

The *Stepping In and Out Game* enables us to re-code an old fearful or traumatic memory so that our body gets the message, "Not Now, No Longer Real, Past and Not Present, Non-Threatening, Not-Dangerous, Not about the Real Me," etc. The Game sets up many, many frames for the fearful content that forbids and prevents us from stepping in because it recruits us to keep *Stepping Out* of the fear and *Into Resourcefulness.*

What are these frames? Among them are frames that send the following messages to our neurology:

- Just Observing and not Participating
- Watching with Dispassionate Interest
- Watching at a Distance
- Watching from my more Resourceful Self in Today
- Watching as if an Editor of the Old Movies
- Taking control of my watching ... watching it as a black and white snapshot, and an old movie, as a movie I can forward to a Scene of Comfort and Pleasure
- Taking control of the old Movie by Rewinding it from the Inside
- Rewinding it and washing Comfort and Pleasure backwards into it
- Taking control by teaching my brain to go from Fear and Trauma to Comfort and Rewind

With all of those messages setting the frame for *how to think and feel* about things, is it any wonder that it completely reformulates the old fear?

The *"Anchoring"* Game

Linking things together, or "anchoring," provides a very powerful neuro-linguistic tool for managing states. We mentioned this in Chapter 10 in the Game for Swishing the Brain. Now we want to turn the anchoring process itself into a Game. This basic NLP pattern provides a way to take a very proactive stance toward the emotional states you experience in life.

As a user-friendly version of Pavlovian conditioning, *anchoring* allows us to take emotional states, thoughts, memories, imaginations, and even skills and set up new kinds of *associations* between these experiences.

Pavlov discovered this when working with his laboratory dogs. He observed their unconditioned response to meat powder which activated their saliva glands. To this response, he attached the trigger of a bell. He rang the bell when their neurology was salivating to the meat. Later, when he rang the bell, the dogs salivated. The *bell* got connected to the state of eating. He found that he could *condition* them to salivate to the sound of a bell. Today we talk about "ringing someone's bell."

That's the Game set-up. All we have to do is associate one state of mind-emotion-physiology to some stimuli. If we do, we can *condition* our neurology to *respond* to the trigger with a more empowering state. If it can happen to a simple dog mind, it can happen to you!

By the way, this description gives us a neuro-linguistic understanding of how we get fear states connected to all kinds of non-dangerous situations in the first place. Access state of fear, ring some bell (connect some other trigger) and presto ... thereafter the new trigger can do it alone.

At one level *meaning* means "connection, association, and linkage." What does something "mean" to you? What does criticism, small spaces, embarrassment, risk, etc. *mean* to you? It depends on what you have *connected* to those words or referents.

Once you create the linkage, it *anchors* the experience to that state. We use the term "anchor" because that's where you have cast your mental-emotional and neurological anchor and it holds the structure in place. Let some time and repetition and habituation pass and then the "meaning" becomes not only your frame of reference, but your frame of mind. You frame everything in terms of that association. That's the rule of this Game which makes it powerfully destructive and/or empowering. It all depends upon *what* you have anchored.

Once set, anchors *trigger states*. Fire the trigger, and the experience (the emotional state) comes back. We can anchor in every sensory system as well as in the language system. The key factors in playing this game are:

- Intensity: Anchor at the peak of an experience so you have lots of neurological energy for the association.
- Purity: Make the anchor distinct, discrete, and specific so that the association is clear and distinct and not easily confused with something else.
- Uniqueness: Make the anchor unusual, precise, distinct, and replicable.

How do we play this anchoring Game?

1) First, design your desired behavioral response. What state of mind, emotion, and body do you want to reproduce at the snap of a finger? Confidence, courage, calmness, mindfulness, stepping back to check ecology, strength, assertiveness, etc. What Game do you want to play when some fearful object comes into view? What language game, behavioral game, interpersonal response, etc. do you want to produce?

What cue would you like to use as your trigger for this state?   It could be a word, internal image, external image, sound, music, smell, touch, etc. You could use a gesture of your hand, a particular smile, the rolling of someone's eyes, memory of Donald Duck's voice, etc.

2) Catch or elicit the desired response. You can either wait until you naturally go into the resourceful state or you can call it forth intentionally. Whenever you catch yourself in the resourceful state, link or anchor it to a new stimulus. Give yourself permission to really *"feel this"* (the resourceful state) while you link it to the gesture, word, picture, smell, etc.

If you want help with this (and it's always good to have someone else anchor you when you first play this neurological Game), have someone set the anchor when you go into state, whether you go there naturally or whether you recall it fully and re-experience by your memory or imagination. As you go back in your mind to a time when you felt that resource, remember it fully ... and at the peak of the experience, link *that* with some new stimulus.

If you are working with someone to set the anchor, add a visual (make a face or gesture), sound (unique tonality, way of saying something, sound effect), sensation (touch), body posture, or word. Use *unique* triggers when you anchor and use all of the sensory systems to create redundancy.

3) Use the new stimulus and connect to the target situation. Practice "firing" the anchor to see how well it brings the state back. Think about something neutral, how many light bulbs in your living room ... and fire the anchor. What happens?   It is set when the anchor brings back the thoughts, memories, images, feelings, etc.   Keep refreshing the anchor over several days until it becomes automatic and unthinking. It will.

Now think about the target situation where you want lots of that resource (confidence, calmness, courage, etc.) and as you think about that—fire the anchor. Tell yourself, "And I can *feel this* whenever I think about *that...* " Then enjoy the feeling. Repeat until you're pleased with the speed and quality of the anchoring.

If you are anchoring someone and have set the anchor, invite that person to think about the fearful object and just as soon as they do fire the anchor and say, "and you can *feel this...* about that."

4) Test. Interrupt the resource state, think about something else, and then re-trigger the stimulus. Does the response come back? Is it strong enough?

Have you ever faced a fear in a courageous way and just did something that worked out wonderfully and you felt proud of yourself? Recall that until you are there again. If not, then imagine what that would be like. As your body feels that courage, repeat the word "courage" in a way that sounds strong, firm, and confident. Repeat the word calmly and slowly so that with every repetition of your breathing, you feel yourself becoming even more courageous in just the right way now... And let it reverberate in the echo chambers of your mind.

The *>Insert> Resources* Game

Here's another Game to play that will transform fears and create a sense of mastery. It's more advanced than the previous Games. It's a Game where you stop the mental movies in your mind, the ones that scare the hell out of you, splice in a powerful resource, then start the movie up again and notice how the inserted resource transforms the old movie.

The Game Set Up

There's a funny thing about the way we *think*. Namely, we think mostly by making movies inside our heads. We don't do this in any real or literal way, it's just a *seeming* sense (something philosophers call phenomenological). And that's precisely the point. As we think about fifth grade, Washington crossing the Delaware in 1776, Robin Hood in England, the Romans and Greeks of the first century, our heads seem to be running movies– movies full of sounds, smells, sensations, and things. As a species, we are inveterate *movie-makers*. We think by recalling and re-presenting inside of our "minds" various scenarios so that it seems like we are seeing, hearing, feeling, smelling, and tasting things again.

Obviously, we don't do this *literally*. I say *obviously*, yet I realize that it's not so *obvious* to some people. Apparently some people, not yet fully informed by modern brain research and the neuro-sciences, don't know that we do not actually have little movies or pictures, or sounds or sensations or tastes or smells occurring *in our brains*. It only *seems* like we have these internal movies running in our minds. It only seems like we are having those sensory experiences. And yet our bodies don't know this. Typically they respond to the movies in our mind as if they are real. So, in the final analysis, all we have *up there* is an exchange of neuro-transmitters, peptides, the exchange of ions and positive and negative charges at the molecular level of neurological activity, the activation of cell assemblages, and other bio-electro-chemical processes. When that happens, our bodies move and feel.

So what *actually exists* up there and what we *sense* represent two different levels. Our *sense level* provides us our *conscious* way of *representing* things. This refers to our *mapping* about things. We *map* it so that it seems like and feels like a reproduction of our sense experiences. If you have studied philosophy, you will recognize this as *phenomenology*. What we actually have to do with, consciously, involves the *phenomena* that we *experience*, that seemingness of our representations.

Regardless of what we call it, we all experience our *thoughts* as the internal *re-presenting* to ourselves of what we have seen, heard, smelled, felt, and tasted *on the outside*. As noted before we describe such thinking as our *sensory representational systems* (the VAK). Now the good thing about all of this is that by thinking about our *thinking as internal movies* and as a way we *encode* our understanding this gives us a new Game for *taking charge* of our brains to transform our everyday fears.

The Rules of this Game

What happens when we pause a movie so that it stops? Rent a movie and try it on your television set sometime. When you stop your movie, it holds a frame still and all you see is a snapshot. The same thing happens when you take an internal film of a fear or anything else, and stop it. It turns that movie into a mere *snapshot* of your thoughts. Try it. Imagine something fearful and freeze frame it.

What happens?

In *stopping the movie* you create the effect of solidifying your pictures. As you engage in this freeze-framing, your mental thoughts or images become more static... more solid, more two-dimensional, do they not? When you do that, then what happens? Do you not then respond to them as if they were more static and dead, less alive and dynamic?

Great. Now you know one of the rules for how we're going to play this game. Since all of our mental constructions are just that, *mental constructions*, internal mappings, we can stop them, turn them down, white them out, etc.

Here's something else you can do in your head when you don't have anything better to do. Since you stopped the movie, freeze-framed the slides, you can now visualize the space between one frame on the screen of your mind and the next image as individual snapshots. Whether the movie was moving at a clip of 32 images a second or 64 images, as you slow them down and then stop them, you can pry open a space between a couple of the frames.

How easily can you stop a fearful movie and allow yourself to become aware of *the space between* the frames? Play with this for a bit. Speed your movie up, then slow it down. Speed it up, slow it down. Now stop it. Dead in its tracks. Frozen. Static. Now move apart two of the frames where the movie is the scariest. Send your awareness to *this space* between the frames, to the ... *Void* of the nothingness in between the frames. Got it? Great.

Now in that *pause* ... inside that pregnant pause embedded inside the frozen frames when you stopped, in your mind, with the knowledge of the previous picture ... and of the upcoming picture, now *in that void* where you now have a place into which you can stick in an entirely new image... in that space, what image could you put into that void that would thereby *totally transform everything* in the movie? What would make it an entirely new and different movie? What would empower the characters of the movie (mainly you) to experience a new and enhancing ending of the movie? I wonder just what would *you* like to stick in there? And what would someone else like to stick in there?

So, in that *Void of the Pause* ... we could actually embed all kinds of things... then later, when we rewind the picture a bit, and then let it go forward as our pictures normally do, then all of a sudden a whole New Image, and even an entirely New World, could magically pop into existence.

The "Sticking Great Scenes into Your Terrifying Movies" Game

This Game involves *stepping back and out of* an internal movie, stopping the movie dead in its tracks, and then, from a higher level, *bringing some resource* (coded as a part of the movie) to bear upon the original movie.

To play with how this language pattern works in stopping a movie we invited some people to experiment with it. They ran an internal mental movie, and then they stopped it abruptly. They did this just to see what would happen. For some this *minimized* the negative feelings connected to the internal memory.

When one person stopped the movie, all of the frames that occurred before the place where he stopped it simply collapsed. It was kind of like a train wreck. All of his frames crashed into the void. However, to our amazement, he could still get the old unpleasant movie to run. That led me to try some additional framing (or meta-stating) processes so he could completely blow out that movie.

Once someone knows how to abruptly stop a movie, I invite him or her to insert a spiritual resource like a representation of Love, Oneness, Being, God, Jesus, etc., into the stop. Once inserted into the movie, the person then lets the movie play out to the end. The rules of the Game are simple: first identify and feel the spiritual resource. When you get to the scenes of fear, insert the Resource Clip, then re-run the entire movie from the beginning with the Insert inside it. Playing this >Resource Insert> Game has made a lot of difference for every one who has taken the time to play this Game.

How the Game Works

If you're into explanations and like to read the technical and theoretical foundations for how a process works, read this section. If such doesn't interest you, skip this section and go to the next section, "People Who Have Played The Game."

As an engineer, Alfred Korzybski studied the structure of human experiences. He compared the *structure* of our primary states, which are so full of emotions and energy ("first-order abstractions") with our higher or meta-states ("second-order abstractions") which seem so much more stable. He used the analogy of *watching a movie.* In watching a film, we can focus on *experiencing* its drama and movement or we can focus on stopping the movie and gaining understanding of its *structure, form,* and *nature.* Content and Structure. Lower experience and higher experience.

When our internal pictures operate as a dynamic and ever-shifting *movie,* he wrote that—

> "... our 'emotions' are aroused, we 'live through' the drama; but the details... are blurred. ... The picture was 'moving,' all was changing, shifting, dynamic, similar to the world *and* our feelings on the unspeakable levels. The impressions were vague, shifting, non-lasting, and what was left of it was mostly coloured by the individual mood...
>
> "But if we *stop* the moving film ... and analyse the static and extensional series of small pictures on the reel, we find that the drama which so stirred our 'emotions' in its moving aspect becomes a series of slightly different static pictures, each difference between the given jerk or grimace being a *measurable* entity...
>
> "The *moving* picture represents the usually brief processes going on in the lower nerve centres, 'close to life', but unreliable and evading scrutiny. The *arrested* static film which lasts indefinitely, giving *measurable* differences ... allows analysis and gives a good analogy of the working of higher nerve centres, disclosing that all life occurrences have many aspects... The moving picture gives us the process; each static film of the reel gives us stages of the process in chosen intervals."
>
> (*Science and Sanity*, p. 292, British spelling)

In this passage Korzybski, commenting on the nature of our *internal abstractions,* separated and sorted two kinds. He noted how they correspond to two levels of brain processing. The ever shifting nature of the lower levels (thalamic processing) and the more static nature of the higher levels (cortical processing) corresponds to our primary level states and our meta-states.

> "The thalamic regions ...are a vestibule through which all impulses from the receptors have to pass in order to reach the cortex" (p. 290)

Here the *dynamic* and shifting nature of data creates in our experience the highly affective nature of "thoughts," namely *emotions and somatic responses.*

> "The cortex receives its materials as elaborated by the thalamus. The abstractions of the cortex are abstractions from abstractions and so ought to be called abstractions of higher order. ... The receptors are in direct contact with the outside world and convey their excitation and nerve currents to the lower nerve centers…" (p. 290)

The *thalamic* thinking at the lower level needs to be "re-educated" by the "development of poise, balance, and a proportional increase of critical judgment and so 'intelligence'" from the higher levels. These higher-level abstractions "have *lost* their *shifting* character" and "are further removed from the outside world." (p. 291)

Korzybski noted that the lower level of brain processing, the thalamic processes, corresponds to the quickness, fluctuations and movement of data. This leads to more emotionality, reactivity, and inability to control "thoughts." He said that when we send this thalamic material up to the higher levels of brain processing, we abstract one or more levels from it and can slow down our images and develop greater control over them. This makes our pictures more solid and real.

From an engineering point of view, he wrote about translating static data to dynamic data and vice versa. In this way a person develops choice and control over running his or her own brain. What does all of this have to do with the *"Inserting Resources" Game?* Everything. In that Game we tap into the power and usefulness of both dynamic and static images. We begin with the dynamic flow of "thoughts" —stop the internal movie, insert a new awareness, and then put it back into a dynamic form which will then reactivate new, different, and more resourceful emotions.

People Who Have Played the Game

Several years ago, the father of a young lady, Alethia, shot himself and ended his life. At the time of the shooting, Alethia was in the house and saw her father's body immediately after the shooting. Her memory of this traumatic event gave her the content to play a Game in her mind-emotions for years which created a variety of problems for her. She kept running this old movie in her mind, using it to torture herself and making herself feel really terrible.

When she learned about the *Insert Resource Game,* she started up the movie, ran it a bit, and then stopped it midway into the horror. She then picked out a resource that she thought would change everything (an image of Jesus). After inserting that frame into the other frames, she ran the movie again. This time it felt different, she said that she had "a knowing that my spiritual resource was there all the time."

Upon finishing the first running of the old movie in her mind, she ran the entire movie another time, now with a conscious awareness of seeing *this new image pop in* just at the point where those images really assisted her. Alethia reported that by becoming consciously aware of this presence, it allowed her to see her deceased father being ushered into heaven. She later reported that this procedure removed "much of the negative emotions that had been associated with the memory."

"Sticking God into Your Movies"

David engaged in an incident during his teenage years that has bothered him ever since. As an adult he continues to run a very clear movie of a confrontation between himself and his parents that puts him in some pretty unresourceful states. When we found out, we asked him to run the movie of himself and his parents and the discussion.

Like the others, he stepped back, began the movie and then stopped it midway, inserted a new resource and then let the movie play to the end. It was a great Game move. The procedure immediately lowered his negative emotions. He then went back and ran the movie from the beginning to the end to put it all together as one piece. As he did, he saw himself, his father, and his awareness of a divine presence in the context of the confrontation.

"Wow. While the content has stayed the same, I see God as 'meta' to us all. And the anxiety that I have always felt is gone. This works great. It's like I have a sense of my spiritual values right in there when I really need to have that awareness."

Updating the Old Movies

Calion chose a really bad scene to test this Game. Though divorced, Calion had endured a horrific marriage with a terribly abusive man. Her memory involved recalling him wanting her to go with him somewhere, but she refused. As she went into the house, he followed and physically assaulted her by severely beating her in the face.

When Clarion described the movie before playing the "Insert Resource" Game, it was clear that she was playing another Game, "Step right into the old Crap and feel all the horrible emotions all over again." She had learned to play that Game in therapy with a therapist of the "Emotional Game" School, "Relive the Bad Times!" They believe you have to keep going through the crap until you get used to it, finish the business, and then your emotional reactions settle down. That's the Game they try to play with every client. That so-called Therapy Game doesn't carry any appeal for us. We'd rather get people *out* of the pain and *into new frames of mind* that will transform their lives.

In questioning her, she mentioned a strange thing. She described the scene of the worst abuse with a "click," "click," and "click" sound. Later we found out this indicated that she was focusing in on each frame as the movie played. Describing it in this way, it seemed that slowing down the frames was making things more real and solid for her. I immediately told her to stop *slowing* the movie down, and *stop it completely.* Freeze frame it!

Funny how we can take a Game designed for transformation and vitality and turn it into something to feel bad about. And yet most of us can do that. We can play the "How Can I Turn this Game into Shit?" Game about other Games. So be careful with your *attitude.* The power of the transformative Games not only lie in the structure and process, but also your intentionality as you play the Games.

As you play out your thoughts about fear and phobias, step back from time to time to notice the Games you're playing with your Games. How much are you focusing on the causations of the fears? How much are you playing a Fear Game about the Game? What are you thinking and feeling about your fears, your internal movies, your confidence that it will work, etc.? *What's your attitude?*

When we slow down painful movies and run them frame-by-frame in an excruciatingly slow pace, we often intensify the horrible feelings and absorb even more of the hurt and pain encapsulated in each frame. In accessing this movie, Calion saw each frame distinctly and clearly and expressed a lot of hurt and emotion while doing this. I told her to stop it.

That's when she began playing the *Insert Resource Game.* After the Game, she described the new movie after placing *her resource* into it.

"I saw a new presence, maybe an angel, come in the room with me and he stood with outstretched arms protecting me from my husband. He can't get to me anymore!"

The actual situation for her was that he had gone to prison a long time ago and he could not get to her. In spite of that knowledge, she had been living in fearful terror that he could. It was just a thought, just her frame, and so just the game that she had been playing. After playing the *Insert Resource Game,* she set a new frame in her mind, a protection frame of a guardian angel. It was a new Game which even allowed her to recall the old scene with laughter. What a change from when she first recalled it as the tears flowed and her face indicated much pain.

Inserting Resources As a "Show Stopper"

The week that we first came up with the Insert Resource Game, Bob took his wife Linda out to eat at a favorite restaurant known for their fish. Bob asked Linda if she would like to try out a new procedure and to play along with it to see what would happen. She raised her eyebrow and cautiously said, "Okay..." He told her a little about the new Frame Game (although we didn't call it that then), and invited her to think about some old internal movie of a negative event at work. Being at the restaurant she played the game strictly inside her head and nodded when she had located such a reel and was ready to let it roll.

Bob gave her the instruction to play it about half way into the movie and then *to stop it* there.   Since the *Insert Resource Game* involves accessing a great resource, he invited her to do that, and to then finish the movie. When he then asked her to play it again to put it all together, she gave a strange response, one that we had not encountered before. She couldn't get the movie to fire-up and run again. "It won't run with that resource in it." Talk about a resource being a real Show Stopper! Now that's some Game to play if you want to lock up an old stupid movie. What resource could you install into your B-rated movie that would cause a melt-down like that?

Bob decided to check out what was going on upstairs in Linda's mind a day or so later. You know how it is with those of us who like to play *Best Games* with people. We've got to check our work. A few days later he checked with her again and the resourcefulness was continuing. Linda said,

> "It was an old thing you know about who was teaching me the Human Resource stuff. Now when I think about that event, it doesn't mean anything at all to me anymore."

When Will You just *Stop it* From Being a Limitation?

Sharon was yet another person we experimented with. Bob met with her for two meetings and then had another one with both her and her 16-year old daughter, Carla.   As a single parent, Sharon raised Carla by herself since she was six years old. When Bob met Carla, he discovered that she had been playing a Game that involved intense anger. She was playing the "I'm as Mad as Hell and I'm Going to Turn it All Loose by Blaming my Mother." What a Game! Of course, Sharon had lost all control of Carla. That became clear when Bob had his second meeting with Sharon.

When he next saw Sharon, the teenager had run away from home. Eventually, she located Carla at the home of a girlfriend who also came from a broken home. When Sharon discovered that the girlfriend was herself in the custody of the Department of Social Services and lived in a group home for rebellious teenagers, she didn't want Carla to spend even one more night with her. Though Sharon had notified the police of Carla's disappearance, they could do little.

So the Game she tried to play was, "I'm Still Your Mother and You're Going to Obey me!" It didn't work out very well. Though she was able to trick Carla out of the friend's house, that only led to a fight between mother and daughter. That's when Sharon lost her temper and hit Carla. And that's when the police arrived at the scene. A new Game ensued. Sharon was under arrest and Carla had to go to her grandmother's in another state. Ah, the Games we play!

In describing these traumatic events, Sharon was running her movie of the confrontations, fights, name-calling, arrest, jail, etc. Though she was playing the movie and watching it as a spectator, it was still tearing her up. Bob got her to play *the Insert Game;* run the movie, stop it abruptly before the fight, insert a resource, complete the movie. Then run it from beginning to end with the resource stuck right in the middle. She did all of that very easily.

What happened? Sharon began reminiscing about how she would have behaved so differently if she realized and felt the presence of that resource when she was actually making the movie in real life. She then described a most interesting insight. She said that on her way over to get her daughter, she had prayed and thought about 'suiting up' for a spiritual battle. Raising her arm up as if holding a sword in her right hand, she said,

> "I put on the breastplate of righteousness and grabbed hold of the sword of the spirit."

Ah, you went as a soldier and was in *that frame of mind,* and so, of course, you ended up fighting, didn't you?

> "Yes, I sure did."

Later Sharon called and apologized to her daughter from a very different frame of mind, and not a suiting up for battle frame.

The frames we set obviously establish the Games we play. This story shows how we can so quickly, subtly, and even unknowingly set a frame by the *metaphors* we use. Lakoff and Johnson (1980, *Metaphors We Live By*) have written extensively about this meta-stating process. Frame yourself with a War Metaphor, and it's easy to play War Games with loved ones, yet those are *not* the Games that produce the kind of payoffs we're usually looking for in relationships.

The Backgrounding / Foregrounding Game

Here's a Game for creating newer and better movies. It falls out from the fact that in every movie, whether a real one we can go to or a mental one in our head, we have something in the foreground and something in the background. These cinematic features come with the territory of the Movie Metaphor.

To play fear and anxiety Games, we have to focus our attention on whatever objects we use to set off our fear and anxiety states. To do that, we have to let that fearful object sing and dance out to front stage on the theater of our mind. We must *foreground* that fear, make it big and foreboding, and let it loom frighteningly before us. We can put all kinds of resourceful thoughts, references, and/or beliefs in the background and that only seems to downplay and decommission such from having much influence.

Fear Games need an object to fear that is close, big, front and center. This describes the typical structure of fear. To really carry off a major phobic reaction, we have to get the object of our fear really in the foreground. The monster has to jump out at us. The lurking dangers have to loom out and fill up the screen.

Could our very skill at *foregrounding* some things and *backgrounding* other things drive and determine whether we play Fear Games or Mastery Games? Yes, you bet. Whatever we put front and center in the foreground will most strongly influence what's "on our mind," and therefore our state of mind. When we're playing Fear Games, we have fearful objects, people, events, etc. as the focus of our attention. It doesn't matter *why* we do it. But if we use past traumatic events to explain and justify why we do it, this just solidifies our foregrounding of fear and makes the problem worse.

Understanding the Foregrounding/ Backgrounding Game

In *Meta-States* we have a basic principle that we use for describing what happens at the higher levels of mind. We say, "Energy flows where attention goes—as governed by the intentional frame." In *Frame Games* we translated that, *The Game's play goes to where the frame determines.*

This shows up in terms of the images, sounds, and words that we foreground and background in our mental movies. Every image stands out from some background. That's what makes an image in the foreground— front and center. It stands out.

NLP adopted from Gestalt psychology the *foreground /background* structure or distinction, and how we shift back and forth. Today in perceptual psychology and cognitive psychology we call these *gestalt shifts*. Our attention moves to the images in the foreground and then back to another possible image that we could foreground but which otherwise remains in the background. Such *gestalt shifts* can powerfully affect our emotional responses.

Figure 10:1
Young Woman/ Old Hag

This is the classic gestalt example of *the Old Hag / Young Woman.* This Picture powerfully illustrates the foreground/background shift that occurs in external perception as we look at it. Research experiments indicate that we can, apart from someone's awareness, create a cognitive "set" which can predispose or prime a person to see one image rather than the other. We prime response potential. Then, either by looking long enough or having someone suggest how they can see the other picture—one experiences *the gestalt shift*. Once that occurs, a person can generally shift back and forth at will. Yet even then, even though we fully know and believe that we can see each picture, we cannot see *both* images *simultaneously*. We can only see one or the other. It shifts digitally. Off. On.

How does this work?

Robert Dilts (1995) explains it in terms of self-organization theory.

> "The picture itself is simply a complex combination or 'landscape' of lines and light and dark areas. The women, young or old, are not really on the paper, but rather in our minds. We 'see' a 'young' or 'old' woman because of the basic assumptions and deep structures within our own nervous systems—what Aristotle referred to as 'formal causes.' To move between the 'images' in the 'landscape' we need to first destabilize our focus on one attractor and subsequently restablize or 'fixate' our attention around the new attractor." (p. 257)

This means that something *attracts* us to "see" the lines and shades in a certain way. Something *pulls us* toward *foregrounding* the "young woman" or the "old woman." To look at one tiny line as a delicate eye lash, and a thicker line as a necklace, and another line to function as a beautiful jaw allows "the young woman" to emerge from the picture. To see the same lines as the form of a large nose and the thicker line as tightly pursed lips invites "the old hag" image to emerge.

In terms of Mind Games, this means that *what we foreground sets the frame* so that all of the other pieces around, under, and in the foreground get organized by that frame. By so *foregrounding* certain elements and using them to construct certain meanings (semantic structures), a *configuration* arises that fits a form, image, and meaning that we *bring to the lines and shades*.

When a person cannot "see" one emergent image, we sometimes point with our finger and say, 'Just look at it this way." "Imagine that this line *is* an eye lash..." "Now do you see it?" Having articulated the details that enable us to *configure* the gestalt (the overall systemic configuration), we can begin to intentionally run *the Gestalt Switch*. We can foreground and background at will. It now becomes a Game and we become the Game Master!

Ah, ha!   What shall I foreground today?

What shall I background?

As we highlight one representation, we by necessity downplay other representations.   As we play one Game in our mind by one focus of attention, that in itself prevents us from playing other Games.   Such highlighting can even *hide* other ways of viewing things.   Lakoff and Johnson (1980) describe this cognitive mechanism as inherent in "categorization."

> "A categorization is a natural way of identifying a *kind* of object or experience by highlighting certain properties, downplaying others, and hiding still others. Each of the dimensions gives the properties that are highlighted." (p. 163)

They even assert that "every description will highlight, downplay, and hide."   As an illustration, they use the following to show it happening at the linguistic level.

> "I've invited a sexy blonde to our dinner party.
>
> I've invited a renowned cellist to our dinner party.
>
> I've invited a Marxist to our dinner party.
>
> I've invited a lesbian to our dinner party." (p. 163)

Now *if* each of these descriptions fits for the same person, then each of these descriptions highlights different aspects of that same individual. So even linguistically, even with words, let alone with images on the inner movie of our mind, we can use words to *categorize* (or frame) the woman in different ways.   Each is a "true statement" in what it asserts, and yet each leaves out and hides other things.   What is highlighted or downplayed depends mostly upon the author's intention and agenda, upon what the author wants to make *salient* (standing out prominently and strikingly), and what the author wants to downplay and hide.

Now does that give you some ideas?

For us, it illustrates how we can *foreground* and *background* information at the sensory based representational level of perception and at the linguistic level as well.   In this, every single statement that we make *foregrounds* certain things as it makes those things salient and it *backgrounds* other things.

Okay, So How Do We Play
The Backgrounding / Foregrounding Game?

Think about something that you find pleasantly delightful. Delightful in that it gives you a sense of personal enjoyment in some way, relaxation, control, achievement, confidence, etc. Now see, hear, and feel that pleasure as a movie in your mind. Do so fully and completely so that when you step into it, all of your neurology glows with it. Be there fully in that delightful pleasure until you know you can easily recover this.

Now step back from that delight and notice what you have put in the foreground of your internal movie. What have you put in the background? If you think you have nothing in the background, look really close to see what kind of a "nothing" you have there. Is it a white screen or a black one? How large is this foreground? How far or narrow does it stretch out?

What sounds are in the foreground? What words, music, tones, and volumes? What smells and tastes? When you *step inside* the movie, what do you feel front and center?

Going through this process will enable you to notice and identify the background in your movies, both the resourceful ones and the limiting ones. Once you've detected the landscape, *shift* it. Fade out the images that you don't need or want to foreground and zoom your mental camera into those in the background. Turn down the volume or tone of the voices or music in the foreground so that you can fully focus on those in the background that bring out your confidence, sense of power, resilience, motivation, etc.

Great Game!

How was it for you, this first time of consciously foregrounding and backgrounding representations and ideas. This is a great Game for mastering fears. This gives you the power to *set the contexts or frames* of your mind. How about that? As long as you see, hear, and feel an experience in whatever configuration of the foreground that you constructed, you will *not* even notice the background. This does not make it go away. It only makes it *un-conscious* as in *outside*-of-awareness to you.

What backgrounding of fear or foregrounding of resources would you like to do? Name your Game? Have you ever felt confident? Courageous? Bold? Centered? Caring? Passionate? What would happen to your fear if you foregrounded those qualities in any old fear movie?

Well, let's try it.

Is there anything that scares you spitless that you'd rather operate from out of one of those resources? Good. Pull it up and let that reel start playing out noticing as you do, what you have naturally and unconsciously put in the foreground. Got it? How far back into the background is your sense of personal confidence, commitment, courage, power, etc.? Look until you find them somewhere in the background of the movie.

Good. Now step back from that Fear Game. As an observer, notice all of the good and wonderful things that you have which you have backgrounded. Notice what you have foregrounded in that experience. Do so in all of the sensory systems: visually, auditorially, kinesthetically, and with language. Now play the *Quality Control Game*. Does this make your life a party? Is this what you want or need? Does this enhance or create balance?

If you're convinced that you don't need to put your resources in the back and your fears up front, then shift them. Put the fears in the background and bring the resources into the foreground. Do the gestalt shift ... allowing background to become foreground and visa versa. Get them dancing, back and forth, back and forth ... round and round they go... and where they stop—you have them inverted, switched around where they will stay.

The Gestalting Game

You now know the Game. So play with your subjective experiences. What are two strong resources, which, if you brought them to the fearful experience, would completely alter that experience forever? As a menu list, you could choose from: faith, courage, relaxation, presence of mind, sense of feeling centered and whole, a loving attitude, permission to feel more empowered than I have ever before in my life, etc.

Next, look for that resource in your Fear Game. Play the sensory-rich fear movie and notice the *you* in that cinematic production. Now,

notice **the *you*** *who has those resources* to handle that with no problem.
It may seem to be so far in the background that you can just barely see
them, then as you continue, begin to let them come forth... closer and
closer... until all you have to do is give them your word to come *forth*
and you know they will.

As you see *the You with all of those resources*, let the foreground of
the Fear Game fade and be replaced by the background of resources in
a quick gestalt shift.   When the resources have shifted in, let them lock
in place... Hear a bolt locking them in place.

How to Mindfully Play the Gestalt Shift Game
Step 1: Detect your Foreground/Background Structure
Whatever "thought of fear or anxiety" comes to mind, *step back
from it* for a moment (the meta-move of observation), and just
notice what you find in the foreground. What's up front? What
stands out?   Next shift your awareness to the background
against which it stands.

Step 2: Become aware of your own Foregrounding/ Backgrounding Patterns
What do you typically foreground in order to do fear? What do
you regularly and systematically background or avoid in order
to experience fear? In other words, what do you "not see" that
allows you to experience fear? It is back there. Look! How
much *flexibility of consciousness* do you have with regard to
these choices? Do they serve you well? Do they enhance your
life?

Step 3: Decide to Take Charge of Your Gestalt Shifting
That we foreground some things and background other things
simply describes one of the factors about how the brain works.
Taking control over the way we run our brain so that we learn
how to foreground resources, solutions, getting things done,
etc., however, describes, how we can use this distinction for
running our brains more effectively. So run the ecology check
constantly on your backgrounding and foregrounding to make

sure that your learned patterns work for you rather than against you.

Step 4: Commit yourself to Foregrounding Resources

If you know that you *can* put in resourceful thoughts, beliefs, pictures, sounds, music, feelings, etc., then make a meta-level commitment to yourself to do so. In your mind, move up and utter a profoundly powerful *"Yes!"* to that resource. "I will make that idea, feeling, sound, music, etc. *stand out* in my mind!"

If what *stands out as salient* in your mind is crap, non-sense, hurtful old pains, old fears, resentments, regrets, etc.—guess what states and meta-states that will evoke in you? Will that do you any good?

Step 5: Swish the Gestalt Shift in

Once you feel strongly compelled to *get away from that(!),* then turn around and intentionally *bring mental and emotional resources to the foreground of your mind.* Do it so that your attention shifts to the new referents. *Swish* it there five times really, really fast. Every time you think of the background junk— see, hear, and feel it fading out to the background as *the new resourceful You, Ideas, Beliefs, etc.* come dancing into the Foreground and really stand-out with triumphant music playing and trumpets blowing!

Debriefing the Game

The term *salient* refers to something *standing out conspicuously, prominently, and strikingly.* From *salire* (Latin), it has within it the idea of *sallying forth* or jumping out. Has something ever really jumped out, in your mind, in such a way that it becomes totally compelling? That speaks about the power of foregrounding.

Given that we can make both representations and ideas *salient* so that they project outward and upward from their surroundings—what would you like to foreground in your mind? What would you like to fade out and vanish into the background?

Similarly for backgrounds. Sometimes background noise, chatter, self-talk, hypnotic lines, etc. occur just below the threshold of *conscious awareness*, but still within the scope of influence. Here you might take notice of things in the immediate background that may have an unhealthy influence on your states.

Old hag, beautiful young lady— what do you see? What do you want to see? What kind of a gestalt shift would you like to experience? The gestalt shift actually explains some of the shifting that occurs in many of the Fear Mastery Games that we have adapted from such NLP Patterns as the Swish and the Phobia Cure.

Summary

- We frame our "thoughts" as internal movies and these Movies set the frames for our everyday Games. The Stepping In and Out Game gives us the power to change our Frame Games to serve our personal effectiveness and resourcefulness. What Movie do you want playing in the theater of your mind? Choose well.

- Similarly the *>Insert Resources> Game* offers a radically new and surprising way to run your brain as you take charge of your internal *Movies*. This Game allows you become the Editor of your Movies and insert clips that make for personal resourcefulness.

- Stepping aside from our thoughts enables us to notice what we have foregrounded in contrast to what we have backgrounded. This gives us the *structural format* of our Movies. *Foregrounding* and *backgrounding* pictures, sounds, sensations, and words operates at a higher level that we can now use powerfully. We can now run a gestalt switch in our brain, step back from the content of our computations, notice our current foreground and background structure, then choose what to make stand out in our mental-emotional world.

- As *map-makers*, we construct and produce our internal

movies, we foreground and background, we edit, run forward, run backwards, etc. This creates the Matrix of Frames in our minds that set up the Games we play.

- You now know how the Games are set up. This gives you the power to choose the Movies you play. It gives you the Game skills for running the clips that support your highest beliefs, values, understandings, etc. Let them now *attract* scenes that increase your effectiveness. Only play Movies that organize your internal world to foreground your values and visions.

- This distinction describes one meta-level structure of excellence that we can use in modeling genius.

- Since your energy will flow where your attention goes and will be governed by your highest intentions, the Rules of the Game that you establish will increase your personal expertise in every realm of life. What frame will you set up to attract the valued experiences that you want?

PLAY FLOWS
WHERE THE GAME GOES
AS DETERMINED
BY THE FRAME

- All of your Games make perfect sense. They are not "crazy," nor are you. They are expressions of the Frames that organize their Rules, Payoffs, Set-up, etc.

- But not all Games are healthy, enhancing, or empowering. Many are limiting, unsane, and toxic.

- The *Play* of a Game will always flow according to the Frames. So make sure your Frames are good ones.

- When you *Quality Control* your Frames, you Quality Control your Games.

Chapter 11

MASTERY GAMES

GAMES THAT MAKE FEAR GAMES REDUNDANT

When children start arguing and fussing over a game, sometimes instead of finding out who did what, who's not playing fair, who's not taking turns, we can make all of that redundant and irrelevant by giving them a much better Game to play. Sometimes we can do the same with ourselves. We can use this same tactic with old Fear Games that we've played. Sometimes, they just become irrelevant. Sometimes we just forget about them because we have gotten passionately absorbed in a much more engaging Game— a Game that empowers and enhances life. That's the design of the Games in this chapter.

Map Updating
If "the map is not the territory," but just a way of mapping the world,

just a frame that sets up a Game, then if we find that a particular map or frame initiates Fear Games that we don't need, then we can devote our attention and energy to *updating our map* to play a more refined or enhancing Game.

Ignoring this step makes attempts at "change" hard, painful, difficult and even impossible. Trying to change feelings, Games, old ways of navigating while still living under the old rules, makes "change" tough. It makes it a hundred times more difficult than it needs to be. It makes it a distressful ordeal. It can be done, but we would not recommend that approach unless you have plenty of time and money for years of therapy! Yet once you're convinced of the absolute utter futility of living in the present by referencing old fears, you're ready to try a much more efficient approach.

The Time-Lining Game

Playing with our sense of "time" was a Game developed by the original developers of NLP. It proved so useful that James and Woodsmall (1988) wrote a book (*Time Line Therapy*) on how to use it for therapy. Ten years later, we (Bodenhamer & Hall, 1997) wrote another book *(Adventures with Time Lines)* about it, extending and expanding the model with Neuro-Semantics.

Now the nice thing about *"time"* is that it doesn't exist. Yes, that probably sounds really strange, but "time" as a thing does *not* exist. It does not exist "out there" at least. You have never walked out onto your yard and stumbled over a hunk of "time" that someone left in your yard. "Time" is not *that* kind of thing. "Out there" in the dynamic, ever-changing world is movement, activity, change, or in a word–*events.*

We create "time" as a concept in our mind and measure it by comparing the changes in one thing (earth moving around the sun) to other things, for example, how fast a runner completes a race, how long it takes while standing in a line, etc. Since "time" exists in the mind, it's easy to play with it— to tweak it, twist it around, make it serve our ends, and enhance our life.

Of course, some people have a *bad relationship* to "time." Imagine that. What a strange thing! Yet it's true. Just listen to them.

"I don't have enough time."

"Time is against me, it's not a friend, it's against me."
"Time is pressuring me." etc.

Of course, if "time" was a thing, we'd grab a hold of it and teach it a lesson for doing such mean things to these innocent people. But it's not a thing that we can get a hold of. It's a mental map that we construct in our heads. That's why people in different cultures have different cultural maps and frames about this concept and so develop different relationships to the way they handle "time" and the arrangements of the events in their lives. They play Time Games that differ from our Games.

The Time-Lining Game involves using our typical ways of thinking about, representing, encoding and believing about "time" so that we live in the now with an eye on the future rather than torture ourselves by living too much in the "past." The Fear Game that a lot of people play which keeps them locked into fear, and fearful signals of danger and threat, involves playing "The Past Trance."

Recognizing map from territory enables us to *come into the now, into this moment,* and re-orient ourselves to the world today rather than use the past time-frame as our reference point. If we play the *Past Frame Game,* then we use and focus on old fears and old events as our current frame. Our fears often arise as products of past dangers, but dangers that no longer exist.

When we shift to playing the *Live in the Now Game,* we shift our reference. We now use fear as a legitimate emotion if there is some current danger or threat that we truly need to fear. This leads us to a new kind of sorting:

What do I have to be afraid of right now?
Does this *fear* serve me as a signal of a true danger or threat?
In what way is it a danger? A danger to what?
What resource would serve me to face and master this current situation?

If we have typically focused on the past, looked for the worst case scenario and then stepped into those representations, then we undoubtedly have *the Old Fear Game* down pat. If so, then we have the know-how to make ourselves miserable at any given moment. We can probably even do it all the time. Often we do. Yet, if something fearful did happen in our past and we now live our mental life there by constantly recalling that event, then we are playing the game of living our life in the fears of the past. This is *the Old Fear Game.*

It is the *Past Trance Game* and it involves encoding today's events inside the frame of the Past. This allows us to use all kinds of present day triggers to remind us of past hurts, dangers, threats, embarrassments, traumas, etc. If you want to play this Game, then set the frame:

"The past determines the future."

"The experiences you've been through destine you to the emotions you'll experience in your future."

The Future Catastrophe Game gives us a chance to also use our "future" "time" frames of beliefs and values to scare the hell out of ourselves even before the dreaded terrible things happen. All you have to do to set up and play this Game is to begin to imagine all of the terrible and horrible things that could happen to you in the future, or to any one you love. Imagine the awfulness of it vividly, dramatically, and be sure to *step into the horror movie fully.* That should do it.

Living Resourcefully in the Present Game

If you don't care for those Games, don't want to play them, and truly do want to master your fears, and the general spirit of fearfulness, then play the *Living Resourcefully in the Present with an eye on a Compelling Future Game.* How does that sound? Would you like to play that one?

How to Play *the Present Moment* Game
Step 1: *Come into the Now*

> Use your sensory equipment and open your eyes, ears, skin, etc. and access the most intense "uptime," or sensory aware, state possible. Let your "mind" go as you come to your "senses." In a relaxed and comfortable way, do this daily for 5 or 10 minutes until it becomes a habit of living in the now. As you do, consider all of the values and benefits of being able to live in the now. This will help to validate and confirm the value of this Game.

Step 2: *Establish Some Robust Frames for the Now*

Set up some enhancing frames that validate living in the now.

"This day and time is the only 'time' that I really have."

"I'll take no worrisome thought for tomorrow."

"Time is just a concept, the 'past' and the 'future' are but concepts."

Step 3: *Frame the Past as Useful Learnings*

Frame the events that you've been through as valuable for learnings. Then search through them for valuable lessons, significant points, truths to live by. When a memory arises, play the "What can I learn from this?" Game. When you have sucked out all of the learnings, then let it go.

"It was just an experience ... thank God it's over."

Step 4: *Frame your Future as Open-Ended*

Frame the events that you have not yet experienced, but want to experience, as the open-ended future that you get to create every day in every moment.

"The *future* will be is made out of the actions, thoughts, beliefs, frames, etc. that I create today. So I will use every day to establish the direction and orientation that will pull me toward a compelling future."

"Since the *future* does not yet exist, I refuse to borrow worries and fears about possible time-lines. I refuse to waste my energies on worrisome fears but will instead focus my energies on what I can do today to secure a more enticing future."

Playing *Living in the Present* Game enables you to focus your mind on *the now*. This builds up the ability to concentrate. Focusing on the sensory world of the *now* reduces the contamination of "the past" and "the future." When you live in *this moment*, you have memories but you are not thinking about them. Michael Colgrass (2000) describes this in his book on performing with confidence in terms of how dogs think. "Everything is now, right now." This is living in the moment.

"If they run into a bear they'll remember their last encounter with a bear and respond accordingly. But they don't anticipate meeting the bear–that's the difference. ... To a dog, a misstep is a gone the moment it happens because the dog is already paying attention to the next moment. There is no 'mistake' because there is no past. And there's no fear, because there's no future. There is only now ... and now... and now." (pp. 86-87)

In this Game, we give total focus on the moment, relentlessly. Every moment is "a new now." Take a step and experience it ... it's a New Now. Take another step, another New Now. Move to the right, to the left, a New Now. It's a great way to move through the world being fully present in this moment, alive to the people and events of this now... and not drag old fears with you. This frame invites you into a fresh new Game.

The *"Time-Line"* Game

Some events *have already occurred* and so are past, and some *are occurring right now* in this present moment, and yet other events *will occur at some later time in the future...* Since we are aware of this, aware of past, present, and future *events,* we can make a meta-map as we think about these three time tenses and the Time Zones they create. As we *step back* from our representation of events in these three dimensions, we can imagine a line or path that connects them and that's how we invent our *Time-Line.* It's easy. We grew up looking at historical time-lines in books, from the first century, through the Dark Ages, the Renaissance, the Industrial Age, and into Modern times.

We can and do use this same format with our own life. Since you've been dressing yourself and washing your face for a long time, think about doing it last week, last month, last year, two years ago, five years. Think about doing it today. You did, didn't you? Think about it tomorrow, next week, next month, next year, two years, five years.

Whew! What a journey, and all around dressing and washing your face! Feel cleaner? Now step back. Float up, in your mind, above yourself ... and notice *where in space* you have a sense of the events of your past, your present, your future. If you were to draw a line through these locations, what would that "line" look like?

Most people have a left to right line ... left is where they put things of the past, the present is in their current position, and to the right they put future events. Many people put the past behind them and the line comes right up to and through their body and on out in front of them. My line arches at a 45 degree angle coming from my left ... and back, it comes to my present position but doesn't enter into my body, then it moves on up to my right, still at a 45 degree angle and out from my right side and up toward the ceiling. I sense it like a ribbon that weaves my past into my present into my future.

There's all kinds of arrangements, configurations, figures, and forms. Some have a boomerang configuration. The line starts out in front, to the left and comes in to the body ... kisses the skin and then like a boomerang goes out in front on the right side. Some have spirals, circles, paths, etc. Lines dominate probably due to the lines we looked at and memorized in schools. It was an easy way to code events over "time."

As you step back and notice how you know the difference between then, now, and yet to be... notice location in space. Let your body intuitions guide you. Point your finger to where past events seem to be. Then point your finger to where future events seem to be. It's all a map and an invention anyway. None of it is real. And it changes!

Notice how thick the line is. Is it a path? Notice it's shape and configuration. Notice its color, form, density, its clarity or fuzziness, its width and height, its intensity of life (dim or bright). Notice if it has a sound track and the qualities of the sound track.

When you have it, now you can really begin to play! Float above it. Just float up out of your body and look down to see your time-line stretching out over the years... zoom back to a wonderful time and place and notice it... if it was really wonderful, float down into it and enjoy it... again... then zoom up *on* the line to the now.

Float up again and this time zoom forward a year, five years, ten, etc. Stop and look down on that future you... Imagine a compelling future event that you really want to occur and know that it's possible, and go there and enjoy the pleasure of what that will be like... And look back toward your past, to the now ... and notice the steps that brought you here, and learn.

The *"It's Never too late to have a Happy Childhood"* Game

If "time" does not exist "out there," but operates as an invented mental concept, and if we can form and reform it so that it empowers and enhances life, then there's nothing that stops us from re-inventing our past and commissioning it to become a positive reference point (a positive frame of reference). Well, is there? Is there anything stopping you from having the happy childhood you always wanted?

"But it's scandalous to alter memory that way!"

Really? Does that mean that all of your memories are totally accurate and pristine? Don't believe it. Your wet brain doesn't work that way. Unlike the fairly stable chips that you can encode 0 and 1 on, your wet brain is made up of ever-changing cells in an ever-active nervous system full of bio-electric charges, the exchanging of ions at the molecular level, and the spurting of neuro-transmitters and neuro-peptides all over the place. The wetness of your brain and the ever-active neuro-networks create the situation that all of your current day learnings and experiences continually influence your memories.

So, what does all of that mean?

It means that the "past" never was the way you now remember it! It also means that the *past* that we carry encoded in our minds is always changing, is continually changing. Every time we think about some event of our past, every time we talk about it, etc., it changes. That's why "talk therapy" can work. The Talking Game, the Hypnosis Game, the Therapy Game, these and many other games *change memories.* Memories are *that* fluid and changeable. The "memories" that we carry inside our neurology are very different from the more static forms of information storage that we use.

To play the *Change History Game*, pick a memory that "the very thought" of it initiates unpleasant feelings. Got one? Good.

Now float up and over your time-line and go back, all the way back, to a time and a place where that memory occurred. Good. And now go back even a little further, say 15 minutes prior to the event ... Floating ... floating back ever so gently... and from this higher perspective just look down on that Younger You prior to the old trauma or hurt.

Now pick out as many resourceful states of mind, body, emotion, understanding, skill, etc. that would have totally transformed that old situation. Access each and every one of these resources, one at a time, stepping into them fully... Stop and do this. Access confidence, then a solid sense of yourself and your value, etc.

When you have these resources accessed and amplified so that you feel totally centered, focused, clear, strong, courageous etc., then float down into that moment, that moment 15 minutes prior to the event, and be there again ... but this time with this difference. Be there with all of these resources and looking into your future, knowing that in a moment you will step forward and race forward ... in super fast time... up to the present ... letting all of those resources change everything that has been ... transforming your memories ... imagining the difference those resources would have made and letting your memories change for the better... Ready? Go. And bring those resources with you up to this moment.

Figure 11:1

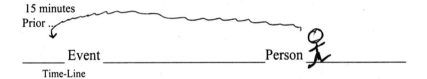

Good. Now just be with those feelings, knowing that the change that you have initiated will continue to reverberate backwards and forwards in time... giving your memory of the past more resources to reference... And just let it keep transforming... even in your sleep this evening and in the nights to come.

The *"Getting Over the Past"* Game

How can some people mentally live in the "past?" Though the "past" no longer exists and is done and over, they keep going back there–in their mind– and playing the old movies. In that way, they "live" in the past." They use the conceptual past time frame (their memories of previous events) as their sorting filter as they move through life. They relate to the events, people, and situations of today, not as *today*, but strictly and only in terms of previous understandings.

To use the past time frame in this way is to use it as an internal governor for what one focuses on (previous hurts, fears, and dangers) and how one focuses attention. When we do this all the time and that frame becomes "the frame of mind we wake up in" every morning, it becomes our attitude and world view.

That happens because whenever we continually repeat a meta-level pattern, we install that pattern as our mental filter or *frame*. It becomes the governing pattern of our life. If that repetitive meta-pattern involves fear, then it fills up our mental and emotional world with fear. It programs our matrix of frames to attract more fear to us. It can even fill up our world with multiple levels of fears: afraid of our fear, afraid of being open, fear of repeating our past, fear of being vulnerable, of making a mistake, of being laughed at, etc.

If that's the structure of *Living in the Past*, then the key lies in changing our frame of reference. Suppose that you find a "problem" as you think about your past, a problem that won't go away? What then?

Play the *"Getting Over the Past" Game*. After all, it is past. Done. Finished. It's not occurring now. It could only be occurring now if we're encoding it as occurring now. And if we're doing that, we only need to detect how we're doing such, and stop it. Putting a stop to that will allow us to create another coding, coding today as now and the future as open to new possibilities, not based exclusively upon what has happened, but what we want to happen and what we will commit ourselves to making happen. It's just a different way to think and live; a different Game to play.

Step 1: Discover the fear's root cause or source

Suppose you knew the root cause of the fear and suppose that when you identify that cause and disconnect from it, doing so will cause the fear to completely disappear, when would that have been? Would that root cause have occurred prior to, during, or after your birth? Just float back, in your mind, until you find the answer to this.

Step 2: Float back to the source on the time-line

As you float back ... letting your inner knowings take you there, nod your head when you have an approximate location of the root cause. Good. Now float up above your time-line of that source thanking the unconscious part of your mind for having brought you to this place.

As you gently float up over the event, now just observe in a calm and mindful way that Younger You down there in that situation... Is this the source of the fear— the source which, if we transform it, will completely release you from the fear so that you can get on with life?

Step 3: Access Resources

From this calm observer position, consider all of the learnings and resources that you've developed over the years that would transform that old source of fear... and access them, one by one, letting them grow and intensify. And you have probably learned something even from this experience... and you can notice those learnings and even develop new learnings now... Learnings that you can use as resourceful Frames of Reference for how to live effectively...

Step 4: Float back a little further

Now as you keep intensifying all of those powerful resources, just imagine floating back another fifteen minutes or even an hour before the event that was the source of the fear. Now with those resources gently float down into your time-line 15 or 60 minutes prior to the event. ... good.

In just a moment, I want you to look into your future and to do so knowing that from this point of view, when the source event has not yet occurred then it doesn't yet exist. Where is it? It is nowhere. And where are all those fearful emotions that it evoked? Nowhere. So, now look into your future from this point of time ... and what do you see?   ... That's right. Nothing.... just a future wide open to all kinds of possibilities. None of the old trauma is in your future, is it? The event, the emotions, the limiting beliefs, all of that has disappeared, hasn't it?

If you sense any of that, being here in this point of time, you can let all of that go, fully... forever... can you not? Wouldn't that be nice? Nice to just let the emotions go. ... as you breathe in and out deeply...

Step 5: *Take the empowered resourceful step into the new future*
Now with all of your resources ... when you're ready, step forward into your yet unformed future ... and just let your resources transform any and every event that arises as you move into the future and through those events and then zoom up to the now... with your resources knowing that you're disconnecting the old fears and their sources.

Step 6: *Pace the resources into the future*
Now that you have let the old fears go and the reference points of the past so that they don't figure into your thinking or emoting, imagine taking your resources into your future with you into any and all times and situations that you'll need them.

Move forward into your future noticing how your resources can transform other situations that would have otherwise triggered fear.

Step 7: *Test the game*
Now, would you like to have the old fears back? Well, try to get them back, try as hard as you can ... to re-experience them.

How the *Getting Over the Past* Game Works
This Game works by recoding *how* and *what* we think about "the past" (i.e., events and experiences that have already occurred). As we frame such using the following ideas and beliefs– we enter into a new world:

- The "Past" is completed and finished.
- Past experiences are just experiences that we've been through, not who we are, and certainly not our destiny.

- The "Past" is just a map of what I remember and the meanings I gave to those events then.
- Using the "Past" for learnings instead of reasons to feel bad is an intelligent use of those events.
- The term "The Past" is just noun-like language and not a real entity, it's just a nominalization (Chapter 12). If it misdirects my mind so that I treat such as if solid, real, entity-like, and unchangeable, then I shall speak of such using verbs to use a more accurate map, "the events that have happened..."

The Game also works by giving us a way to "go back" in our mind to those previous memories and re-code them with more resourcefulness and pleasure and to then use such as our reference points.

The "Place of Pure Potentiality" Game

The following Game uses a Time-Line process to provide a simple Game (i.e., procedure) for eliminating fears, and even unwanted beliefs. Yet inside of this Game we have yet another basic Game, *"Taking Different Points of View" Game.*   This sub-game is played by taking each one of your fears through the five perceptual positions which we designate as: Self, Other, Observer, System, and God.

In the *Taking Different Points of View* Game, we begin with the First Perceptual Position which means thinking about the fear from one's own eyes, body, etc. From first position, we look at the world from *our own* point of view. In first position, we do not take into account anyone else's position. We simply think, "How does this affect me?" All of our primary fears and anxieties emerge from first position. We create fear, anxieties, and phobias by associating into experiences of fear. We begin here, but we do not stay here. In fact, staying here *is* the problem. Every time we think about the fearful event or object, every time we recall the terrifying experience, we think about it from this position. It's as if we're stuck in this role and can't play any other role. All of that is about to change... for the better.

This sub-game revels in the fact that we can look at an experience from many positions. Doing that offers tremendous potential for managing our states, taking control of our emotions, and enhancing our communications.

Second position refers to seeing things from another person's perspective. It means walking in another's shoes. It means taking into consideration how something looks, sounds, feels, etc. from the other's point of view. In second position, we imagine entering the other's body and look at ourselves through his or her eyes.   This gives us an imagined sense of what it looks like and sounds like from the other's point of view.   Second position develops our ability for empathy. It increases our flexibility when we're involved in conflict with someone. Second position increases our appreciation of the one listening to us; how we're coming across.

Third position means perceiving from a neutral or meta-position. It's stepping outside the system and looking at ourselves and the other interacting and seeing the larger context.   While just observing or witnessing without being involved.   *Fourth position* does that yet further, seeing cultural frames of many levels and layers. It sees things in family systems, economic and political systems, education systems, etc. *Fifth position* does this yet further and takes, as it were, the "God" or universal position.

Now for the play.

How to Play the "Pure Potentiality" Game
Step 1: Step out of your Fear Game
You know the first position of your fear. Identify that and then begin to suppose that you communicated your fears to someone brave and courageous. As you step out of that "first position," step into the point of view of a caring and resourceful other person. From this new perspective, notice the higher level Games that this allows you to play. What happens?

Step 2: Step Into the Position of the Brave
Now step into that person's perspective. See, hear, and feel what that courageous person sees, hears, and feels about the description you give of that fear. Stay with this and just notice it ... and notice it from the perspective of someone brave and courageous.

Step 3: Step Outside the System

Third position refers to stepping out of both first and second position and into the position of an independent observer. It's like stepping out of a movie so that you can watch the movie. Since you did that many times in some of the previous Games, this step ought to be pretty easy and familiar. Imagine it fully this time to get a full description.

In a sense, third position facilitates our stepping into, and then operating out of, a position of objectivity. Just observe. As we step back to just observe, we can notice how a conversation or event looks to someone totally uninvolved. It's like being a director of a movie. It's like watching a play. It's like looking over a busy mall from a balcony five floors up. We can see both the *Us* in that situation experiencing the fear, the Caring Courageous person listening to us, and the entire situation—whatever that entails.

Step 4: Step Way Out Beyond All Systems

Fourth Perceptual Position refers to the "we" perspective of an entire system. We do this by stepping aside and adopting a system's point of view. We may step into the system level of a business, a government, a nation, the planet, the universe. We do this with our fears by stepping outside our immediate environment and life and looking at it from our family's point of view, our work, our resourcefulness as a person, or from the system of our social contexts. When I step into a systems perspective about my health, how do I think and feel about being controlled by a fear?

Step 5: Dance To a Time Before Actuality

Fifth Position refers to the universal perceptual position. This perspective provides the widest and largest level perspective of all, the God point of view . Fifth position is the highest meta-position and allows us to take on multiple perceptual positions and rapidly shift between them to increase our flexibility. With fifth position we can even over-view things through time, seeing things as they progress over time.

Dancing in and out of these positions, especially into fifth position frequently is sufficient for eliminating fears. This is especially true for people who have or can create a spiritual resource as they experience the fifth position. Suppose, for example, that you believe that you were "in the mind of God" prior to being conceived and born. If so, then a statement like the following from Jeremiah the prophet could become a frame for a whole new Game.

> "Before I formed you in the womb I knew you, before you were born I set you apart; I appointed you as a prophet to the nations."

Using this idea as a spiritual concept along with the fifth position enables us to see ourselves prior to our conception and prior to any and all fears and phobias. Step into that mind-space. Mentally go to the place where you were prior to being conceived, there in "the mind of God," and notice all of the possibilities that emerge prior to any fearful event or traumatic experience. Notice just how resourceful you feel when you step into that place.

As you think about your time-line, and have a sense of where your past is and where your future goes out to, float back along that time-line, and go back, go all the way back ... back beyond your teenage years, your childhood years, the times of your preschool, and even float back into your mother's womb, and then prior to that, to conception and before ...

Step 6: Move to the Place of Pure Potentiality

And as you come to the place of *pure potentiality,* whether it is in the mind of God or in the Void of nothing prior to your existence, stop and experience *pure potentiality* ... fully and completely. And as you do, just notice that this is a place before all emotions, all fears, anxieties, phobias, and hurts. They haven't happened...

And given the nature of this being a place of pure *potentiality*, begin ... while you are in this conceptual place to create and welcome all kinds of new frames of mind and frames of meaning that will guide you in all of your life ... guide you without fear or anxiety...

Step 7: Zoom To the Now with the New Potentialities

And when you *feel those fully* ... then zoom forward along your time-line bringing them with you, and re-experiencing all of your life with them ... letting them transform all of your days and experiences and come right up to the now.... and stop... and enjoy the new frames of mind that you can take with you into every future day.

Summary

- How about a Mastery Game that just doesn't leave you any time for the Fear Games? Suppose you get playing and having so much fun in making your life empowering that you just forget to freak yourself out? That's what the *Living Resourcefully in the Present Game* was all about.

- As a symbolic class of life, we relate to the concept of "time" and do so in such ways that make life enhancing or limiting. Now we can play some Time Games that will put an end to the Past, install a Happy Childhood today, and create a Compelling Bright Future. We can play numerous Time Games that put an end to Living in the Past and for Constructing a Happy Childhood at any time.

- Here are Resourceful Games for your mind and body that will leave you without the time or desire to default back to the old Fear Games.

"IT'S NEVER TOO LATE TO HAVE A HAPPY CHILDHOOD"

- We can play the "Change History" Game today because "the past" does not exist. Not in actuality. At best it only exists as an idea in our minds. In actuality, the events are *past*. Gone. They are not happening now.

- What mental and emotional Games do you play with past events? What Games do you play with the Concept of "the past?" Do those Games enhance your life?

- Would you like to play some New Games with your Memories of the Past– Games that will free you from where you have been and empower you to move on to where you want to go? You can.

- Get the Frame and you can Play the Game!

Chapter 12

THE NOMINALIZING GAME

How to Turn Fears
Into Big Unsolvable Monsters

Games in this Chapter:
The Demon Entity of "Fear" Game
The "That's Who I Am" or Identity Game
The *Describe What You are Doing* Games

Suppose we wanted to play a sci-fi type of game, a game where we take something common and ordinary and give it the aura of the demonic, of alien entities living inside your mind and heart and body and ready to break out at any moment to terrify the hell out of you and others and bathe your mind and emotions in total horror! Wouldn't that be fun? Suppose we wanted to play a *Game of Horror* with our own emotions.

How would we do it?

How would we structure the Game?

What would be the rules of the Game?

Easy. We can do it linguistically. We can do it with *words*. The seemingly simple tool of language gives us this power to turn an emotion into a Monster or a Demon. All we have to do is to take the action words (verbs) that describe actual mental and emotional processes and turn them into static labels (nouns). This will freeze the activity so that we snapshot the processes at one point in time and can then treat them as "things." So here goes:

Verbs that describe processes–

> *Fearing, feeling afraid, breathing heavily, thinking about all the terrible things that could happen.*

Noun-like words (nominalizations) that freeze action into labels (in italics)–

> "I have a problem with *Fear*. Sometimes when I least expect it *a Panic Attack* comes upon me."

After we reduce and freeze the actions, we can then relate to the Labels as "the last word" about our subject, as "permanent and unchangeable" and as an Entity in its own right. We call this linguistic distinction "nominalizing" and the end-results, nominalizations. It comes from the idea of *naming* or nominalizing a process.

Best of all, we can do it with the experience of *fearing*. We can reduce the mental, physical, and emoting processes in such a way that they seem like "Things." Suddenly, there appears a new creature, Fear. It's like a thing or Entity.

> "I have this problem with *Fear*."
>
> "My *Fear* controls me and makes me act in ways that sabotage my own success."
>
> "If it weren't for an *Anxiety*..."
>
> "I have this *Panic Disorder* and...."

In these expressions, who would have ever guessed that *fear* (as a verb) refers to a *way of thinking, feeling, and acting*? Nominalizing transforms all of that. It makes Fear seem like a thing, What a great trick of language! It sets us up for a major delusion. Now let the Games begin!

The *Demon Entity of "Fear"* Game

Now you would think that the psychological community would know better than to be seduced into this Game. You would think that, if anybody would know better, psychologists would by all means *avoid nominalizing "Fear" as a Thing* (and Entity!) and being recruited to that Game.

But no. Many of them, perhaps most, do not.

In fact, the situation is even worse than that. Psychologists, psychiatrists, and mental health counselors are among the key players in *"The Demon Fear"* Game. Sure, there are a few in psychology, those with training in NLP, Brief Therapy, Reality Therapy, Rational Emotive Therapy, who know better and won't play such Games. But most psychotherapists have been fully recruited into the Game. This is not a slam against psychologists. It is rather a slam against a Fear Game that undermines personal resourcefulness and prevents many from mastering their fears.

They even have a Game book that sets it all up. It's called the *DSM-IV*. Ooouuu! Spooky name. And true to form, many mental health professionals worship at the foot of the *Diagnostic and Statistical Manual* (DSM) as if it were the Bible for the field of psychiatry. This is the Diagnostic Manual for mental, emotional, and personality disorders. The American Psychiatric Association swears by this book. If you want to read about The Demon Fear Game, read this book. It will treat Fear as a thing, even as the Bogy Man.

Are you unfamiliar with the "labeling" (naming) of the DSM-IV? The following gives you a little taste of the kinds of descriptions that you'll find in the *American Psychiatric Association Diagnostic Criteria* (1994). The following provides examples of how the mental health field plays this Naming Game.

As you read, consider each of these descriptions as some of the *Fear Games* created by the medical model. It's their way of trying to make sense of things. The descriptions are almost like descriptions of how to play these Games. Highly suggestive people can read such descriptions and cue their bodies to access the states like fear and curiosity. Watch out that you don't do that.

To understand the very different approach we take in *Games for Mastering Fears* we offer the following from the section on Anxiety Disorder (DSM-V, pp. 393-394). Just notice how these descriptions seek to invite you into a trance (recruit you to the Games) because they assume that descriptions are real and that they point to real "things." Implied also is another idea, that is, that the people who suffer these distresses are victims.

Don't believe any of that. They are not real. These are just Game descriptions— structured Games that people learn to play; structured games that they can unlearn.

"A *panic attack* is a discrete period in which there is the sudden onset of intense apprehension, fearfulness, or terror often associated with feelings of impending doom. During these attacks, symptoms such as shortness of breath, palpitations, chest pain or discomfort, choking or smothering sensations and fear of going "crazy" or losing control are present.

Agoraphobia is anxiety about, or avoidance of places or situations from which escape might be difficult (or embarrassing) or in which help may not be available in the event of having a Panic Attack or panic-like symptoms.

Panic Disorder Without Agoraphobia is characterized by recurrent unexpected Panic Attacks about which there is persistent concern.

Panic Disorder With Agoraphobia is characterized by both recurrent unexpected Panic Attacks and Agoraphobia.

Agoraphobia Without History of Panic Disorders is characterized by the presence of Agoraphobia and panic-like symptoms without a history of unexpected Panic Attacks.

Specific Phobia is characterized by clinically significant anxiety provoked by exposure to a specific feared object or situation often leading to avoidance behavior.

Social Phobia is characterized by clinically significant anxiety provoked by exposure to certain types of social or performance situations, often leading to avoidance behavior.

Obsessive-Compulsive Disorder is characterized by obsessions (which cause marked anxiety or distress) and/or by compulsions (which serve to neutralize anxiety).

Post-Traumatic Stress Disorder is characterized by the re-experiencing of an extremely traumatic event accompanied by symptoms of increased arousal and by avoidance of stimuli associated with the trauma.

Acute Stress Disorder is characterized by symptoms similar to those of Post Traumatic Stress Disorder that occur immediately in the aftermath of an extremely traumatic event.

Generalized Anxiety Disorder is characterized by at least 6 months of persistent and excessive anxiety and worry.

Anxiety Disorder Due to a General Medical Condition is

characterized by prominent symptoms of anxiety that are judged to be a direct physiological consequence of a general medical condition.

Substance-Induced Anxiety Disorder is characterized by prominent symptoms of anxiety that are judged to be a direct physiological consequence of a drug of abuse, a medication, or toxin exposure.

Anxiety Disorder Not Otherwise Specified is included for coding disorders with prominent anxiety or phobia avoidance that do not meet criteria for any specific Anxiety Disorders defined in this section (or anxiety symptoms about which there is inadequate or contradictory information).

Panic Attack Game

What's the Game set-up of requirements (criteria) that qualifies for a 'panic attack?' The DSM-IV offers this. There has to be a discrete period of intense fear or discomfort in which four (or more) of the following symptoms developed abruptly and reached a peak within ten minutes (p. 395). If you can rack up that many symptoms, you qualify to play the *Panic Attack Game.* You don't just have a case wherein you accessed a strong fear and amplified it, you are the victim of a "Panic Attack." That will payoff in a lot more attention, interest, focus, and in terms of excuse power, you'll have a lot more clout than if you just had a fear.

    (1) Palpitations, pounding heart or accelerated heart rate
    (2) Sweating
    (3) Trembling or shaking
    (4) Sensations of shortness of breath or smothering
    (5) Feeling of choking
    (6) Chest pain or discomfort
    (7) Nausea or abdominal distress
    (8) Feeling dizzy, unsteady, lightheaded or faint
    (9) De-realization (feelings of unreality) or depersonalization (being detached from oneself)
    (10) Fear of losing control or going crazy
    (11) Fear of dying

(12) Paresthesias (numbness or tingling sensations)

(13) Chills or hot flashes

What are some of the key features in having a bonafide "Panic Attack?"

> "Individuals seeking care for unexpected Panic Attacks will usually describe the fear as intense and report that they thought they were about to die, lose control, have a heart attack or stroke, or 'go crazy.' They also usually report an urgent desire to flee from wherever the attack is occurring. With recurrent attacks, some of the intense fearfulness may wane. Shortness of breath is a common symptom in Panic Attacks associated with Panic Disorder With and Without Agoraphobia. Blushing is common in situationally bound Panic Attacks related to social or performance anxiety. The anxiety that is characteristic of a Panic Attack can be differentiated from generalized anxiety by its intermittent almost paroxysmal nature and its typically greater severity." (p. 394)

The DSM-IV game book also offers a description of the diagnostic features of a "Panic Disorder."

> "The essential feature of Panic Disorder is the presence of recurrent, unexpected Panic Attacks followed by at least one month of persistent concern about having another Panic Attack, worry about the possible implications or consequences of the Panic Attacks or significant behavioral change related to the attacks. The Panic Attacks are not due to the direct physiological effects of a substance (e.g. Caffeine Intoxication) or a general medical condition (e.g., hyperthyroidism). Finally the Panic Attacks are not better accounted for by another mental disorder (e.g., Specific or Social Phobia, Obsessive-Compulsive Disorder, Post Traumatic Stress Disorder or Separation Anxiety Disorder)." (p. 397)

"That's Who I Am" Game

Did that scare you? Reading the foregoing materials from the *American Psychiatric Association Diagnostic Criteria (DSM-IV)* may give you some idea about how the psychotherapy business plays many of *the Identity Fear Games* as they turn experiences into "things" and then treat those labels as the very identity of those persons. When mental health professionals know how to use such descriptions tentatively as a diagnostic tool and without labeling, they can put the DSM-IV to good use. It can assist a therapist in diagnosing a disordering process and direct him or her with regard to giving the appropriate treatment.

[We won't belabor this here since we have a book on this subject, *The Structure of Personality: Modeling Personality Using NLP and Neuro-Semantics* (2001).]

Here we only want to identify one of the stupidest and scariest Games that therapists and others can play, that is, using a description of a process to Name a person and make it who they are. In *the Scary Game* of *"I Am..."* we take an emotion, an experience, a way of processing information and transform it into an Identity (hear screams of terror in the background, the screams in the bathroom scene of the Bates Hotel!!). It is scary. And its a way to lock a person into a Fear Game that they can't escape.

Through years of actual psychotherapeutic practice we have observed far too much of this kind of a thing going on. People have been severely damaged by having such labels stuck on to them. What's fearful about that? Namely, that the person then identifies him or herself with these labels and the "problem" solidifies into the person's mind as who they *are.* "I am a Phobic." "I suffer from a Phobia Disorder."

When that happens, a process (i.e., phobicing, panicking) becomes frozen not only into a "Thing," but also into an identity label. This naming or nominalizing makes the experience a "Thing." When that happens then the person loses all sense of the experience as a set of actions, processes, and games. That undermines a sense of personal ownership, responsibility, and empowerment. Labels lead to victimizing Games.

When this happens it invites people into some of the scariest Games of all. They then become afraid of *who they are,* afraid that they lack potential, afraid that they are fated to being a failure, etc. These describe the domain of meta-fears and Meta Fear Games which we'll explore in some later chapters.

The *Describe What You're Doing* Game

William Glasser, M.D. and psychiatrist left Psychoanalysis and founded Reality Therapy. In his book, *Control Theory* (1983), he wrote about the power of language on experience and noted the influence of terms and labels on how we experience things. He described how he would not allow any patient to use any emotional term or psychosomatic term as a noun. He demanded that they all speak about their experiences as *verbs*.

This may sound as if it is just "semantics." People generally say that as a way of saying, "It's just different definitions" and therefore it is not real. "It's just different words for the same fact." Actually it is "semantics" and as such, it is more than a matter of words. It is a matter of *neuro-semantics*. After all, the semantics or meanings that we give to things greatly influences how we experience things and the states we are induced into. That's why there is magic in turning labels about processes back into verbs. Doing so enables us to see and recognize the dynamic structuring involved in our Games, especially in the Fear Games. As the verbs then restore the processes to our view, we can recognize the framing involved in such activities as depressing, anxietying, panicking, heart-attacking, head-aching, angering, fearing, etc.

Talking this way may sound strange, especially at first. Yet it enables us to more accurately *describe what we are doing*. My suffering from depression occurs because I am depressing. My bout with rage and anger arises because I am angering and raging. My attacks of Anger and Panic arise because I am fearing, scaring myself, and panicking. This more dynamic language enables us to more accurately *map processes as verbs*. This avoids and prevents the nominalizing and reifying of terms that creates the Demon Entity of "Fear" and so prevents us from entering into that delusional world.

Accurately describing what we are actually *doing* enables us to play the *Ownership Game*.

> "Okay, I admit it, I frighten myself."
> "I panic myself by thinking about horrible things that might be and then blow them out of proportion so that they loom large in my mind."

At the same time, it supports us in recognizing the role of *interpretation* and *meaning appraisal* in our lives. That's because events, triggers, and stimuli do *not* mean anything in and of themselves. We cannot truly say, "He scares me." Or even, "Being out late at night in a dangerous part of town scares me." That assumes "fear" exists out there rather than emerges as an interactive part of our mind-body (neuro-semantic) system.

> "I respond with fear to X because I think about it in Y terms, using Z references, and the following thinking patterns."

If you think that this is "just semantics," then try it. Talk this way for a couple of weeks and notice the transformations that it initiates in you. Next time you're tempted to say, "He scared me..." shift to "He got a response from me." When you do that, you *foreground* your response, cue your brain that everybody would not so respond, but that you have learned that particular response. As you foreground this, it reminds you that you also have the ability to choose to learn a different response if that one doesn't enhance your life.

There are not "negative events," there are only our *interpretation* of events as negative.

Summary

- Labels are not real. They are not things. They do not define people and they are never the last word about human reality. The danger with psychiatric labels, like those from the DSM-IV, is that we can forget this and think that they are real, that they define who people *are*, and then get them to play out Games of fear and victimhood.
- Fear, as an emotion, as a way of thinking, as a way of responding and reacting to events, is *a process—a Game.* It's something we *do*. This gives us the structural question, "Just how do you *do* your fear process?"
- And when you know the answer to that, you can stop it and learn to do something more enhancing.

Chapter 13

GAMES FOR MASTERING META-FEARS

Games in this Chapter
The Mind Swishing Game
A Miracle Happened Overnight While I was Sleeping! Game

Feeling afraid of a specific event, person, situation, or external referent in our world provides us the informational value and signal that all emotions provide. This makes them useful. We can use them as *feedback* about the relationship between our model of the world and our experience of the world. The emotion as such tells us that we need to adjust one or the other, or both. And the emotion also provides us the energy to make some adjustment.

Yet ultimately, an emotion is just an emotion. Nothing more. We visited this understanding earlier when we described the frames for playing *"It's Just an Emotion" Game.* (Chapter 8)

However, when we *react* to any of our *reactions* of thought or emotion with *fear* and begin to fear ourselves, our states, our emotions, our thoughts, etc., we begin to dread and feel apprehension about a meaning, an idea, a concept, what we may become, what we may find, etc. When this happens, the "fear" becomes something more than a primary level fear. The fear itself can become a *meta-fear*. A *higher* level fear ("meta" means higher, "above," "about,"). Then, the higher fear becomes *a taboo* against ourselves, corroding, and weakening ego strength so that we make ourselves "an enemy to reality," to human experience, to our fallibilities, to ideas, etc. This can lead to repression, psychosomatic problems, unsanity, weakening of our personal power, etc.

Such "fear" puts us at odds with ourselves. Constructing "fear of self" can take so many forms: fear of our sexuality, fear of our assertiveness, fear of our passions, fear of being a fallible human being, fear of being vulnerable, fear of sadness, fear of excitement, fear of the idea of getting fat, fear of the idea of being rejected, etc. These are all meta-fears. They indicate a higher level of fear processing and framing.

When we begin to *bring fear against ourselves* and against our ideas, feelings, awarenesses, etc., this starts an ongoing process that can, and often does, worsen with time. It's a basic meta-stating process that we construct in our minds. And we do it so easily. We reflect back onto ourselves with fear so that we end up fearing an experience and what some *idea* about something means.

Consider that. We come to *fear* what something *means*. Then, because "fear" makes us freeze, fight, and/or flee—we experience these basic Survival reactions (the Stress Survival Game, Chapter 3) to ourselves, to our feelings, to our ideas, etc.

Yet *this kind of "fear"* (if we can even call it that at this level) begins a corroding and destructive process. In *Meta-States* trainings, as well as the basic books, *Meta-States* and *Dragon Slaying*, we constantly emphasize the potential for destructiveness that can occur.

> *When we bring negative thoughts and feelings against ourselves (or against the thoughts and feelings of some state), we create "dragon states." Doing this sets up self-conflicts, incongruencies, and puts us at odds with our own selves.*

These kinds of "fear" do *not* respond well to the *Stepping In and Out Game* (i.e., the classic NLP Phobia Cure). Why not? Because we are not afraid of an external referent. Our fear is not a primary fear, but a "fear" (dread, dislike, upset, stress, anger etc.) of *what something means*. It is the fear of an idea, fear of one of our experiences. As a meta-fear, it is a mental frame of reference for how we think about things. It creates neuro-semantic states that are higher than primary states. For this kind of so-called "fear," we need reframing. We need to set a new frame (i.e., to meta-state ourselves) with some resource that creates a higher level structure that allows us to face, accept, appreciate, own, etc.

the idea, experience, state, or whatever.

This explains why the so-called "paradoxical" intentions and prescriptions typically work so well here. We feel them as counter-intuitive, yet they work at a higher logical level.

> "Try really hard to freak out when I say this word, mention this idea, etc."
>
> "I want you to fully embrace and welcome your fear ... as you do, listen to it and notice what informational value it has for you. What does it say?"
>
> "As you look with the eyes of appreciation at that idea or feeling that you've been afraid of, just for a moment, look beyond the immediate things it does and look for its higher values and intentions. How does it seek to serve you?"

"The Me For Whom Fear is No Problem" Game

With the Swish Pattern we have a tool by which we can exchange memories or replace the visual images of deleted memories. In *Using Your Brain For A Change* (1985), Bandler describes this as a process (Game) for working on specific behaviors which a person may no longer want. In terms of eliminating many different kinds of unwanted habits (i.e., smoking, nail biting, etc.), this pattern has proven very effective. Therapists and coaches have also used it effectively to get people to swish away negative images and replace them with positive images.

Given the value and usefulness of this pattern, we have here turned it into a Game, a frame game, for eliminating fearful images and swishing the brain to a Courageous Self for whom the fear is "No Problem!" When you play this Game with your brain, you set up a new direction for your brain (or the brain of another).

The set-up for playing the Mind Swishing Game involves several pieces. It first involves identifying the old negative image. This will be the key player in the Swish Game, so you've got to get some image that gives you problems. The image could be a picture, sound, word, feeling, or combination of these. Whatever it is, the image needs to cue you to feel really bad, scared out of your wits, unresourceful, and trigger you into some piece of stupid behavior, that kind of thing.

Next, we will identify the new positive image. If you had a deck of cards and could pull out or create a card of the Ideal You— just imagine that card. Give it color, depth, richness, and add in all of the facets of the most resourceful you. This could be the desired image that you will use to trigger the new Game and enable you to be at your best, operate from your best, and give you a great place to go.

The actual *mind swishing* aspect of the Game will occur so that you move from the cue image for the old problem state toward the image that triggers the desired state. Then, with all of that set up, we will tap into the internal motivation of feeling disgusted with the old and longing for the new. This will pull on you to want to move to the desired place, but doesn't quite put you there. This will leave you with an internal pull and tension to get there.

With this set-up for the Game, we will then play it several times and that will set up a repetitiveness so that the Game habituates, leaving you stuck in a state of thinking and feeling resourceful. Now that you know the process, are you ready to play? Good, here we go.

How to Play the Mind-Swishing Game
Step 1: Identify a fear that you wish to change

What do you fear that's really stupid to fear? What fear have you had enough of and don't need to take counsel from? Identify that fear. Pick a fear that really doesn't serve you well, doesn't enhance your life, in fact, puts the damper on life. Toward what would you like to respond differently than how you presently respond?

Step 2: Identify and develop a fear trigger

What about that fear scares you? Welcome it into your awareness for a moment and just notice how it scares you. Do you experience a fearful picture, uneasy feeling, or some terrifying sound? How do you know to play the Fear Game? Since it's a response to something, what is that something?

If you were going to teach someone else *how* to play the Fear Game that you play, so that you could get a day off, how would you coach that person to play this Game? Does the cue come from some external source? Then see that image. As you attend to the Fear Game, notice all of the factors that set it off: what you say to yourself about it, how you feel, any smells, memories, etc.

When do you play this Fear Game?

In what context, with whom, where, etc.?

What do you see, hear, and feel that starts the Game?

What makes you play this Game? What cranks things up so that you become really terrified?

If you don't know how you play the Game, then just guess about some cue and pick it to see if you can use it to play this new Game.

Make a large, bright, image of what you see just before the fear begins, a picture that you actually see from your own eyes (we call that an "associated" image). Does that set off the Fear Game?

Step 3: Form and develop an image of the Bold & Fearless You

The next step in this Frame Game is to identify *the Me* for whom the fear trigger would be *"No Problem."* Doing this allows you to become an inventor of yourself, an editor of the mental movie in your mind.

Make a picture of *the You* who has so many powerful resources in the face of that old fear trigger, that this *You* would have no difficulty at all facing and mastering the situation.

How would you see that You with these desired skills and powers? (For example: see self relaxed, looking confident, look of strength, etc.)

What would you look like without the presence of the old fear? How would you look as you engage in the new desired behavior?

Make a picture of that *You* as if you were a movie director and editor. See it on the screen of your mind. Now step into that desired state of being and notice how powerful it feels. Is this enough to do the job? Is this enough to play a Game of courage, fearlessness, boldness, etc.? Do you like this?

Now step back out and leave that wonderfully powerful *You* there.   Yeah, I know, it sucks... but we're doing this for a purpose.   What purpose?   To pull on your neurology from your imagined future self... so that it pulls on you moving you always in that direction.

Step 4: *Make sure this new Bold You and the state it puts you into is ecological*

To make sure you have this setup just right before doing the mind-swishing, run your desired Self and state through the following questions.

Have you stated and pictured your outcome in a positive format?

What will you see, hear, and feel when you have your outcome?

Does your desired state depend on you, and you alone?

Where, when, how, and with whom do you want this outcome? Do you want this outcome all the time, in all places and without any limitations?

What would you lose if you accomplished your outcome?

What do you have now, and what do you need to get your outcome?

How will having this outcome affect the lives of those around you?

Step 5: *Do the Mental Swish Game*

Using the triggering picture or movie of the fear, make it really bright and large so that it fills the screen of your mind.   Make sure you have stepped into it fully so that you see it from your own eyes.

As you close your eyes, just see in front of you that image in your present life that triggers the old Fear Game.   Now into the lower left corner of this picture, shrink down your desired Self image, the you for whom the Fear Game would be no problem and put it as a small, dark picture.   Good.   You have the Game setup all ready. Now its time to play.

With the large bright picture of the fear trigger which contains that little tiny dot of the Resourceful You, now let this picture quickly fade out... zoom back into a nothingness that's dark so that it shrinks and becomes small, dark, and very dim *and at the same time,* let the tiny little dark dot of the Resourceful You become large and bright as it fills the mental screen space of your mind. Do this very quickly. Let it happen very quickly ... in the space of one second. Because brains like to go fast, the quicker you let the Game go, the better. Let the old picture *swiiissshhh* out and the new one *swiiissshhh* in... you can even hear it *swiiissshhhing.*

When you've swished your mind, clear the screen and repeat this game five more times. Clear the screen each time, that's important. Teach that old brain of yours *where to go!*

Step 6: *Playing the Mind-Swishing Game Using Other Features*
Sometimes some people just don't score enough points with size and brightness and distance. They need to play with their brain in a little different way. If that happens, then play with the sound quality and tones of voice to see if that gets you the points you want so that you can score a home run in Courage.

Step 7: *Testing the Game to see if you Win*
Now let's test for results. Did you score a point in the play? Let's find out. Try really hard to think of that triggering picture and see if it can get you to play the old Fear Game. Try really hard to do this. Try *not* to immediately swish over to the new Resourceful You image.

Step 8: *Stick the results of the Swish into your future*
So do you like the new Game? Would you like to immediately swish your brain to the Resourceful You for whom the fear trigger is no problem and then play out your life in a resourceful and courageous way? Then imagine moving through the days and weeks of your life doing just that... And notice how that

transforms things. Do you like that? Are you fully aligned with that?

Explaining the Swish Game

Why does the Swish Game work?

Because it does not leave you at the final step of the old Game but takes you one step further. It sends your brain on to yet another place, to the place where you represent your best resourceful self and as it leaves you there, you begin to experience and feel that resourceful you for whom the old fear is "No problem." The Game gives you the ability to send or "swish"your brain to that next step.

After all, brains go places. Brains connect things. They link one thing with another. It's no surprise that a fearful object triggers fear. That's basic association. The brain thinks about an object and it triggers fear. The Swish Game *uses* this knowledge by linking yet one more thing to our state of fear, namely, an identity frame: The game trains your brain to actually link the object to a picture of the new resourceful you.

"What if a Miracle Happened?!" Game

Here's a game you can play to master fears. For just a few moments, suppose that you pretended that after you went to bed, and sometime during the night, somehow, in some unknown way, a miracle happened that took away all of your fears and fearfulness and that you woke up in the morning full of courage, boldness, fearlessness, etc.. So when you awaken in the morning, you simply begin to live your life in a way that demonstrates that you have somehow awakened to life *the day after the miracle...*

Imagine that one! Go ahead. Give yourself a chance to really imagine this miracle frame.

If you do, this means that you will wake up, as it were, from the miracle and move into the day. It means that as you do, you will discover that the fears you had experienced and had worried about will no longer be there .... Go ahead and dream this dream and imagine it fully and completely... how you live life the day after the miracle...

As you do, let the following creative questions engage your

imagination.

> How would you know that a miracle has occurred?
>
> What do you see, hear, and feel as you live life without the fear?
> Suppose you didn't tell anybody else that a miracle had occurred during the night. How would they sense the difference?
>
> What would they see, hear, or feel that would cue them about the miracle?

Asking The "Miracle" Question

In *Brief Therapy* Steve de Shazer (1988) popularized the use of "The Miracle Question." He based this question on his theorizing about the human mind and how we construct our realities. He got many of his ideas for this application process from the hypnotic work of Milton Erickson.   Having based this *miracle frame-of-reference* upon Ericksonian processes, it offers a creative and generative perspective. In fact, entire books and interventions have sprung from this simple question.

In this Game, de Shazer used Erickson's presuppositions that people have the resources they need, we should start with the person's current reality (i.e., pace their model of the world), and that when we "prescribe the symptom" this empowers people to take charge of their own responses. ["Prescribing the symptom" means asking someone to perform the symptom consciously and intentionally.] This sets up the Game Plan. In using *the miracle question,* we empower ourselves or another to experience a radically useful shift in thinking-and-feeling —a shift to a solution focus.

> "Suppose that one night there is a miracle and while you are sleeping the problem that brought you into therapy is solved: How would you know? What would be different? How would your husband know without your saying a word to him about it?" (1988: page 5)

Not only does this question redirect us to *solutions*, it also directs us to specific sensory-based descriptions of what the solution will look like, sound like, and feel like. If you played with the question, did you not experience this?   It enables us to start thinking and talking about the evidences of such a solution in see-hear-feel indicators.   Doing this enables us to stay out of the fuzzy kind of thinking that contributes to "problems."

As we now turn this into a Game for mastering fears, we can apply it to our experiences of fear and even to the general attitude of fearfulness. We can use the miracle question as the frame for a Game that we can use in multiple contexts. For example, we can use it as an exploration question for therapy, as an imaginative problem solving solution for business, as a way to generate more creativity for management and consulting work, and much more.

The "Hey, A Miracle Happened Overnight While I was Sleeping!" Game

When you play this Game, you use the creative thinking that's involved in pretending. Start with the "As if..." frame of reference so that you can begin to pretend that there are solutions and then let your imagination run while wondering what they are and how to find them and how they would work out. Pretending in this way enables your brain to play a particular Game, the *As If Game.* It actually gets your whole neuro-linguistic system into action, and it then invites you to get so involved in the fun that you forget that it was all made-up. Frequently, when that happens, our brain-body system begins to think it's real and so actualize or "real-ize" the new skills and attitudes.

The Game setup flows from something wild and crazy:

> "Let's pretend a miracle happens tonight while you're sleeping, and when you wake up in the morning, the fears, anxiety, panic, spirit of fearfulness, and all of the problems due to fear (being intimidated, inability to be assertive, take risks, etc.) are gone; they are just no longer there. I wonder how you will discover the miracle? What will let you know that it happened? What will be the first clues of it? Or will someone else first recognize the difference in you."

To recruit someone to play this Game, to engage this pattern fully can occur by simply asking another, "So you really just want a miracle in your life that will make everything better?"

> "Right! That's all I want. Just a miracle."

"Okay, let's go with that for a little bit... imagine that a miracle happens tonight and... as you step into that miracle, how will you recognize it when it happens?"

Step 1: Identify the Fear or the Fearfulness
About which we'll Imagine a Miracle

What do you fear that doesn't serve you well at all? What object or event invites you into a state of fear, triggers it, an object which if you didn't fear, you could cope and master that situation much better?

What prevents me (or, you) from getting on the highway of life and living in a vital, happy, and ferocious way? What holds me (or you) back from letting go of this fear fully and completely? What thoughts-feelings (beliefs, states) do you need to explode into tomorrow with grace, power, love, passion, and confidence to replace the fear and anxiety?

Figure 13:1

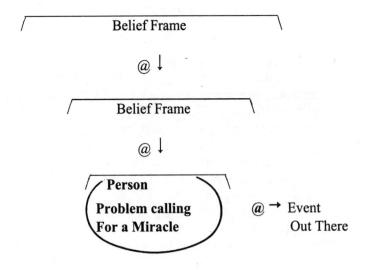

To play this Game with some of the higher level fears (the meta-fears), use the following elicitations to get the meta-fear and then ask this question:

> What conceptual category do you really *do not* like? With regard to ideas, events, and experiences in life, what will you say when you use the sentence stem, *"I don't like...."?*
>
> Fill in the abstract concept with various nominalizations (i.e., fear, phobia, anxiety). You could even have a fear, dread, or apprehension of such higher level conceptual categories as cause, time, relationships, justice, power, dependency, independence, manipulation, etc.
>
> "The idea that really rattles me is..."
>
> So what do you say *stops you,* or gives you problems?
>
> Do you fear a sensory-based constraint "out there" (e.g., not enough finances, angry boss, inadequate degrees, heights, snakes, etc.)? This would be an actual object or event.
>
> Or do you fear some category of interpretation (i.e., authority figures, *dislike* "time" pressures, *feel* inadequate due to a divorce, *feel* stuck in some past trauma, fear the possibility of getting a disease, being filthy, etc.)?

Step 2: Identify your higher level frame games

With this step in the Game, you now move to a higher level and get to play the *Meta Game* as we access and activate our higher-level thoughts-and-feelings *about* the primary level fear. We do this to flush out the executive level ideas that support and sustain the fear.

> What do you believe *about* this problem, emotion, fear, etc.?
>
> What does this mean to you? What other meanings do you give to it?
>
> What significance does it hold for you?
>
> And if that's true, what does that mean to you?

Step 3: Sketch out the Meta-Level Game Structure as you Head for the Ceiling

> Every Game has a structure. So we begin by identifying the meta-level states of thoughts-and-feelings *about* the lower level

thoughts-and-feelings. What are the meta-states and frames in this Game that structure and form it so that it functions as it does? Diagram the meta-levels embedded within higher levels.

Figure 13:2

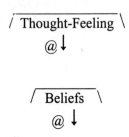

Step 4: Quality Control All of Those Meta-Beliefs
Once you have the Game set-up from Step 3, now run the Game Quality Control Check on it. Ask, "So this really makes life a party, right?"
This checks the thoughts-and-feelings *inside* of thoughts-and-feelings in terms of ecology, balance, vitality, health, etc. It checks to see if you're playing a Game that's even worth playing.

> Does this kind of thinking-feeling about the fear trigger really help you in living your life?
> Do these mind-frames make life better for you? Do they enhance things?
> Does this game empower you to experience more resourcefulness?
> Would you recommend this game to your children? Loved ones?

It doesn't? (Get a great big "Hell, No!" response at this point. When you do, amplify it out of the roof so that all of the neurological energy congruently communicates this *"No!"*)

> I don't believe you, you really need to live this way, play this Game, this is good for you!

Step 5: *Imagine the Opposite*

So you really are sick and tired of that Game? (Get a Meta-YES! response).

You really do want a different life?

You really do need a miracle?

Good. Let's play a Game. Close your eyes. Imagine that night has come and you have retired to bed. So, sleep... really sleep ... in the growing knowledge that this night will be a very special night. So just relax and dream away... fall asleep more deeply than you have ever before. Because this evening something very special is going to happen. But you won't know how or why it has happened.... because that's the way miracles are, they are *miracles*. Unexplainable happenings that just happen. And suppose that tonight a miracle happens that changes everything from the fear and fearfulness that you've lived with up until now and that in the morning you will wake up and be thinking-and-feeling in a completely different way, without the fear.... and just be with these thoughts, the feelings that they bring, and the excitement of anticipating what life without the fear would be like, because you can...

Good, now in just a minute you will be waking up to the day after the miracle, but before you do, you can begin to wonder, really wonder what that will be like. How will you know? What will you do? What will you feel in that day after the miracle. But for now you can keep sleeping and enjoying the miracle... and in a moment, when I snap my finger you can wake up without the fear.

Step 6: *Waking up to the Day after the Miracle*

Now as you take your time to adjust and to look around this room with new eyes, the eyes that no longer see fear, but see life in bold and courageous and resourceful ways, I want you to identify the first thing that will let you know that a miracle happened in the middle of the night when you were sleeping. So, how will you know? What will first let you know?

How are you thinking-and-feeling on this day after the miracle?

What state or states will you be finding yourself in?

Who will be the first to notice, you or someone else? What will they notice that's different?

Now as you move out in the world this day after the miracle, what beliefs about yourself, about that old fear object, about the world support this new resourceful state?

And what state does this experience presuppose?

What supporting meanings and values and identifications empower this new way of operating?

Step 7: Stick the Days of the Miracle out into your Future

Now that you have stepped out and into the miracle state so fully and completely, and having accessed all of the supporting beliefs, values, decisions and states-about-states that empower this experience... Do you want to keep this? Do you like this? Is this a much better frame for living? A much better Game?

Good. So just allow yourself to fully enjoy vividly imagining yourself moving into tomorrow and the days and weeks to come with this resource. Are you fully aligned with that? Does that feel congruent to who you are and what you're about?

Debriefing The Game

Did you like that Game? We play it in our trainings all the time to give people a way to totally step out of "the kind of thinking that creates the problem," to give a person a chance with a brand new kind of thinking. To play this Game you simply *step into the miracle,* experience the grace, assume the reality, and then use it to re-orient yourself to a new future that you will realize in the coming days. Do you need to earn so many brownie points to deserve the miracle? Of course not.

Just *step into the miracle.* Just represent it fully and completely until your neurology feels it. Just send those "miracle" representations to your brain so that you can then use them for new self-definition as you move into tomorrow.

But is this real? Does this really work? Aren't you just fooling yourself?

Ah, so you don't want to play, eh?

Remember, we're inviting you to do this so that you can *give yourself a chance for a new way of thinking and feeling.* Do this to access the states of confidence and courage (or whatever other state you're going after). Don't do this to prove to anyone that you already have such confidence and courage. It's not for that. *That* would lead to faking it and being dishonest with yourself. This pattern gives you the chance to *give you the chance* to try on a brand new way of thinking.

Want to ruin it completely?

Here's how. Tell yourself, "What I'm doing is not real and I'm not really experiencing a miracle and I'm not really building a new pattern, I'm just acing 'as if.'" A discounting frame of mind like that can tear apart the most creative patterns for transformation.

Rabbi Zelig Pliskin (2000) says that it takes courage to act "as if" you had courage. He quotes a person who used this technique.

> "I found [the interviews] too nerve wracking. 'Call on your inner courage,' I was told. 'My inner courage is so weak that it can't speak above a whisper,' I replied. ... During this time, I read that if you act 'as if' you were joyous, this increases your actual level of joy. ...
>
> The next day I was resolved to go for at least three interviews. Each time I walked through the door I would say to myself, 'I am now going to act 'as if' I had tremendous courage. I will feel the way I would feel if I had total confidence. I will walk and talk the way I would if I were to have intense courage.'
>
> I still didn't feel as strong as someone who is naturally courageous. But this did give me a greater feeling of courage than I ever had before . I guess that this helped me make a better impression on the person doing the hiring, and the third interview was a success." (pp. 78-79)

If you're not naturally courageous, then be *un*naturally courageous, and do so repeatedly until it becomes habitual so that you can then easily forget that you turned it on as an experiment.

The Laminating States Game

When we create a *gestalt,* this refers to creating a *configuration* of a whole that is "more than the sum of the parts." In terms of our mind-body-emotion system, we can create a much more complex state, a state of mind and emotions that is more than the sum of the parts. When this happens, various elements come together in such a way that from the many interactive parts in the system, something new emerges, something more than the sum of the parts. We call this a gestalt state. Courage is such a state. The parts of courage do not explain the overall feel or nature of courage. So it is with resilience, proactivity, etc. "The whole is greater than the sum of the parts." In a *gestalt state* we have one or more levels of states upon states (hence, meta-states). In the Game of framing and outframing a primary state, we have set in motion a new and higher state.

How To Play:
Step 1: *Identify elements and components that you want in the batch*
What are the elements and components which you will need to make up a rich and vibrant state of the desired gestalt (i.e., optimism, seeing opportunities, courage, etc.).

What higher and more complex mental-emotional game would you like to play?

How would you like to customize this mind-body game so that it seems compelling enough to create "courage" (or, optimistic motivation, resilience, or some other gestalt) for yourself?

What do you need to think, feel, know, value, and believe so that this gestalt emerges for you?

Step 2: *Access and amplify each resource*
Use small and simple examples of each quality as you access each state, and apply to the situations. Keep layering the states with more resourceful states, resourceful beliefs and ideas until it seems like something new is or has emerged. Access feeling calm at a beach, access the feeling of confidence that you have when you think about the ability to scramble eggs, access the sense of being assertive when ordering food at a restaurant.

Step 3: ***Apply to your primary situation and put into your future***

As you access each component, apply that resource to the primary fear situation always aware that at any moment the neuro-linguistic alchemy might occur producing some new emergent property from the system of interactive parts. Keep future pacing this enriching resource to how you think, perceive, feel, talk, and act at work, home, in relationships, or wherever.

Step 4: ***Install by making an empowering decision for it, then meta-Yes! it***

Are you willing to make this your program for this situation? Would you like it as your way of being in the world in place of the old program of fear and anxiety?

As you imagine moving forward with this gestalt state, notice how it will or could affect your self-definition in a rich and positive way. Do you like that? Will you keep it as yours?

The Courage Game

The design of this Game involves engineering the higher-level state of mind of *courage* and to then commission it to operate as our frame of mind. This enables us to program it as the frame of mind to wake up in .... for the rest of our lives.

How would you like that?

There are a variety of components that we can put together and mix up to create the overall configuration that we call "courage." This means that there are a variety of ways to create a batch of courage. In establishing *the Courage Game* for yourself, you will have many ways to set it up. Yet how you set it up will determine how you'll texture and qualify the game. For instance, you could have:

Risky Danger

Joyous excitement of fear (or in spite of fear)

Boldness to take risks in reaching objective

Overwhelming sense of one's desired outcome or value

Not-caring a at all for what others say or think while moving forward

Rejecting concern about embarrassment as irrelevant

Play around with this meta-level construct of courage to bring other states to bear on it as you set various frames. See the chart for giving you lots of ideas in the Game set-up. Try on different variations just for the fun of it. It will give you many ideas about how to *texture* your courage. After all, there are many, many kinds of courage. In the chart, the first parenthesis ( ) identifies a higher level state of mind to bring to interface with the lower state. This will let you discover for yourself how the higher frames organize, modulate, and drive the primary level game.

(Noble) courage	(Outrageous) courage
(Ferocious) courage	(Clever) courage
(Gentle) courage	(Charming) courage
(Delightful) courage	(Authentic) courage
(Easy) courage	(Humorous) courage
(Ambitious) courage	(Soft-hearted) courage
(Dignified) courage	(Wise) courage
(Embracing) courage	(Loving) courage
(Reverent) courage	(Innocent) courage

How to Play:
Step 1: Access a primary state of fear
What is some object that you fear that you do not need to fear? What is an object of fear that doesn't make up a "reasonable" fear and regarding which you want to respond with courage? Menu list: An audience, the elevator, getting a no, making a fool of yourself, your boss, etc.

Step 2: Recall and use a previous courageous referent
Think about *a former unrealistic fear* that you once had and which, at some time in your history, you then took the courage to face. In some way, you developed enough boldness to "face that fear," enough passion to "walk into the fear" without letting it paralyze you, enough of a compelling desired outcome so that you "put the fear in its place."
Menu list: Facing the fear of public speaking, riding an elevator,

asking someone out for a date, volunteering for something new that you really want to do, asking for a raise, etc.

Step 3: *Flush out your current frames and meta-frames*
How do you think and/or feel about that fear of that object?
How well does this serve you?
Have you had enough of this old fear dominating your life?

Step 4: *Design engineer the higher frames for the Game*
Experiment with such resources as boldness, passion, compelling outcome, etc. Keep bringing these higher-level states of mind-emotion *to bear on* the lower abstractions to see what new configuration arises. These will set up and establish the game, how to play it, the texture of the Game, etc.

Figure 13:3

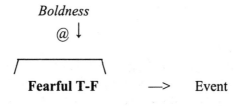

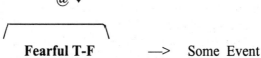

Step 5: *Check out the overall gestalt configuration*
Did courage emerge when you framed the fear with boldness? How much of it do you have? Do you need more of it? Do you need to tweak the experience in some way to make it even

better? Does this give you enough of a frame to play the game?

Figure 13:4

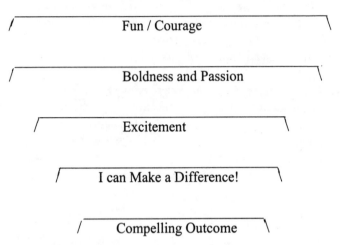

Step 6: *Keep recycling*

Continue to cycle through this process (meta-stating) as you design engineer until the desired gestalt emerges and you have all the mind-emotional-body ingredients to play the courageous game.

The "Drop Down Through" Game

Here's an idea. What would it be like if, the next time you're in a negative emotional state, instead of staying in that state and wallowing in it, or struggling against it as if trying to extricate yourself from quicksand or fighting a mortal battle against it, you just *dropped down* through it? What would that feel like? What if the *bottom just fell out* of that emotion and you found yourself dropping into thoughts, feelings, awarenesses, or state below it? Now wouldn't that be weird? And fun? Are you Game to play?

Most of the Games so far have played with the *going up elevator* metaphor. Now we want to play a different game, the *Drop Down Through Game.*   You can find this pattern in various NLP sources, having come from that model originally (James, 1989). We liked it so well that we put it in our book, *Time Lining: Patterns for Adventuring in "Time"* (1997, pp. 247-257).

The frame that sets up this Game says that we imagine using a kinesthetic feeling of free falling so that we sense falling downward, ever downward, continually through all of the fearful, hurtful, traumatic, angry, frustrated states until we find a resource state.

How to Play:
Step 1: Identify an initial event to the fear (or negative emotion)
What is the problem? What brought that about?

What is the root cause of this problem, which, when you disconnect it fully, will cause these negative emotions to completely disappear and free you for the kind of life, resources, and excellence that you desire?

When was the first time you felt this emotion?

Step 2: On your time-line, return to that first event
Be with that emotion (fear) for just a moment and get a feel for it ... what it feels like ... what you experience with it ... good ... now as you float up over your time-line and back into your past, let your unconscious mind be your guide to bring you all the way back to the first time you feel this feeling ... and just follow that feeling to other times and places where that feels familiar... all the way back....

And as you go into your past ... and find yourself coming upon the original event for this feeling ... then notice that event and notice that you have also mapped it in such a way that you gave it lots of meaning, lots of power, and that you don't have to do that any longer, in fact as this awareness grows, and you know that this journey to that old feeling will be the last one, just drop down into that event again.

Step 3: Identify and preserve valued learnings
And as you now re-visit that old event that you mis-mapped, just notice what you felt ... and most especially the things that

you have learned from that situation that you want to preserve. And notice what else you might need to learn from this event ... and you can wonder, "What can I learn from this?" What have you learned that will now allow you to let this go easily and effortlessly?

Step 4: Drop-down through

Now in just a moment I want you to allow yourself to drop down through this emotion as you *do a kind of kinesthetic free-fall through it* and I'm sure you know what it feels like when you suddenly feel the floor drop out from beneath you or that you could know that feeling and as you sense it, then as quickly as you can... Just *drop down through that feeling* ... and what is the emotion below this one? What would you call this feeling that lies beneath the first feeling?

Step 5: Keep repeating the process of dropping-down through

Good... and let's do it again... very quickly just drop through that feeling to whatever feeling lies beneath this one. And what feeling do you now find?

Continue this process until the dropping through brings you to a "void" or "nothingness," to some unspeakable stage of experience and just stay there in that void or nothingness ... often there will not be any words to describe this experience. It's jut a sense that there's nothing there. And so as you just notice it, wonder what you will experience when in just a moment you come out the other side of the nothingness to a different set of feelings and experiences, those that are more positive. When you do, keep dropping down through those positive feelings. Do this until you visit two to five positive emotions.

Step 6: Solidify and confirm as time-line resources

And as you stay with those positive feelings of love, purpose, oneness, make snapshots of what this state of mind looks, sounds, and feels like... because this feels very resourceful, doesn't it? And would you want more access to this?

Step 7: *Take the resource into your time-line*

As you hold this resource constant float back up and bring it with you fully so that you can put it into the time-line itself as a memory of your past ... and now with this inside your past memory ... move up through time with it, letting it change and transform your history ... let it touch and spread throughout your life in all the appropriate places, fully releasing any and all negative feelings, and letting the resource initiate a chain of events that makes you more and more resourceful as you quickly zoom up to today on your time-line.

Step 8: *Test for the transformation*

As you now look for or try to sense the old emotions ... have they fully disappeared? Will you use that old event as a reference point for understanding your present or future anymore?   As you think about that, does the resource now come to mind?

How much more would you like the resource to come to mind so that you have it even more fully?

Step 9: *Stick it into your future*

As you look out into all of your tomorrows, see that future in terms of having fully resolved those old feelings and issues and notice how your future seems to open up to you now ...   Do you like this? When you experience anything in the future that might remind you of the old feelings, do you now have that resource available? What symbol of that resource could you use to always remind you?

Jeremy began with his fear state and when he dropped down through it, he discovered that he was in a state of worry—worrisome apprehension about this. It felt tight and cramped. When he dropped down through that, he found himself in anger... frustrated and angry and peeved about loses and personal inadequacies, and below that he found futility... a vague emptiness and meaningless and hopelessness.   Below that was nothing. Darkness, a void– just nothingness. And below that, a sense of innocence... a know-nothingness that made everything possible. And below that, joy... an innocent sense of delight. And below that, love.

In tracking that process, we detailed the series of states that Jeremy kept dropping down through:

1. Fear
2. Worry: worrisome apprehension
3. Anger: a frustrated anger about loses
4. Futility: questioning the value and meaning of it all
5. Nothingness: the void
6. Innocence: possibility
7. Joy
8. Love

So what's below that innocent possibility, Jeremy?

"Joy... an innocent sense of just pure delight.   I feel like giggling. It's so ... ah... I don't know how to describe it, freeing and fun ..."

And being with that, drop down yet further... what do you now find?
"Love..."

Good. And just drop into that love fully and be there with it ... letting it touch and transform you... letting it get into your eyes, your face, your mouth, your mind... letting it permeate and renew you...   How's that?
"Great."

So with all of this in mind and body, consider that original fear... Can you even find it? Search hard for it...   Experience it fully with all of this...   Good. And what happens. What happens to your sense of panic? Can you play the old Panic Game when you are inside of this resource?

"No. Not at all. The old fear seems so meaningless and irrelevant now."

In playing this *Dropping Down Through* Game, people will typically move down through a series of states, each one embedded within the previous state. The sequence of embedded states generally range from dropping into two to seven or so negative states, then one or two void states, then 2 to five positive states.

> Brandy began with abandonment, dropped into scared, then lonely, helpless, the nothingness of a blank or void, God.
>
> Susan began with confusion, dropped into shock, then found fear and worry below that, then into specific fears (fear of dad, fear of losing house, fear of being arrested by the police), then into the Nothing, then into safety, then light and love.

So, what's below your fear? Do you know? You don't have to, you know. You only need to just feel the fear and to then *drop down through* it ... fully ... falling... that's right... and more, just falling until you find yourself below it and what's there? And what is that like? And when you *drop down through* that, what is there?

The Mind Back-Tracking Game

Throughout this work we have presented and used the basic NLP and NS map-making principle that governs human experience. We build our maps from our experiences. It's not always logical or reasonable to do, but given the nature of our embodiment, the nature of the kind of nervous systems and brain that we have, it's what we do. If that's what we do, then when we find that we have mapped something in a wrong, stupid, ridiculous, toxic, or unuseful way, then we need to get back to the experience out of which our map came and remap. Don't we?

This is what we do when we use the Meta-Model (Chapter 14) to explore and question the linguistic structures of our maps. The *Clarifying Questions Game* enables us to take the everyday expressions of our language and examine them to find the maps and the frames that we've created. We know that the frames create the Games.

This fits the Cognitive-Behavioral models in psychology and psychotherapy, of which NLP is one. That is, that behind every emotion lies a "thought" (alias, a frame). This "thought" may involve an understanding, awareness, sensory representation, belief, value, decision, etc. Being aware that *"beneath"* (or *behind*) every emotion lies a thought comes the idea of "back-tracking" to the thought out of which it came (Ellis, 1976, Rational-Emotive Therapy, RET, and Beck, 1976). These psychotherapy models search a client's thinking patterns and evaluative judgments to find the source of the emotions and behaviors. We have been doing that here in terms of finding the frames that drive the Games.

We describe this process in terms of the *Levels of Thought* (or mind) in the Meta-States model (Hall, 1995/2000). Taken from Korzybski (1941/1994) this simple model describes how our nervous system models things. After all, that's what our neurology does. Our neurology takes things from the unspeakable territory which we can't reach by words and abstracts (e.g. summarizes) those energy manifestations into neurological transformations (nerve impulses, neuro-chemistry exchanges, etc.) and maps things. That gives us a neural map *of* things. Eventually, we start using symbols and words *about* those maps. That gives us maps of maps. Korzybski *(Science and Sanity)* speaks about semantic mappings (frames) and semantic reactions (games). He even suggested a semantic experiment to discover the "meaning" of any given term. The effect of the experiment leads a person down further and further into the deep structure, into deeper levels of neurology...

> "Here we have reached the bottom and the foundation of all *non-elementalistic meanings*— meanings of *undefined terms*, which we "know" somehow, but cannot tell. In fact, we have reached the un-speakable level." (p. 21)

What does all of that mean? It means that sometimes we need to go back to the territory and the experiences and start the mapping all over. Sometimes we need simply to re-map in new ways that are more appropriate and accurate.

Think of the *Dropping Down Through Game* as a backtracking. In this process, we backtrack to the neuro-linguistic constructions that actually form, structure, and drive the Game. As we imagine going back or "dropping down" to a lower, or prior, level of abstraction, the *Dropping Down Game* assists us in releasing negative emotions. We *drop down* to the experience out of which we made the original mapping.

That Game used the metaphor of *falling* and going *down,* and as you probably suspect, not everyone likes that metaphor. For those who don't care to think of returning to their original mapping in terms of "dropping," we now playfully introduce the metaphor of going *behind* things. In this way, others can use this same process.

The Kinesthetic Stepping Back Game

If you are familiar with one of our earlier books, *The Spirit of NLP* (1996/2000), the next process may remind you of the *Kinesthetic Stepping Back* technique in that book. That process involves beginning with some negative emotion (say, fear) and stepping back from it on our time-line. When we do that, then we can see it from a prior perspective, see it before it happened. It's weird, but just a neuro-linguistic Game. That means that out in front of us we see, as if from a spectator's point of view, our Future Self in a fearful state. How about that? By stepping back from that state in this way, we access or step into another state, into the state just prior to the negative state. And we step back into a state in which we feel more resourceful because we have not yet stepped into that fear state. This lets us play the *Resource Game,* as we ask,

> What resources would change that future experience, would make it less fearful, less distressful?

Asking this question enables us to elicit just the right resources. So that's what we do. Right there and then. We can access a wide variety of resources (i.e., calmness, confidence, self-esteem, sense of power, etc.) and fill up that space in that step with those resources. Neat Game, right?

Well, if it worked with one step back, how about a second step back? Yes, we can step back again and now see our prior self accessing resources for changing the then future step into the fear state. Here we can again imagine additional resources that would help. And so on it goes. We continue to move back on our time-line, stepping back and associating into more and more resources as we move back, and gain increasing perspective on our future path.

By the time we back up several steps we backwards engineer a pathway of resources. Imagine that! Now as we look toward our future, we see step after step into resources. Wouldn't it be nice to walk that line now? Hey, why not? If you have a coach who has helped to elicit each step, then invite that coach now to do his or her thing—coaching you to walk the line to step through the resourceful time path into a more resourceful future, stepping into each resourceful state fully ready to bring all of that to the fear state.

All I have to say about that is, "Watch out fear state!"   So get ready, get set, go... *move forward in time* with those new resources and let the old path change as you move up to the present. Now commission this entire process to completely re-organize your memories and resource references and to use this for the rest of your life.

Backtracking into Resources

If you liked that, backing up or back tracking to the cognitive-behavioral state out of which the fear, frustration, dread, worry, etc. came is a similar process.   In it we ask, "Where does this state come from?" Then we go there. We start with fear (or any negative emotion) and then back up. From where did the fear arise? From a sense of hurt. Okay, go there. And where did that come from? From a sense of feeling inadequate. Okay, go there. And where did that come from? From feeling out of sorts. And that from not feeling very much alive or vigorous, and that from feeling a little tired, and that from feeling okay with self, and that from feeling passionate about a project and that from feeling committed to a vision. Great. Stop.

We've just backed up from a fearful experience and lots of "down" feelings all the way back up to where things are just fine. We've back-tracked. In doing so, we saw where things went astray. We saw where we got off target, where things started going down hill. We took too much counsel from being tired and feeling out of sorts. We have *all* the resources back there to deal with fear.

This pattern as a Game uses the realization that states come from states. That states arise from thoughts and feelings, and from states of health and neurology. Then by backing up we can see where we need new resources to give us more leverage over the ups-and-downs of life and over other processes.

> "And, behind that thought whirling in your mind lies another thought.... So as you allow yourself to notice ... what thought do you find back there?"
>
> This directional question swishes the mind backwards and offers a profound and simple way to go back to a void of nothingness, or to other more neutral

states, or even to more positive resourceful states, and
to then walk through the pathway of time in a new and
different way.

Lights, Camera, Action! Let the Game Begin

Susan was in her mid-fifties, came from a strong religious faith and
loved NLP concepts and patterns. Yet to maintain her own health and
sanity she chose to leave a marriage of 38 years. Why? Because the
marriage had been filled with multiple affairs and addictive behaviors
in her husband.

In her recovery and healing, she began reading *Dragon Slaying*. Yet
as she did, a dragon surfaced that she knew she had to slay. It wasn't
one to merely tame; she needed to completely eliminate this one. It was
a dragon of fear— Fear of taking care of herself, Fear of ending a long-
term marriage, Fear of the finality of the separation, Fear of her future,
the Fear Dragon breathed fiercely down upon her.

*"Susan, behind the thought that you are having a hard time dealing
with the finality of the separation and divorce after 38 years of marriage
there swirls another thought in the back of your mind ... now as you
notice the thoughts, feel free to describe them and flush them out.*

"I feel afraid... I feel afraid that I'm really here because of an
addiction, that I am or have had a sexual addiction to my
husband and that it's been a sick thing, a disgusting thing."

*And, behind, the thought of being totally addicted, sexually, to your
husband lies another thought, what is that thought?*

"I am not sure I can trust you with that because you are a man."

*And, behind the thought that you cannot trust me because I am a man
swirls another thought. What is that thought?"*

"My mother taught me well that I am not to ever trust any man."

*And, behind the thought that you are not ever to trust men, and that
this is scary, what thought lies behind that thought?"*

"That I trusted my husband, and mother was right about not
trusting men. I'm afraid of not knowing what to do. What am
I going to do now"

*That's a good question. And behind that question you have another
thought, do you not?*

"Yes. I am a very sexual person and I don't know how I am going to deal with this now. And right now I am going to confess something ... that I have thought about being with another woman. And, I'm afraid that I have made a big step by confessing that thought. I can now understand how people can think themselves into homosexuality."

And behind the thought that you have thought of being with another woman whirls another thought, what is that thought?"

"That it is unacceptable to me. I need to know how to accept my sexuality without feeling it is addictive, and not feeling like it is bad. I couldn't have sex with another man until I get this straight in my mind. Because when I have sex with my first husband, it wasn't love. He didn't love me. And, it wasn't my love for him either. I was just addicted to sex. And that's what I'm afraid of."

Susan, behind that thought lies another. What is that thought?

"I want to have a relationship with a man who is full of love and full of sexuality."

And, behind that thought, what thoughts arise?

"I think and hope that I want us both to be healthy and godly, and I know it is out there. I know that there is a man out there for me. I believe that God has great things for us. I already know that. The devil has been putting these negative thoughts in my mind to mess things up. I am not going to let the devil get the victory."

And, Susan, behind not letting the devil have the victory, what thought is there? ... Susan paused ... she became speechless, and I figured that she had moved back to a place of nothingness, or a void of some sort.

"Is this the place of pure potentiality that you talked about? Is that what this is? It's so weird and yet so wonderful."

That's right, Susan, go fully into the place of pure potentiality and enjoy it. And, as you are there in pure potentiality, what do you now know? What resources does this bring to you?

"Confidence. I know that I'm going to love again, and marry again and have a husband who will share lots of things with me,

even NLP. It is going to be unreal how many lives we are going
to touch."

With this, Susan began to get so excited that she actually got up and
began walking around. ... *Are we through?*

"No, I have one more thing. I really struggle when I try to
accept the pleasurable things that life offers me.

Good, so what thought lies behind the thought of enjoying life?

"Well, I feel guilty, I feel like I don't deserve to enjoy life."

*So, behind the feeling of guilt for letting yourself feel pleasure, what
thought lies behind that one?*

"Maybe ... ah, that I don't deserve pleasure. I don't deserve
pleasure because I have made such a mess of my marriage. And
I don't deserve pleasure because I was just as wrong as my
husband... "

And, what thought lies behind that thought?

"I have to accept responsibility for the failure of this marriage.
I have always blamed him, and said that he is the guilty one.
Now I have to accept part of the guilt."

*And, Susan, what thought lies behind accepting your part in the
responsibility?*

"Well, I'm thinking that I am forgiven for what I did wrong ...
that I can't make any more choices for him. And behind that I
sense Pure Potentiality!"

Saying this caused her to light up like a morning-glory.

"And I have forgiven myself."

And you have slain that dragon?

"Yes, and my castle is all white."

Summary

- As we move beyond fears that refer to actual things, we move to the meta-levels of fears. We begin to fear ideas, meanings, emotions, and higher level concepts. We fear our fears and then those meta-frames become our governing frames.

- For meta-fears, *Swish Your Brain* to "the Me" for whom this or that fear is no problem. Talk about a powerful and generative Game that transforms more than just a particular problem, Mind-Swishing creates a new orientation and direction in life.

- So does the Miracle Game. Imagining life in the days and weeks after a miracle does something weird to the nervous system. It sets up a self-organizing influence that invites the miracle "as if" frame to attract a new way of moving through the world.

- If *the Quality Control Game* gives us incredible leverage over sick Games, the *Laminating Your State Game* enables us to actually install new qualities into our Games. That allows us to play Gestalt Games and cook up a batch of Courage with just the right flavors to our liking.

- *The Drop Down Through Game* changes the metaphor and allows us to let the bottom fall out of a Game so that we can see what's below it, and what's below that. *The Mind Back Tracking Game* does the same thing, using another metaphor. These Games take us to the place of pure potentiality—and what a Game that sets up!

- All fear is not the same. The nature and wonder of meta-levels lets us know that. As fear moves up each level, it becomes more and more of a dragon or a demon to us. You have just discovered some of the Dragon Slaying and Taming Games that you can play ... and yet there are more to come.

PART IV

ADVANCED LANGUAGE GAMES FOR MASTERING FEARS

Though *advanced,* the following chapters will have a special appeal to those who are curious about how we can actually language fear states into existence, and use language to master such fears. These chapters take you into the heart of both Neuro-Linguistics (NLP) and Neuro-Semantics (NS).

Chapter 14

THE GAMES OF LANGUAGE

Games in this Chapter:
The Specificity or Precision Game
The De-Nominalizing Game
The Blame Game/ The Un-Blame Game
The Meaning Game/ The De-Meaning Game
The All-or-Nothing Game
"But It's my Modus Operandi!" Game
The Fuzzy-Wuzzie Game

Chapter twelve introduced the idea of scaring ourselves by nominalizing. We have it within our power to *name* emotions, experiences, ideas, etc. and *transform* those processes into seemingly Monstrous Entities. How does that work? It works by *the symbolic nature of language* and how, in human experience, *language* governs experience and neurology. That's why this work is based upon neuro-linguistic and neuro-semantic models.

Yes we know that we have not yet described *Frames* or *Games* fully. That comes in the two chapters that follow this chapter. We will get to that. But first we want to introduce how *language works in neurology* and some of the Language Games that we play. These Language Games either increase the terror and fear or they decrease them and give us tools for mastering our fears. When you understand how we linguistically *structure* the Games of life that we play, how we do it, how words map out our sense of reality, and how words create personal limitations and empowerment, you'll know how to change the Fear Games by how you talk to yourself and others.

Without this understanding, people live deaf and blind to the very mechanisms and forces that create their fears. Without realizing the neuro-linguistic power in our words, people drug themselves with anti-anxiety pills while they *keep turning up the fear* by the way they talk. Without an appreciation of how much language governs human consciousness, they fall into delusions and think that their fears are functions of external events, situations, and people. This then leads to adopting some of the worst possible coping mechanisms, and yet the very mechanisms that "seem" and "feel" most natural. Namely, avoidance, denial, refusal to face reality, refusal to confront, "just wanting peace," etc. Without an appreciation of their own role in languaging, they junk one of the most effective tools they have at their disposal for recovery and for taking charge of their own brain and managing their own states.

Language as a Game

Since the symbols we use to process and convey information describes one of the ways that we act and interact in the world, we can think about our use of language as a Game. Many philosophers have. Wittenstein was perhaps the first to think about language as a Game. From research in child development and studies about feral children during the early years of life, those who don't learn how to play the Language Game can't develop their human potentials. When I wrote my dissertation, I focused on *Languaging* and especially about the magic of language in therapy. In that work, I briefly alluded to the research on feral children, children lost to human society during the formative years of language development (six months to four years). These are the unfortunate children who become lost to their families and who are raised by wolves or other wild animals.

Over the centuries, numerous such children have been found. What's interesting here is that those who missed the imprint period of human languaging were never able to enter into the human experience. They were never able to handle *symbolic life*. They ate with their hands and were never able to eat with silverware. They grunted and signaled, but never talked. Most died in their teens.

These extreme cases show to what extent human consciousness is *languaged*. We talk, speak, and dialogue our way to our way of life into existence. Listen to a person in terms of the words, symbols, ideas, beliefs, and language patterns that a person uses. Such reveals the way that person thinks, reasons, values, etc. and the internal experiences that person has and the internal world that that person lives in. Language is *that* crucial. *How* and *what* we say forms and molds our emotions, skills, experiences, possibilities, limitations, etc.

And, *change your languaged world and you change.*

This highlights the heart and soul of what Alfred Korzybski discovered and formulated in General Semantics and what the NLP and Neuro-Semantics models focus on in creating patterns for working with our languaged consciousness. After reading this chapter, one reviewer said it was too deep. He thought it would be over the head of the average person and so he suggested we eliminate it. Because we disagreed, we got busy simplifying it as we could.

> [If you want the full version, see *Communication Magic*, 2001 (formerly, *The Secrets of Magic*, 1998, on the Meta-Model. This is an updated version of the original NLP books, *The Structure of Magic I & II,* by Bandler and Grinder, 1975, 1976.]

Language as a "Reality" Builder

Language drives all of our mind Games, all of our emotional Games, and all of our inter-personal Games. Language has *that* much influence in our Frame Games because we use language to set up the Games, name the Games, describe the Games, keep score, and understand the Games. Also, Games thrive on the linguistic labels we use.

Some Games, in fact, not only thrive on language, but are mostly *Language Games.*

Language and language Games begin by how we "think" using our sensory references. At the first level, this enables us to *re-present* to ourselves information that we have seen, heard, felt, smelled, or tasted and so keep replaying old scary movies. At the next level, we think by coding our understandings in words. This enables us to scare ourselves with *ideas*.

Have you ever done that? Have you ever gone beyond scaring

yourself with sights and sounds to scaring yourself with *ideas*?   The best horror movie directors and writers know how to do that. Hitchcock was a master at that. It wasn't what he showed you that was so scary, but *the ideas he implied*. So with many of the most fearful things on the old Twilight Zone series. Having ants or bees swarm all over one is scary enough, but "being a failure," "throwing away everything you worked for during a lifetime," "losing your most loved and precious one," "being lost forever," etc. —these are much scarier things. And for the most part, you can't see them, hear them, feel them, smell, or taste them. We only know about them through words. Words that encode scary *ideas*.

By words we can take all of the sensory pleasures and delights of a summer day at the beach, an experience involving specific sights, sounds, sensations, and smells of the ocean, the wind, the waves, the sand, etc. and we can encode them all linguistically in a phrase like, "a relaxing day at the beach."   In this way, words give us symbols of sensory experiences. Yet they give us more. We can use that reference experience and classify it as "relaxation," "resourcefulness," "being centered and integrated," etc.

If we can do that with a positive experience, imagine the horrors we can create if we use a painful and distressful experience! There's no end to the levels of torture, dread, worry, anxiety, judgment, hate, regret, etc. that we can build up. There's no limit to the maps of pain and danger that can scare the daylights out of us. Talk about coming equipped with an exquisite torture chamber.   We certainly have that in the higher levels of our mind! And we do that with, yes, you guessed it—*words*.

Linguistic symbols and structures give us the power to operate frames and frames within frames for even more complex Fear Games, or for Resourceful Games. We can use words to evoke a neurological re-experience of a horrible experience, and then we can crank it through the ceiling depending upon the conceptual ideas that we frame that experience in.

Given that words function as maps of experiences, words can provide us schemes, models, or paradigms; the frames that establish our Games. Yet words can be used in ways that go beyond merely mapping various territories. We can create word symbols for things that don't exist, can't exist, and then use them to evoke corresponding neurological responses. It's in this way that we can *talk* ourselves into panic attacks, paranoia, worry, and all kinds of fearful states—states that have no correspondence with anything.

Is such fear real then? Depends on what you mean by "real?"

As *an emotion,* you will experience the "fear" as neurologically real. This is the way it is with every emotion. Inside our bodies, we always experience our "e-motions" as *motions* derived from our *evaluations.* So, whatever we experience "emotionally" we experience as neurological events of our body. There, and to that extent, our emotions are real. Every emotion, after all, is a reflection of the relationship between map and territory (or experience). But as an indicator of what exists out there or what one should do, emotions are often inaccurate, wrong, not real, and not useful.

Add a Word and Change a Reality

When Nancy called for a consultation and brought in her list of things that she wanted "fixed," her fear of water was at the top of the list. We told this story in *Mind-Lines* as an example of how just a *line* can sometimes quickly change a mind and transform a life.

What about water are you afraid of Nancy? How does that pose a problem to you?

She talked at first about some past experiences with water that she didn't like. Then, after dancing around the thoughts and emotions zooming in and out of her awareness, she said, "I will drown and die."

So you're afraid of water because you fear you will drown and die...?

Yes, that's right. I know it sounds funny ... crazy... but that's what I think.

So tell me this, what would happen if you died to the belief that you are afraid you are going to drown and die?

[Long pause... face flushed ... then a smile spread across her face] Why, I could enjoy water! ... [Then laughing] ... Well, that blew that one out of the water, didn't it?

What "sense" did that statement make? How is that logical or rational? Why did Bob say such a thing? Why did he play on the idea of "death" and bring "death" to bear upon the thought?

It really doesn't matter. It worked. Not only did Nancy get free from her fear of water but also her fear of heights. That fear was installed one winter when she was eight years old as she rode in the back of her dad's car as they crossed over a high bridge. The iced over bridge led to her dad losing control of the car so that they spun around and around on the bridge. And although they did not crash and although no one got hurt, as she became scared, she attached the feelings to "high things" and to the fear of water. And that connection of that old emotion and that *idea* of high things and to water remained for 40 some years. Then one day in 1997 a few lines changed her mind and so transformed her life. What a difference to her life today. Today she drives without fear along the high cliffs in the Alpine Mountains.

The "Specific" Indexing Game

NLP itself began as a language Game. Linguist Dr. John Grinder used the T.G.—Transformational Grammar—model to figure out the magic of three world class and renowned therapists. Grinder played an academic Game (called "modeling") with his associate, Richard Bandler. And out of that mix they created a linguistic model which they called "the Meta-Model of language." At the time Transformational Grammar was the cutting edge model in linguistics and so they used it to study *how people code meaning* at various levels of the mind, and how the "deep structures" of experience   are transformed into everyday expressions at the "surface structure" level.

When Grinder and Bandler came upon three therapeutic wizards who were using language in "magical" ways, they explored the very structure of that magic. They wanted to know how these world renown therapists could create such fabulous transformations by *just talking* to people. Out of their exploration, they developed a model *about* how we use language to model or map reality, hence *meta*-model. From the gestalt elegance of Fritz Perls, the systems thinking of Virginia Satir, and medical hypnotism of Milton Erickson came a model about how to use *language* to map reality in ways that enhance rather than impoverish our lives. The model enabled people to play new and more effective language games.

The Meta-Model first of all enables us to play the Game of *High*

Quality Information Gathering. You only have to use the powerful questions of the Meta-Model and you can gather high quality information. The questions enable you to use language to clarify language and to create precision in communication. It also invites and evokes the person we question to reconnect his or her language with the experience out of which it came, thereby inviting new mapping.

Why is that important?

Because we are linguistic creatures and live so much of our lives in language and according to language. We use words to define what's real, possible, valid, etc. It is with words that we encode our ideas about what's threatening and dangerous. As we do, we create our programs or frames for when and how to go into fight/flight states. This means that we can access states of fear, dread, anxiety, etc. just with the words we use. This often happens in the most innocent of ways. We happen to use some words that presuppose threat, danger, or fear in some way, and suddenly we find ourselves in a neuro-linguistic state of fear.

If language and linguistic encoding of thoughts can create fear, we can use this same tool for getting free from fears that dominate in our lives and mastering fears that are irrational and non-enhancing. When you know this, you have moved a long way to becoming a master of your fears, your emotions, and your states.

To play this Game you only need to *index* whatever you, or another, says. *Indexing* refers to asking for more specifics. We ask for more specifics when we index:

-     The Time— When?
-     The Place— Where?
-     The Person or Persons— Who?
-     The Process or Processes— How?
-     The Reasons and Understandings— Why?

It's as simple as that. Of course, to master this domain we will want to learn as much as we can about the neuro-linguistic processes at the root of language processing and how to language ourselves and others most effectively. That's where the Meta-Model comes in. This higher level model *about* language mapping provides the linguistic tools to enable us to get to the experience behind, below, and above a person's words.

After all, whenever we speak, we do not give a complete description of all of our thoughts behind our words. We only give summations or general narratives. We do that in part because we are not able to fully describe things and, if we were, we would never finish our description. Nor can any verbal description exhaustively say everything about an experience. As speakers, we will always have a fuller representation than what we put into words.

Our thoughts have levels. There's the fuller representation of all of our frames of reference and then there's the surface expression. Much of the fuller experience isn't even conscious. Much of it lies at levels *prior* to language; some lies *beyond* words. We use the questions of the Meta-Model to more fully explore the referent experience. The questions elicit or evoke the speaker to provide or create a fuller map. Things deleted are restored; unsatisfactory generalizations are re-evaluated; distorted mapping is recognized and re-mapped.

The "Specific" Game of Indexing enables us to undo our former map-making that suffers from things left out (deletions), conclusions prematurely jumped to (generalizations), and maps out of wack with reality (distortions).

What does the Meta-Model look like? Made up of a dozen linguistic distinctions, the model identifies semantically ill-formed maps in language and offers a sets of questions to work them over. We "work" the map "over" by putting it to the test. We find out how well formed it is. Does it make sense? Does it give us words that allow us to make an internal movie. That's the Game.

> Can you track over directly from the words to an audio-visual movie of the referent?

If you can't— you lose a point. Fluffy map. Non-specific. Unclear. Use that as a cue to *ask the specificity question.* The respondent then has to *make the verbal map clearer.* If he or she does that, add a point! Clarity. Precision.

Sometimes, to answer the question, the speaker has to "go inside"and recall the referent experience. In this way, this model recovers the missing information.

How to Play the Precision or the Representational Tracking Game

Step 1: Listen for the actual words that used and examine them in terms of how well they actually map reality "out there."

Words are only as good as they provide a good *mapping* from the way the world is to our mental pictures and images of such. As you listen, notice statements that you can't track over to the mental screen in your mind. If the words don't let you see, hear, feel, taste, and smell the referent experience, wonder curiously what's missing, what's over-generalized, what's twisted. Require that your brain use specific words that can connect with the see-hear-feel world out there and that your higher level conclusions, beliefs, and understandings can be connected to the empirical world.

> Is something left out? What? Unspecified nouns, verbs, relations, etc.? If so, inquire.

Check for other mapping problems (generalizations and distortions.)

> Has something been too generalized?
> Has a conclusion been too hastily drawn?
> Has a process been distorted so you don't know how it works (cause-effect)? Do you know what it means or how it came to mean a particular thing (complex equivalence)?
> Do you know how they know or have information about another person (mind-reading)?

To play this Game, stay in *sensory awareness*, don't allow any projecting of your meanings or references onto the other's words. Adopt a "Know Nothing" frame of mind.

Step 2: Question everything vague or ill-formed.

Any time you don't know how a mental map works, ask about it. Explore the specifics, index the details.

> How do you represent this 'rejection?'
> Where did you get that information?
> Does it always work that way?

What have you presupposed in this mapping?

Is this an over-generalized map?

Step 3: Continue checking for areas of un-clarity and ask for more precision.

The Game continues until you obtain sufficient information to adequately represent the meanings (yours or another's) in your movie so that you can then run a Quality Control of the Game itself.

Does this mapping and the Game that it initiates enhance my life and empower me as a person?

Is this a positive and enriching Game, one that I would recommend to others?

Does this map and the Game that it sets up enable me to go to the places that I want to go to?

The Clarifying Questions Game

We could equally describe these questions as *the Clarifying Questions Game.* By simply asking lots of indexing or specifying questions, it sorts out and even deframes our linguistic constructions of fears. This shows that the mapping wasn't legitimate in the first place, but poorly modeled. Most debilitating fears are those that immobilize us with uncertainty.

How big is the potential negative consequence?

What can I realistically expect?

What past experiences am I really responding to?

Do I need to use that past experience as my reference point?

What really is the cue that triggered my response of fear?

What else could have played into my fear getting triggered?

What else could that cue have meant?

How else could I have interpreted it?

To what degree could my own attitude have created the event?

How have any of my actions contributed to this experience?

What are my typical expectations about this trigger?

What effective actions can I take?

I asked Joseph about the fears that he claimed were a panic disorder. He told me that he felt dreadful anxiety about his performances in college and that they were debilitating him and ruining his life. "So you're not going to school any longer?" I inquired.

> Oh yes. I'm going, but I feel fear everyday and lots of anxiety, and I live in dread about having a panic attack.

So you don't have panic attacks?

> Well, I almost do every day. And by the time I get home, I'm exhausted with all of the fear and anxiety.

So do you have the attacks of panic?

> Well, not exactly.

You just fear that you will.

> Right.

And you're still going to class, taking the tests, completing the assignments, and doing all of the things you need to do to complete the courses and graduate?

> Well, yes, but I keep thinking about having to get up in two of my classes and report on my research projects. I fear that I'll have the panic then and that will ruin everything. Then I won't get into graduate school.

You tell yourself all of *that*? You lie to yourself with all of *that* nonsense? My God, no wonder you feel ready to freak out. I would too if I fed my brain that kind of crap. I bet you even use a fearful tonality when you think those thoughts and miss out on the fun of saying all of that in Miss Piggy tonality or Elmer Fudd stammering.

> But it's the truth.

You mean you *really believe* that making a fool of yourself in a class will keep you out of Graduate School? What, you think everybody who goes to Graduate School is beyond being fools? I've been there ... I can tell you. They let fools in! 'They do suffer fools gladly.'

> But I get so anxious, so nervous... what if I forget everything?

Ah, the *What ifs... Game!* Yes, that's a good Game to play in your head if you want to freak out. But I think you have an even better one going. I think you're playing the *I've Got to be Perfect and Flawless* Game. I'm guessing that you're playing the *Compulsive "Have To" Game.* You tell yourself that you "have to" get straight As. You "have to" excel at everything. Am I close?

> But that's just the way it is.

Ah, you're going to do the *But this is Absolutely Real and Seriously Real* Game with me, huh? And sure enough, we could go there and have a Battle of the Games—a Frame War. But let's say you win, does this way of thinking, this way of talking to yourself —about how real and serious and black-and-white, and all the rest... does this way of thinking empower you, enable you to be at your best, make studying at the college level a party, infuse you with courage and confidence?

Well, no. It doesn't.

Are you ready to stop it? Would you like to play a more confidently courageous Game? And one that you might have fun playing?

The Fuzzy-Wuzzie Game

A simple linguistic distinction (from the Meta-Model) describes deletions. These include simple deletions and deletions that compare things without any indication as to the standard for the comparisons. *Deletions* can leave lots of expressions very vague, fuzzy, undefined, unspecified. Words that lack a referential index or unspecified nouns, verbs, adverb, adjectives, etc. enable us to play the Fuzzy-Wuzzie Game. The aim in this Game is to keep everybody guessing what in the world you're talking about. You get points by increasing the Fuzz Factor.

You can play Fear Games with unspecified verbs that vaguely describe non-specific actions. Use words like *hurt, upset, injure, threaten, concern* without providing any specific referents. As you leave more specific details out, it enhances the Fuzz Factor.

"I feel abused just being near him; he's so hurtful."

"Since I moved here, my fear has grown worse and worse."

You get points for playing this Game by deleting as much information as possible and eliciting others to fill in the blanks with their own hallucinations! The more others have to guess and engage in guessing, the better a player of the Vague Game you are. Count points for misunderstandings. That's another sign of this Game. So is conflict, resentment, hurt feelings, etc.

A Fear Game Player says:

"I'm afraid of getting involved with anyone. I was hurt really badly in my former marriage, and I don't think I will ever get over my fear of being hurt again."

Using "hurt" as an unspecified verb is worth a point. Texturing it with a little bit of Allness scores another point ("anyone," "ever"). Three points for the Blame Game (the cause-effect: previous hurt—>afraid of getting involved again). The person missed out on a big five pointer, "I'm just not cut out for relationships" (Identity Meaning Game which comes from the linguistic distinction of Complex Equivalence).

The Precision Game, of course, blows this Game to smithereens.

> What hurt do you fear? Hurt with regard to what? Hurt in what way? Did you not play any role or responsibility in the process of the hurt? Have you not developed any resource for coping with the possibility of hurt in the giving and receiving of love?

The All-or-Nothing Game

With the distinction of *Universal Quantifiers* we can play the All-or-Nothing Game. This allows us to turn *one* event or situation into a *forever and ever, world without end* event. Pretty nifty, eh? It allows us to *blow things way out of proportion* and to make a *big deal* out of otherwise mundane situations. Always great for adding some drama to life (pain is included).

When we describe the quantity of a thing, we measure its size, length, endurance, weight, amount, etc. Doing this with things makes lots of sense. It gives lots of folks jobs. It fuels science, mathematics, engineering.

Doing this in the realm of mind, however, takes us to a very different kind of place. It initiates a very different Game. So quantifying something *universally* means framing something as always and forever for everybody to be something, or conversely, it can never, at no time, for no one be valid.

To play this All-or-Nothing Game, just attach an universal word or term that universally quantifies something. Doing this, you will set the frame of Absoluteness. While doing this, feel the God-like power of the generalization of allness! Say it in a bellowing, deity-like mode.

> "After the IRS audited my taxes, I'm always scared about taxes and government. They're all out to get you. They don't care for working people at all."

"Being abused by my dad and brothers growing up, I now know that all men are abusive; that's why I'm afraid of all men."

What a Game! Throw your weight around with these allness words *(all, never, every, always, none)* and you can get a fight going in minutes, sometimes seconds. When you play the Allness Game, you do not leave *any* room for *any* exceptions. You have uttered the *last* word about it. "That's *just* the way it *is*."

Now to mess up this Game and rain on this parade, you have to be a little devilish as you use the Allness words and play the Game right back in another's face. Challenging the Allness Game typically brings out the absurdity of the Game.

> *ALL* men are abusive? Really? There's not a single male on the face of the planet? *Never* has been?
>
> So you have *never* met a man who did *not* abuse ... and abuse women at *all* times?

People who play the All-or-Nothing Game effectively hold onto their fears. Justin said,

> "I have a fear of dying. I'm afraid I'll have a heart attack, an aneurysm and end up bed ridden. I am afraid I am not healthy, that I will get cancer. I have *always* felt that something might be wrong with me."

What a convoluted Game: the Allness Game, the Meaning Game, the Blame Game—Games layered on Games. This gives the Games great staying power. The language Games played out here provide *no* chance of recovery. It *is a* closed case, a foregone conclusion. Hopeless. The Fear Game *totally* dominates. There's nothing wrong with this kid's brain. He simply has the strategy to this Game down pat.

"But It's my Modus Operandi!" Game

Now linguists like to play the Game of inventing jargon for linguistic distinctions. That used to be true with a vengeance for folks in the Transformational Grammar field. They're the folks who brought us "Complex Equivalence" and "Nominalizations." They also brought us *Modal Operators*.

Don't you like that one? *Modal Operators*. Has a nice ring to it. But, hey, why not go back all the way to Latin and get the original?

Modus operandi. Now that has some zing to it! Your *modus operandi* is your M.O.—your *style* of operating, your *mode* of operation. Cool.

To play the *Modus Operandi* Game, you have several choices: Necessity or Desire; Possibility or Choice. What Game do you want to play? What *way of being in the world* do you want to adopt?

> The Necessity Game: I have to, should, must, need, etc.
> The Choice-less Game: I don't have a choice
> The Desire Game: I want to, wish, desire, etc.
> The Possibility Game: I can, am able to, am capable, etc.
> The Choice Game: I choose to, decide, select, etc.
> The Impossibility Game: I can't.

With modal operators we describe, format, frame, and language our *mode* for *operating* in the world. We get to frame our Matrix world.

> Do we operate in a mental world of laws: should, must, have to?
> Do we operate in a world of *opportunities:* possible, possible to, can?
> Do we operate in a world of *obligations:* ought, should?
> Do we operate in a world of *empowerment:* dare, want to, desire, etc.?

The modal operator terms define the boundaries of our model of the world and our style of operation. To tell what Game a person plays, just listen to the way people talk.

> "I can't stop my panic attacks. My doctor says I have a chemical imbalance."
> "I want to stop the worrying and fearful apprehensions, but I can't stop thinking that way."
> "I don't have a choice. Given the traumatic events I've been through, I can't control the fear."

These Fear Game Players keep the game going by this language. These are not innocent words. Nor do they operate innocently. Not at all. They are part of the conspiracy! They frame and format the world these people live in, and will until they change that languaging. We play the Games we do by the words we use. Fear Games thrive on words that describe and frame limits.

To blow this Game out of the water, use the Precision Game questions again:

What would happen if you stopped panicking?

Do you like the frame your physician used on you?

What stops you from panicking yourself?

Does your not having choice enhance your life?

"I have to let this fear go."

What will happen if you do not let the fear go?

What would happen if you did just *let go* of the fear?

How would your life be then?

I know you can't, but if you did become courageous, how would you know?

The Blame Game

The Meta-Model has a distinction that we call, Cause-Effect. This refers to our mapping of cause, contributing factors, influence, etc. The more a person has a scientific or engineering perspective, the more we use the idea of cause to suggest responsibility, ownership, proactivity, etc. Yet many people take the idea of "cause" and immediately jump to the conclusion that it equates with *blaming. Of course,* that's their equation (or Complex Equivalence). This then leads them to playing the Blame Game.

Consider:

"You scare me to death!"

"You always make me afraid of taking a chance when you talk that way."

"I don't like your tone of voice, it frightens me. I'm afraid you're going to do something rash."

These sentences imply *external causation.* They suggest that external triggers, tones, words, ideas, etc. *make* or *cause* another person to experience the state of fear. By implication, this language suggests that the speaker has no choice in how he or she will respond. The responsibility is placed on some external source. Yet as it frees the speaker from his or her own response-power, it blames the external source.

This is the "The Devil Made Me Do It" Game. It implies that other people and external triggers can exercise psychic powers over us.

We play the Blame Game with a set of special words:

Cause-effect words and statements: *make, cause, force, etc.* Any active verb will do to imply causation.

Causational Effects: *if then statements, as you... then because,* Directing attention to an external source: *you, they, it.*

Now to ruin this Game, you have to ask challenging questions that call this external focus into question:

How specifically am I causing you to feel fear?

What processes am I using to make you have these feelings, thoughts, or responses?

Do you have no choice in how you respond?

So you have to have this reaction to this stimulus?

So you are totally powerless and helpless, a victim, to external triggers?

So I can absolutely play your keyboard and you can't do anything about it!?

These questions ruin the Game because it invites the person to re-think and re-map. It thereby empowers the person to assume response-power for his or her own feelings, thoughts, and responses. This facilitates a more proactive response. When people frame themselves as being "at cause," the Blame Game is over.

To play the Victim of the Blame Game, we have to *refuse* to own our own powers and frame the things that we experience as the effects that others cause. We also have to pretend to be the cause of effects on no one else, not even ourselves.

We set up the "I laid all my fears and anxieties at your feet; you are the cause of them!" Game by framing all power to be "out there." We have to blind ourselves to our personal neuro-linguistic powers of thinking, emoting, speaking, and behaving. The Game ceases, however, the moment we open our eyes to these innate powers. Questions from the Precision Game can help with the eye-opening:

Do I really want to give others or this person the power to scare me to death?

How can events that happened years ago cause me to feel fear today?

Why am I affirming and validating my fear?

What if I said "**NO!**" to my fear?"

Does this way of thinking really serve me?

The Meaning Game

The linguistic distinction called *Complex Equivalence* provides a neuro-linguistic game for creating meaning out of diverse elements. To play this game, grab any event, person, object, activity, etc. that you can see-hear-feel in the outside world. Any trigger will work. Now grab a state of mind or emotion and cram the two together. This makes the two equivalent and while it seems like a simple equation, the complexity is that the two come from different dimensions and realities. As a formula, the game generates—

$$X \text{ (external thing)} = Y \text{ (internal state/ significance)}$$

This is the human Game par excellence. We play this Game all the time. We create Complex Equivalences every time we take an empirical part of an experience (one you can see, hear, feel) and treat it as equivalent to some internal state (thought, idea, feeling, memory, imagination, etc.).

You get points in this Game when the external cue immediately and automatically evokes the meaning.

> "I was in a car accident 30 years ago, so fear of driving is just part of my life now."
> "I suffered lots of embarrassments when I was a kid, that's why I'm so fearful and timid now."
> "Seeing people upset or angry means I've done something wrong and that something bad is going to happen."

Ah, the mental equations that we create by linking external behaviors with internal states! What a Game. To play this Game, there are lots of language forms that really make it easy:

> Equation words: *is, are, am, that means, equals*, etc.
> Relational orders: link external phenomenon with internal phenomenon.

To ruin this Game, to pick up your marbles and go home, simply run some of the Precise Game indexing questions in Columbo fashion.

> Specifically how does being in a car accident 30 years ago

(external behavior) mean fear of driving has to be your ongoing
state for years without end?

How does that work?

Does that mean any and every experience with strong emotion
attached to it forever locks you into some state?

Has that happened with every strong emotion you've ever felt?

Has anyone else ever experienced a car accident without
developing a fear of driving?

Or has everybody in every car accident always fallen victim to
'fear of driving' thereafter?

Does this equation enhance your life?

Have you given yourself permission to attach new meanings to
the old triggers?

Would you like to?

What new meanings would you like to attach to the old
triggers?

Who would you be if you did?

Here are lots of ways to ruin semantic constructions like that. If we
glue the old meaning construction together with words, we can unglue
them with words that tear apart or deframe. This is the Deframing
Game.

The Nominalization Game
"Who's Been Frozen in Time and Space?"

We all play *the Nominalization Game*. This is the Game that we
play as we move through life *Naming* and *Labeling* things. We look at
some process or action and give it a name. When we do, it's like
touching it with a super-ice finger. It has to freeze in space and time.

Look, what is that?

"That's an insult."

"That's a put-down."

"That's motivation!"

"That's determination."

"That's failure."

This Game has been played so long and so pervasively, that the
dictionary writers, seeing how we name things and *nounify* them, have

defined a "noun" not only as a tangible object, a "person, place, or thing," but has included such mental processes as an "idea."

The De-Nominalizing Game
"Behold, You're Unfrozen!"

Like the Game of tagging people and they have to freeze, we can also unfreeze these words and labels and restore them to life. We un-name actions and processes and recognize them as verbs. To play the *Verbifying* Game, you have to first find a frozen verb.   To do that, use the Noun Tester. Can you put the referent on a table or in a chair? *Real* nouns are tangible objects, "persons, places, things." *False* nouns are in disguise. They sound like nouns, "motivation," "failure," "self-esteem," etc., but they are not externally real.

"I have a problem with *relationships*."

"My *self-esteem* is at a low point. Too many *failures* I guess."

Yep, here are some nominalizations. Frozen pieces of actions that now look like and sound like things. Let's unfreeze them.

Tug at the word to see if the verb will fall out. "Relationships" ... relate... ah, the hidden verb. Now play the *Precision Game*: Who are you relating to? When? Where? How? Why? To what end?

"Self-esteem..." esteem. What are you esteeming? How? By what criteria? When? What stops you?

"Failure" .. fail.

Sometimes you have to dig deeper to find the hidden verb. You might even have to find out the origins of the term. The verbs of some nominalizations occur in another language. "Spirit" ... breath ... to breathe.

Unmasking the deception of nominalizations can be lots of fun. It's like strip poker. You keep challenging the nominalization to get it to undress so we can see its naked verb. A nominalization hides a process. Here's another way to test it. Does it fit into a saying like, "an ongoing_____." If so, it's a nominalization. "An ongoing relationship" makes sense. An ongoing baseball does not.

The De-Nominalizing "Fear" Game

Run the Un-Freezing Game on fear and anxiety. Can you put "fear" or "anxiety" on a table? In a chair? No? Ah, then you probably having some set of actions frozen in time and space. Does it fit into the "ongoing" phrase? "An ongoing fear" and "an ongoing anxiety." Does that make sense? Yes it does. Bingo! Nominalizations.

Detection phase ended. Now tug at the words. See if you can wrench a verb out of them. "Fear" ... "Anxiety" .. anxious...

Ah, tough words. They don't unmask easily. Inside of anxiety is the idea of choking, originally it came from the word for "to choke..." This reveals the kinesthetic sensations typical with feeling anxious, a holding of the breath, not breathing fully, feeling a constriction. Inside of "fear" as a noun is the verb fear, "to fear, to be afraid..." to think and feel endangered, threatened. Ah, the verbs! The mental, emotional, and physiological *actions*.

Okay, so we've *elicited a verb* from the nominalization. Now what? Oh, yes, the Precision Game.

> What are you evaluating as dangerous or threatening?
> How do you know to make that evaluation?
> Do you always think this way? Feel this way?
> What if you didn't?
> What stops you from stopping the old pattern?
> Do you have to?
> Does everybody respond this way?
> What resource would make that response unnecessary?
> How would you prefer to respond?

These indexing questions typically enable a person to create a new map about a situation. Most situations do not need the fear response. Those that do can be tempered with other responses: calmness, clear thinking, decisive choices, clear valuing, etc.

The very Game of returning the false "thing" back into a process reduces its power over us. When we nominalize mental and emotional processes, we give ideas and emotions too much reality.

"I suffer from Panic Attacks."

That fits the same format we use when we're dealing with true objects, "I suffer from wolf attacks." "The dragon attacked me and scorched the scene."

"I was doing fine last night until the panic attack occurred. It really got me. In fact, I had to call for an ambulance and go to the hospital."

This is the Thingification Game that the DSM-IV plays so very well, but mostly to our detriment. Its category, "Panic Attacks," treats it as a thing, as a disease, as something to be medicated for.

The case study in chapter one provides a sample therapeutic "language Game." The design of the conversation was to tear apart the "thing" called a Panic Attack, to un-freeze it, and to thereby take away so much of the power that had been attributed to it. Justin had been giving all his power away to his fear by the way he had been thinking about it. His conceptualizing of the problem empowered it.

[By the way, "problem" is a nominalization also. The verb inside it? "To cast before." We create "problems" by casting all kinds of things before us... Fear of rejection, fear of being laughed at, etc.]

When we pulled apart the structure of his "problem" we discovered that Justin was *engaging in some actions,* some mental actions in his head by which he was creating his fear experience. That's how it always happens. That's how we all do it. Even panicking ourselves with future anticipations expresses our mental and emotional powers.

Justin had developed the skill of *stepping back* in his mind to an old LSD trip that went bad. By *associating* into that old movie, and running the language frames he did, he cranked up the sense of threat and danger. He pushed it to overload. Then, presto! Out popped a full blown panic... or, now that we know better, panicking. He was engaged in panicking.

This describes how "Panic Attacks" work. They always involved representing an event, memory, anticipation, idea, or concept in such a way that it cues the body's defense mechanisms.   In that sense, it is "real" inside the person's mind, the way he or she processes images (usually of traumatic memories) and then languages it with semantic toxins ("This means I'm losing it, I'm a loser, I'll never amount to anything, I'm defective, etc.). And it is "real" in the sense that it certainly sends those messages to the brain so that it gives instructions to the nervous systems to freak out.

Nominalized "things" like fear, panic attacks, anxiety disorders, etc.

are not externally "real." They do not exist "out there" and get into the body. They are rather neuro-linguistic processes. They describe our internal programs or strategies for creating our fear experiences.

If you can't break the nominalizing habit, then at least choose some ways of thinking, imagining, conceptualizing, etc. that will serve you really well. Pick such nominalized experiences like peace, love, joy, faith, calmness, confidence, courage, resilience, resourcefulness, etc. They'll provide you much healthier Games; Games that will leave you feeling energized and alive.

The Cartesian Logic Game

Cartesian Logic gives us an excellent way to challenge our thinking, especially the irrationality of most of our fears and anxieties. To use it as a Game, simply run a fearful idea through the four Cartesian Logic questions listed below. If you process your internal logic through these distinctions and experience no internal conflict with your answers, then your thinking reflects an ecological perspective. If you can't, the questions expose and vanish the irrational thoughts.

The Game set up is to use the following questions for processing a thought or a piece of mental logic.

1) What will happen if you keep your phobia?
2) What would happen if you do not keep your phobia?
3) What wouldn't happen if you keep your phobia?
4) What wouldn't happen if you did not keep your phobia?

Let's illustrate with the idea, "I almost drowned 30 years ago. It was that experience which caused this phobia I have."

1) What will happen if you keep your phobia?

Well, I'll remain fearful of water, not be able to go near water, not be able to enjoy swimming pools, beaches, rivers, etc. I will look like a fool around people in certain situations, I will be treated as a mental case.

2) What would happen if you do not keep your phobia?

It would free me to enjoy more things, and not have to think about water so much, about whether I'll be near a pool or something. It would increase my self of personal control over my own self.

3) What wouldn't happen if you keep your phobia?

> I won't go on vacations near water, I will not develop personal confidence or master my fears. I won't develop the skills for handling situations.

4) What wouldn't happen if you do not keep your phobia?

> If I don't keep my phobia of water, I won't have to worry about things so much, and won't have to think of myself as a wimp, and won't have to explain about my near-drowning trauma anymore.

Summary

- *Language* empowers us to create higher frames and hence higher Games that can serve our personal empowerment or make life a living hell. The choice lies in how we talk to ourselves and others.

- Language skills, as suggested in this chapter, give us the ability to deframe Games, especially Fear Games, that undermine our effectiveness and create debilitating feelings.

Game Set-Up

Distinction	*Statement —>*	*Question*
1. *Unspecified Nouns* (Simple Deletions)	"It really scares me."	What specifically scares you?
2. *Unspecified Relations* (Comparative Deletions)	"That's much scarier."	Scarier than what? Compared to whom, what?
3. *Unspecified Referential Index*	"They rejected me."	Who specifically rejected you?
4. *Unspecified Verbs*	"I felt tortured by that..."	How did the torture work?
5. *Nominalizations* (Verbs turned into Nouns)	"Fear controls my life."	What are you fearing? How does fear control you? What fear controls your life?
6. *Universal Quantifers* (Allness)	"I always get scared when..."	Always? There's never been a time when you didn't?
7. *Modal Operators* (Operational styles, modus operandi)	"I have to be afraid of him. I can't help it.	What would happen if you did? What would happen if you did not?
8. *Lost Performative* (A statement that deletes the speaker)	Only fools ignore fears.	Who says that? When? Where? Under what circumstances?
9. *Mind-Reading*	You're afraid of doing that!	How do you know that I'm afraid?
10. *Cause-Effect* (Causation statement)	She really scares me.	How does she scare you? What action triggered your fear?
11. *Complex Equivalence* (Things on different levels equated)	He has a frightening tone.	How do you know the tone means that?
12. *Presuppositions*	Everybody in my family has these kinds of fears.	So you're assuming your fears are genetic?

Chapter 15

GAMES FOR MASTERING HIGHER META-FEARS

The Semantic Reaction Games

Games in this Chapter:
The Semantic Reaction Game
The "But I Have to Salivate!" Game
The Word Phobia Game
The "I Could Have Had a Moment of Consciousness" Game

There are fears, and then there are really high level fears. There are fears at the primary level, then there are *meta-fears*. These are our fears about ideas, concepts, anticipations, etc. We looked at how such fears are linguistically structured in the last chapter and will describe Meta-Games for handling them in this chapter.

In the earlier chapters, we began with the primary *Fear Games* as we typically think about fears (or more accurately, *fearing*) as strong emotional reactions to specific people, events, and situations. It's fairly easy to test external things for whether they are truly threatening, dangerous, or overwhelming. We only have to identify the external object and question it in terms of its potential for danger or threat. We can then inquire as to when, where, degree, area, etc. We can also ask the Resource Question,

> *"What resource would I need to effectively handle this object or situation?"*

After that we began unmasking the higher level *fears*—the fears that are layered and textured with concepts and ideas. These refer to how we create levels of fears, fears about fears, and fears about all kinds of *ideas*. These meta-fears initiate neuro-semantic states and frames of mind that we can carry with us for a lifetime. And, they initiate more subtle and resistant Games.

Along the way we have also made a distinction between healthy and sick *primary fears*. Doing this empowers us to sort between the Sick and Healthy Fear Games so that we can reject and refuse the first as we welcome and embrace the second. This allows us to play the right kind of Games with fears—as we would want to play with any negative emotion. In the *Healthy Fear Games* we welcome the somatic messages. These are the messages that weigh the relationship between our Map of the World and our Experience of the World, the messages we call "emotions."

The negative, debilitating, and destructive fear games really begin when we refuse to welcome fear, understand it, appreciate it, reality test it, quality control for it and evaluate it in higher level terms such as our goals, objectives, character, social context, etc. The problems we develop in relationship with *fear* usually involve our beliefs, understandings, and feelings about *fear*. That moves us to a higher level. This leads to the higher or semantic Fear Games:

> Fearing fear itself
> Raging angrily at our fear
> Rejecting our fear in judgment and disdain
> Dreading our fear
> Shaming ourselves because of our fear
> It's unmanly to be afraid
> If you accept fear, you'll become fear-dominated
> If you feel fear, you have to obey it
> It's futile to not act on the fear
> Etc.

When we do these kinds of things, we play the *"Let's Create Dragon States out of our Fears"* Game. When we do, it then begins to consume us and fill us with unhealthy, toxic, and morbid *ideas* about fear. Such meta-level frames of mind then establish the governing rules (or cognitive frames) for how to play those really sick Games.

How do we create Dragons? Generally by embracing any idea, feeling, or action that rejects rather than accepts fear. That sets up the

Game. It puts us in a bad relationship to fear. Then we fear fear. Then we close our eyes and minds to understanding it, facing it, and welcoming it. Then we misuse our fear by turning it against ourselves. Earlier, we talked about this being counter-intuitive and paradoxical in nature.

From a higher level of acceptance and appreciation, we can *embrace* the emotion as an emotion (or play the *"It's just an Emotion Game"*), find out about the message in the fear, and then make mindful choices about what to do about it.

The "But I Have to Salivate!" Game

The Semantic Reactions Game is easily detected. Just look for unthinking, automatic, and knee-jerk type of reactions in yourself or others. Have you ever seen such? When was the last time, say, during the last twenty-four hours, that you experienced such? It's really easy to detect because it's so common—so much a part of our experiences as meaning-makers.

To flush out your own semantic reactions, and the "But I Have to Salivate When I see that, hear that, feel that, think about that..." Game, use any of the following questions:

- Are there any ideas or concepts that "get" you?
- What words or terms upset you, rattle your cage, or push your buttons?
- Can people "push your buttons" so that you get into a reactive mode?
- What do they have to say, do, gesture, etc.?
- What can you expect of yourself when you feel threatened?
- What is par for the course when you feel frustrated?
- How well adjusted are you to states of stress?
- Do you like your anger or rage?
- What happens when you feel disappointed for the fifth time in a day?
- How well do you live with shame or guilt?
- Does vulnerability, exposure, embarrassment,

intimidation ever get you?

The Semantic Reaction Game

Korzybski described a phenomenon which he called, *"Semantic Reactions."* This refers to when we react, not to events and physical stimuli, but to *semantic* stimuli—to *meanings.* It refers to how *meanings* (semantics) incorporated as our frames-of-mind and our attitudes then drive our Games. When that happens, *we then automatically and unthinkingly react.* That's a semantic reaction. Like a physical reflex, we respond in a knee-jerk reaction to *symbols.* The meaning has gotten into our body, our muscles, and our neurology so much that we don't have to think about it any longer. We just feel. The meaning has become somatized; it has become metabolized by our body. Now the higher level meanings (frames) completely govern the Games we play and how we play them. We then experience things as if we are "programmed" to react to ideas, words, feelings, etc. that violate our frames. And, in a way, we are.

In a semantic reaction, we use our nervous system similarly to how animals use theirs. We treat semantic stimuli (meanings, frames) as direct signals. Doing this blinds us to the stimuli as *symbols* and so we fail to use our nervous system in a more advanced way so that we have more extensive human possibilities.

Yet precisely because we are a symbolic class of life, to the extent that we set higher symbolic meanings about fear, we can thereby turn our fears into *Fear Frames* about experiences, ideas, concepts, people, emotions, thoughts, etc. So even though we may *not* need to fear those things, if we set such frames, then the very content of *ideas* can become fearful to us. Then our bodies will react as if we were falling off a cliff, being burned, being attacked by a wolf, etc. The experience of these higher meta-fears will *feel just as real as our feelings to true dangers.*

Now in contrast to semantic reactions, Korzybski also talked about the human way to respond. He talked about semantic *responses.* A semantic response arises as a fully conditioned and conscious response because it comes from our awareness and choice. It comes from our *human mindfulness* about things. So instead of blindly and unconsciously reacting as if conditioned by some Pavlovian trigger, we mindfully and consciously respond with choice. What a Game! It's a Game of *Mindful Empowerment*. Want to play? In this Game we use the higher cortical functions of our brain instead of relying on the easier and quicker lower, yet more primitive, Fight/Flight responses of the lower brain.

When we set a frame of fear—the *frame* commissions and organizes our whole mind-body system for fear. That's what higher frames do. They establish self-organizing systems. In doing so, the frames set up the fear itself as an executive level attractor. This enables and programs us to see, hear, and feel *fear* everywhere! It also sets a command to the nervous system so that the "fear" gets into our very muscles. Then we have "fear" as our program for "response readiness." This transforms our experience of fear into the spirit of fearfulness.

When that happens, we are set up to self-evoke panic attacks, panic disorders, paranoid states, states of hesitation, apprehension, etc. How about *that* Game? We can establish a Game of *"Being Totally Freaked out by Ideas, Words, and Gestures."* And we can set up such Games without any awareness that *we* played a part in the set-up. That's the weird thing about it. Once we have the Semantic Reaction Game set up, we then react *as if* external stimuli are "making" us feel, think, act, etc. This blinds us to the role that our symbols and symbolic systems play in cognition.

The Word Phobia Game

During the years when I conducted extensive Assertive Communication Trainings, I found myself surprised at how so many people seemed to suffer from *Word Phobia*. Like the character Marty in the *Back to the Future* movie series who became blindly reactive when anyone called him "chicken," they just "had to react" to certain words, terms, phrases, gestures, etc. In Marty's case, the very question, "What are you? Chicken!?" was such a come on. It "pushed his buttons." He didn't have permission to be thought of as a chicken. He had to prove himself every time. That's a case of semantic reactiveness. I began exploring this as we worked to unplug the buttons and become un-insultable.

Later I began noticing that this idea had even broader applications and ramifications. Other people were not so criticism sensitive, but had other forms of semantic reactiveness. Some had semantic reactions to *new words,* others to *big words,* others to *emotionally laden terms.* At first, I simply would comment, "Hey, they're just words." But what I learned was that *to that person, they were not just words.* They had thoroughly *confused* map (words) and territory (experience). In their nervous system, they really did not know how to distinguish or separate map and territory. They *identified* one (the word or words) with the experience. In their nervous system (neurology) the word seemed real to them. They had so confused the word with the actual deed that the word seemed, felt, and was experienced as if the deed.

Korzybski described this as *animalistic* in order to point out the structure of this process. It is animalistic to the extent that we use our nervous system as animals use theirs. It is animalistic to the extent that we *identify* map and territory as the *same* thing. This *identification* reveals a primitive way of thinking, the lack of critical distinctions. It's also a form of unsanity.

"Un-sanity" he called it, not insanity. To do so does not mean one has become crazy or cannot tell what is real. It means that one doesn't make some very critical and important distinctions and so cannot make the best adjustments to reality (sanity). Consequently, this leads the nervous system to become full of *nervous reactions,* hence "neurotic."

This highlights the importance of the map/territory distinction. We use systems that *stand for* and *represent* something *other than themselves.* The word "three" is arbitrary. So is "cat." So is "computer." Linguistics separates us from the primitive so-called "language" of animals. They use "signs," not symbols. The sound of the growl is *part of the message* of threat. The showing of the teeth is *part of* the message, "I'm ready to attack" or "This is my territory." Dogs do not, have not, and cannot use the showing of teeth or the growl as an arbitrary symbol for something else, "I was thinking about a frisby that I had when I was a puppy."

As a symbolic class of life, who build and experience and evoke *neuro-semantic states* every day of our lives, we use *symbols* (words, language, math, diagrams, formulas, etc.) to stand for other things. The word or the symbol *is never the object it represents.* Whatever you say about something does not create that something. Words are not "real" externally.

To describe a horror movie, a frightening scene, a terrible prospective future is to *just say words.*

- Can you hear such descriptions as just words, as just descriptions?
- Or do the words immediately evoke semantic reactions?
- Have you been using your nervous system (neurology) animalistically?
- Has it served you well?
- Are you ready to come into the full heritage of a human being with higher cortical functions, who can rise up to meta-levels in his or her use of symbols?

Playing the "I Could Have Had a Moment of Consciousness" Game

To really master fears, and to live a life that moves you way beyond a life of having your buttons pushed, your cage rattled, and suffering from unreasonable and irrational fears, etc., we can learn to play a new game, a *Game of Mindfulness.* The following offers a step-by-step way to set up the Game so that you operate from an executive level of meta-mindfulness.

Step 1: *Learn the Map/Territory Distinction until you can Feel it*

Do you know there's an unbridgeable gap between your maps of reality and reality itself? Do you *feel* it in your body?

If you did *feel* it in your body, how would that feel? Pretend that you know and begin to gesture out the awareness that "The map is not the territory," "The map is but a map, a set of symbols *about* the territory." Let your hands guide and formulate your understandings.

Do you know that you always and only deal with reality indirectly, through your maps, frames, and understandings? Do you know that whatever you say or think about anything is just a mapping?

Are you willing to know this and discover this and let this

become a guiding principle in your life?

Step 2: *Invite Consciousness to be your guide*

If *mindful awareness* describes the human way to move through the world, then have you fully and completely decided to make this your modus operandi?

Will you rise above the animal's world of Stimulus —>Response?

Will you find and live in *the gap* between Stimulus —>Response? The gap where you can think, consider, meta-think, take action, become proactive, etc.?

Then say it:

> "No more blind, unconscious *reactions* for me. I will take full responsibility for my thinking, feeling, speaking and behaving. These are my responses. No one 'made' me think, feel, speak, or act as I did. They might have invited me, but I accepted the invitation. If I can do that, I can also turn down invitations to feel fear, operate from fear and take counsel of my fears. Though words may elicit and evoke representations they are ultimately *my* representations, under my executive direction."

Step 3: *Practice running and developing your own brain*

Will you develop conscious mindfulness? Will you decide to run your own brain and to manage all of the higher levels of your mind by accessing a meta-awareness?

Will you commit yourself to learning more about how your brain works and to taking control of your internal movies and the frames you set?

Step 4: *Set standards for your mind*

Will you, from this day forward, stubbornly refuse to take counsel of your fears in an unthinking and mindless way? Will you instead take counsel of your values, intentions, empowering beliefs, and desired outcomes?

Will you play the *Quality Control Game* with your brain and life and set some higher standards for your semantic states?

> "As I realize that taking counsel of my fears is just a bad habit, I will quality control my fears. Some fears I'll respect because they hold me back from acting foolishly; other fears I'll respect as signals of all ideas that no longer serve me and boldly face down from my resourcefulness, confidence, and greater understandings."

Step 5: Practice resource framing

Will you from this day forward, begin practicing accessing your highest resources like confidence, faith, hope, joy, love, calmness, proactivity, etc. in responding to life's events?

Will you play the Game of Personal Resourcefulness and immediately respond to any and every challenge, threat, and/or danger by asking, "What resource do I need to effectively handle this?"

> "As I treat fears as messages and check them out for accuracy, I will live primarily from an empowered state of knowing my self, my values, and by having a bold and courageous vision of what I want to do with my life."

Detecting & Mastering Pseudo-Fear Games

Having recognized that there are a wide-range of experiences which fall under the category of "fear," and that there are also experiences that are meta-fears, we can now begin to recognize that many of the meta-fears actually have nothing to do with "fear." I know this sounds strange, but it's true. We call them "fears," but when we do, we mis-name them. Frequently, we have simply linked or connected an experience to the term "fear" that actually represents just an unpleasant or undesirable emotion. To call it "fear" inaccurately maps the situation. To assume that our label is infallible locks us into an unsolvable prison.

Not only do "fears" at meta-levels differ radically from fear at primary levels, but they typically take on some very different properties.

This means that the very nature of "fear" shifts and changes at the higher levels and takes on some very different semantics.

For example, consider "the fear of public speaking." Polls indicate that this represents a major and significant fear for millions of people. Many people begin to feel fear when they think about standing up before a group of people to make a speech. What are they afraid of? Are there any actual dangers or threats?

There could be. It could be a primary level fear. Fear of losing a job if one is candidating and the speech goes poorly. Fear of being critiqued by a professor and getting a poor grade, flunking a course, having to repeat the course, etc. Fear of reporters misrepresenting one's public position on an issue, of being unfairly portrayed, of exposure of weakness in the ideas or the presentation. Sure there could be some legitimate, actual threats and dangers. Yet even these *depend* upon the semantic significance we give to such. How important is that to you? What is the worst case scenario of danger that it could pose?

More typical, however, are the meta-fears involved in public speaking. Most people are only vaguely afraid of things— fear of criticism, of looking foolish, of being on the spot, of not being fully prepared, of standing out, etc. These are the meta-frames that set up the Fear Games that we play. "But what if I'm not outstanding, brilliant, and dazzling?"

Then there are times when it's not "fear" at all, but some other emotion that masquerades as fear, that's falsely labeled "fear," and that therefore cannot be solved by fear mastery techniques. Such is the following case.

Christopher, a professional in his field of medicine and a corporate business owner who also had lots of training in NLP, called. I knew that he held himself to a high standard and that "walking his talk" was really important to him so that he would not have been the kind of person to have only run the pattern in a half-baked way or to have excused himself with stupid excuses. His complaint? Fear of public speaking.

> "I'm still afraid of public speaking. I don't know what went amiss or didn't work when I did the 'Phobia Cure,' but it didn't work. I felt better for awhile; but I was still afraid. I guess I need something more powerful than that. Do you have

something specifically for public speaking?"

Tell me, how do you know you're afraid of public speaking.

How do I know? Because I get afraid every time I speak in public.

Really? And how do you actually know that you're afraid?

Well, because I get nervous mainly. And my hands sweat and my heart is beating fast and my stomach feels queasy. That kind of thing.

That's all? (I said in a credulous and doubting tonality.) *I still don't understand how you know to call* that *"fear;" that's what I feel when I get "excited."*

Well, it's really uncomfortable.

Yeah? (More incredulity and with a tone of "You've got to do better than that!)

Well, there's the nervous energy. I never start out very smoothly, sometimes I even stumble for my words and I nervously move my hands...

Yeah? That still sounds like it could be excitement and possibly the lack of thorough training in gesturing. What is there about any of that which has to be labeled "fear?" That's what I want to know.

It's *not* fear? But it feels fearful.

That's what I don't understand yet, how do you know it's "fearful?": Do you freeze up and can't talk?

Well, no. I always finish the speech.

Well, maybe you have the fearful cognitions of wanting to run away? Is that what's going on? You really don't want to do public speaking?

No. I do want to speak in public. It's great for my career, it helps me to influence others and that kind of thing. And I'm actually pretty good at it.

Well, maybe you're scared to death of what others' think? Afraid of criticism, afraid of being rejected as a worthless human being? That you'll be disgraced by your incompetence?

(Laughing) No, no. It's not that. I do want to make a good impression. That's why I do the extensive preparations that I do.

So you're not wetting your pants in fear about messing up and looking like a fool?

(Laughing even harder) No. Of course not!

Well, Christopher, I think what we have here is a case of a mistaken label. It doesn't sound like fear to me at all. It sounds like the marvelous excitement of really wanting to knock their socks off.

But I don't like the feelings that I...

That's the problem! (I said interrupting)

You mean I've meta-stated myself with *a dislike of my nervousness* and have falsely mislabeled it "fear?"

Exactly.

And that would explain why the NLP Phobia Pattern didn't work with me? It wasn't a phobia in the first place?

Precisely. You weren't phobic of anything. Did you ever have a traumatic public speaking experience that invited you to set the frame that "Public speaking is dangerous?"

No.

And your thoughts about public speaking?

Well, ah ... that I like it; that it promotes my influence, that it's important in my career, ... and that I don't like being nervous.

Ah, the meta-state structure! You "don't like being nervous." You don't get a kick out of feeling and sensing your whole body reving up and getting ready to let them have it!

Yes, I guess that's it. I have always thought that "nervousness" meant fear and was a bad thing.

Like the first time you had sex. If you felt nervous about it, that had to mean that you were a flop, not really excited, scared of women, that kind of ...

(Interrupting me with laughter) I get it. I get it. You made your point.

Christopher was not afraid of public speaking. He simply had a bad relationship with "nervousness." He didn't like *the experience* or the feeling of nervousness. He also didn't like *the idea or concept* of being nervous. At first, I just coached him into using deep breathing and relaxation to give him the edge on turning the nervousness into managed excitement so that he "had" it rather than it having him (*Instant*

Relaxation, 1998). With the meta-state of dislike of the idea of being nervous because of all the things it had come to mean to him, we reframed its meaning, accessed acceptance and appreciation of his nervousness so that he could "dwell more comfortably in his skin with the fact that nerves sometimes generate somatic energy."

I then played some meta-stating Games with him as I layered his dislike of feeling nervous with several resources. If you have eyes and ears to detect the meta-levels and Frame Games, you can catch *frames* that I set for him:

> *Christopher, since you'll be speaking to a group on Thursday, I want you to use it to see if you can use your managed nervousness and come up with three gestures that you can use to transform it into "excitement." And every time you feel the sensations that you have called "fear," I want you to imagine a resourceful voice saying, 'Not fear, anticipation of how I'm going to knock their socks off!' And as you do that, just experiment with how much nervousness you can translate into excitement, knowing that as you do it is increasing your professional skills as a public speaker.*

When "Fear" is Mis-Labeled

We have found that fear is most often mis-labeled, as it was with Christopher, because we so easily confuse another emotion with it—namely, the emotion of *"dislike"* (discomfort, uncomfortable, queasy, etc.). Christopher disliked a certain set of sensations and had learned, or been taught, or somewhere picked up that those sensations mean "fear." Consider some of the things that you say you fear.

Criticism	Rejection	Insult
Public speaking	Taking a risk	Elevators
Small places	Cold calling	etc.

Now step back from your frames and wonder, really wonder;

> "Could I just *dislike* the sensations, or some facet of the experience, or the *idea* of it and only be confusing *fear* for my dislike?"

Not being turned on about taking on the dislikes and disapprovals of others ("criticism,' "rejection") is a pretty normal response. What if, instead of it being a *"fear,"* your experience really indicates that you do not particularly like it, are not particular drawn to it with total excitement, "Oh, Boy!," or even that you just lack some of the necessary skills to handle that event with grace and dignity.

I worked with a group of agoraphobics a number of years ago. They had (and have) an Agoraphobics Association. That always struck me as kind of paradoxical because they didn't do teleconferencing, they met at the leader's home. That meant they were all able to leave home. They asked me to come out to the leader's house to work with them. Usually, five to seven people would show up. After establishing rapport, I asked,

If you're agoraphobic, how are you able to drive and come here to Ruth's house?

> Well, we're not *as* agoraphobic as Ruth. That's why we have to have our meeting here at her house. She can't leave her house at all, but we can leave ours.

Right. That makes sense. So there's a rating system in how agoraphobic a person may be.

> Yeah. Some people are very agoraphobic and some are in the process of getting more afraid and others are in the process of becoming less afraid.

So tell me, what are you afraid of specifically? What's the worst thing that will happen to you if you leave your house? Ruth, since you're the most skilled at this ability, or "the worst," what scares the hell out of you so much? (I said that with more of a tone of levity than seriousness.)

> Well, I don't know... not when you put it that way.

Well, I mean with all the car jackers here in this small town, there's got to be something that would be the worst possible thing that you could possibly imagine.

> Well, I just get uncomfortable. Very uncomfortable. My heart begins to pound, and I sweat and I begin to worry, 'what if I freeze?' and then I just have to pull over and get my breath and head back home.

Oh, so you do leave home?

> Not really. Not anymore. Just if I have to go to the store for

some food if my husband can't leave work and do it.

Ruth, if you did not have this program inside your head that scared the hell out of you when you left the house, and you had a normal response to leaving home, what would your life be like? What would you be doing with yourself?

Well, I used to work. I was a receptionist and ...

That's what you'd like to return to do?

No, not really. I didn't like that at all.

So what would you do?

I don't know.

Pretend that you do know and just describe what you'd love to be doing.

Well, ah... I really don't have anything that I'd like to be doing.

Do you like what you're doing now... staying at home and all?

Well, yes. I get to do some of the crafts and things that I love to do. ... but it's such a hassle to not be able to go to the Mall or other stores to get supplies.

So you just do without?

Oh no. Larry picks them up for me.

You know, Ruth, it sounds like you have a wonderful life and wonderful lifestyle and that you're not really an agoraphobic at all. You just love staying home, being waited on, and being treated as special for this so-called agoraphobia.

(Stunned silence... Hurt looks...) You just don't understand.

I left the dialogue there and turned to another. Three years later Ruth wrote a letter and said that she was never more shocked, angered, upset, and hurt than by what I had said to her in front of the group that evening. But that it was all true though she hated to admit it, and that she couldn't admit it at the time. She said she had come to realize that she hid her anger, but would fret and stew every Wednesday and Thursday prior to the meetings. And unknown to me, she complained to the others that I didn't know what I was doing and that the group should stop having me come, and that I was making her agoraphobia worse.

That went on for several weeks until two of the other persons confronted her by using the same questions that I had used. And when they asked the questions, she couldn't complain that they didn't understand, and because they were "getting better," they pushed the questions until it became clear that *fear was an excuse.* That the real issue was an unwillingness to take on and accept some of the more unpleasant facets of life, to accept distressful feelings as just feelings, and to face the discomfort through building up more resourceful responses.

In her letter, Ruth said that the moment came when she *decided* to stop calling her experience "fear" and "agoraphobia."

> "Once I dropped those labels, everything was strange for awhile. I kept saying to myself, 'What do I call this?' And eventually I decided to call it, 'being out of my Comfort Zone,' and as I decided that that was okay, then I began asking the questions that you zapped me with, 'What do I really want?'"

Thereafter she began making plans, and re-orienting the focus of her life. She shifted it from *what she didn't want,* to what she did want. She began driving again. She found a job that she really enjoyed, and she re-entered the life "of the normals" as she expressed it.

This doesn't mean that all agoraphobics have this same experience or structure, but it does provide one example of how one person (actually several) mis-labeled their experience, became too comfortable with and in that label, and then began building their lives and identities around a false-to-fact label.

The Double-Bind Frame Game

To play this Game we identify a fear that we *have to have* because "that's just the way it is," "that's the kind of person I am," "that's what's been destined or fated by some experience." "Ever since I nearly drowned, I've been deathly afraid of water. God, it was terrible. I'll never get over it."

The primary experience was the near-drowning experience. We amplify it and crank it out of the ceiling by picturing it as a movie that we play in full color, larger than life, and terrifying as hell while being the tragic victim all over again. Then we frame it inside of various ideas, "It was so Terrible," "I'll never get over it." "Once you've been through a hell like that, it will stay with you for the rest of your life." "I'm just not the kind of person that handles traumas like that well."

Figure 15:1

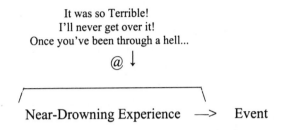

The higher ideas *bind* the Game so that we have to play it, we cannot *not* play it. We play it because it's "who we are." We may even bind it further with even higher frames over those frames.

> "If I were to not feel terrified by that thought, I wouldn't know who I was. I can't even imagine that. I don't think it would be a good thing to dismiss it, that would mean that I didn't learn my lesson."

With each higher frame we have more rules of the Game, how the Game is set up, what holds the Game in place, and the meanings we give to the whole structure. Of course, the power of such a double-binding situation lies in it operating outside of our awareness. We don't see it. We think it is "real," rather than being a map about reality. So, bringing this into awareness implies the Meta-Awareness Game that either deframes it or blows it away.

Fear of Being Vulnerable Game

This is the Game that creates the gestalt of that we call, "shyness. " Inside of feeling and being shy we typically have a mixture of several fears. More often than not we have:

- The fear of making a spectacle of oneself
- The fear of being embarrassed

- The fear of being exposed
- The fear of standing out
- The fear of being independent
- The fear of having no one to lean upon
- The fear of possibly being criticized, etc.

To play the *Shy Game* we need to create several prohibitions in our minds against these things, the awareness of ourselves as socially inept, the belief that embarrassment would kill us, that we could never live it down, that to be open and vulnerable is to be brazen, and that it is bad, etc. The feeling of *inhibition* that a person experiences in being shy can be driven by numerous limiting beliefs.

> "Don't make a spectacle of yourself; everybody will look at you and I'll be so embarrassed."

> "Don't make a fool of yourself; no one will like you and you'll be friendless."

That same inhibition can also be created through an unpleasant experience of embarrassment so that we develop a fear of both the state of embarrassment and the very idea of being embarrassed and what that means.

To play the Shyness Game, it also typically helps if we sense ourselves as *dependent* on someone else, on some idea, role, etc. In this, the lack of independence along with the fear of being rejected, ignored, left alone, or abandoned, supported by personal memories or the stories of others, helps to create the Shy Game.

Summary

- There are fears of the everyday world and then there are the higher fears of ideas and beliefs. There are primary and meta-fears. There are Fight/Flight Survival State fears about true dangers in the world, and then there are Semantic Fears of a higher nature.

- There are also Mastery Techniques for fear at all levels of mapping. So whether it is a fear of a true and legitimate danger, a fear of a pseudo-danger, or a fear of a semantic danger, *fear* as the feeling of threat and danger and a desire to run or freeze may be accurate or inaccurate, useful or unuseful, enhancing or limiting.

- The Mastery Techniques of this Chapter provide tools for refusing the Semantics Reactions Game so that we can play the *Moment of Consciousness Game* as we mindfully choose our reactions, catch Double-Binding Games, and Recognize a Meta-Fear when we encounter it.

LET THE GAMES BEGIN!

Now that you have learned about the Fear Games and been introduced to the *Mastery Games,* the time has come to blow the whistle and let the games begin. Whenever you now find yourself playing a Fear Game and it doesn't enhance your life by warning you of a true and legitimate danger, you can welcome those feelings in, step back from it and Quality Control your thinking and responding. You can now *Name the Games* being played around you and those which others may seek to recruit you to and decide, at a higher level of mind, which Games to play and which to refuse. You can put an end to all Old Horror Movies that various triggers can stimulate and adopt a fully empowered consciousness that gives you the personal confidence, courage, and power to look life in the face and take intelligent risks. *No more running scared for you.*

You also have the ability now to frame "fear" so that you can live your life in a truly masterful way. Now you know that ultimately, *fear* is just an emotion. Whether it accurately or inaccurately cues you about particular actions you should or should not take depends upon the evaluations that create the danger-threat-feelings. You *master* your fears as you understand the cognitions, the evaluations, standards, values from which they arise, and compare them to the sensory based information before you.

Even *fear* of *fear* is just an emotion. True enough, it is a higher level of emotion and yet it is still just the stuff of the mind-body system as it processes information. Recognizing this enables you now to take your neuro-linguistic mapping in stride without over-loading it with too much meaning. It also cues you in to the secret of personal mastery, taking charge of your mapping at all levels. Then you can set the kind of frames that bring out your best and accesses your highest skills.

At the primary level *fear* can be, and should be, your friend. You can make it a useful ally if only you will. You can validate your fears and other negative emotions as legitimate messages, embrace them as such and then gather the necessary information to test the information value that they hold.

Now you know that it is in fear of fear, fear of ourselves, fear of any other emotion, fear of ideas, concepts, memories, imaginations, etc., that you begin mapping fear in ways that do you damage. But now you have the tools and patterns (games) for setting newer and higher frames. Using the NLP and NS models as sketched out in this work, you have a multitude of ways, methods, and processes for truly mastering your fears and playing the Games that make for boldness, courage, adventure, vitality, and passion.

When You Know the Game Plan

Knowing the Game Plan of our Frames and the Games that they generate gives us the secrets for personal mastery. That's the power of knowing a Game Plan.

In 1997, *Psychology Today* carried an article entitled, "Panicked Is As Panicked Does." The article reported that noted clinical psychologist Brad Schmidt had constructed an assessment tool to identify those most likely to suffer a panic attack.

> "His 16-question assessment, designed to measure high-anxiety sensitivity, looks at the degree of fear that people have *about* their anxiety symptoms. On a five-point scale, subjects rate statements such as, 'Unusual body sensations scare me,' 'It scares me when my heart beats rapidly' or 'When I am nervous, I worry I might be mentally ill.' In tests of the assessment tool, subjects who scored at the high end of the scale were more than *six times more likely to suffer panic attacks.*" (p. 17, italics added).

How a person thinks or *frames* things greatly contributes to and influences the *Games* we play in terms of our feelings and actions. Our action and emotional Games follow our frames as night follows day. Where there is fear and anxiety symptoms, we don't have to look far for a person who has turned his or her psychic energy against "self." Close by will be a person who has framed things in fearful terms.

The solution to this?

> "If people understand ahead of time their propensity to panic, they can seek help and learn to control it and react to the onset of symptoms with less anxiety, thereby breaking the panic cycle before it spirals out of control."

Such Frame Game awareness gives us the insight that just knowing about a "propensity to panic" empowers us to take that into account so that we can take effective action. Better yet, it invites us to invent better kinds of games. For example, you can now–

Accept and enjoy the symptoms of fear by playing *the Joyful Acceptance Game*

Appreciate the learnings the symptoms offer us by playing *the Curious Learning Game*

Feel calm and relaxed about the symptoms by playfully playing *the Calmly Relaxed Game.*

Now also you know better than to build frames by which you might *enjoy fear.* Bateson (1972) described this in the life for the Balinese. The following offers a description of how they came to enjoy the thrill of being afraid.

"The Balinese pattern is essentially derivative from contexts of instrumental avoidance; they see the world as dangerous, and themselves as avoiding, by the endless rote behavior of ritual and courtesy, the ever-present risk of *faux pas*. Their life is built upon fear, albeit that in general *they enjoy fear.* The positive value with which they endow their immediate acts, not looking for a goal, is somehow associated with this enjoyment of fear. It is the acrobat's enjoyment both of the thrill and of his own virtuosity in avoiding danger." (p. 174, *italics* added)

Yet using the anthropological studies of the Balinese and how they set up a strange relationship to "a nameless, shapeless fear"and how they let that meta-frame organize their lives, Margaret Mead recognized that we can do the same with more positive emotions like hope, anticipation, and optimism.

"The Balinese attitude might be defined as a habit of rote sequences inspired by a thrilling sense of ever-imminent but indefinite danger, and I think that what Dr. Mead is urging us toward might be defined in like terms, as a habit of rote sequences inspired by a thrilling sense of ever-imminent but undefined reward. ... If the Balinese is kept busy and happy by a nameless, shapeless fear, not located in space or time, we might be kept on our toes by a nameless, shapeless, unlocated hope of enormous achievement. All we need to be sure of is that, at any moment, achievement may be just around the corner, and true or false, this can never be tested. We have got to be like those few artists and scientists who work with this urgent sort of inspiration, the urgency that comes from feeling that great discovery, the answer to all our problems, or great creation, the perfect sonnet, is always only just beyond our reach, or like the mother of a child who feels that, provided she pay constant enough attention, there is a real hope that her child may be infinitely rare phenomenon, a great and happy person." (175-176)

So may you do that... may you let a "nameless, shapeless optimistic hope" ...an urgent sort of inspiration about some tremendous experience always lie around the corner of your mind pulling you into an ever more resourceful and vital style of life.

What can You Say "YES!" To...?

This book has been all about finding and developing the resources so that we can live more fully, bravely, mindfully, and compassionately. To close, consider this question.

> *What can you say "Yes!" to that would completely melt away any irrational fear?*

Find a resource that puts steel into your backbone, that puts passion and compassion into your mind and heart, that lifts up your vision and values .... get that resource and say a most hearty *"Yes!"* to it. Then, with a "Yes!" on your lips, a "Yes!" that arises from your heart, the "No" that fear would utter in your face won't and can't stand a stand to invalidate your hopes and dreams, can they? That's the power of a strong and empowering "Yes!"

May you find and develop the resources in the days and weeks and months to come ... resources that evoke a *"Yes!"* response that will surprise and delight you!

BIBLIOGRAPHY

Bandler, Richard and Grinder, John. (1976). *The structure of magic, Volume II.* Palo Alto, CA: Science & Behavior Books.

Bateson, Gregory. (1972). *Steps to an ecology of mind.* New York: Ballantine Books.

Bandler, Richard and Grinder, John. (1982). *Reframing: Neuro-linguistic programming and the transformation of meaning.* UT: Real People Press.

Bandler, Richard. (1985). *Using your brain for a change.* (Ed. Connirae and Steve Andreas). Moab, UT: Real People Press.

Bateson, Gregory. (1972). *Steps to an ecology of mind.* NY: Ballantine Books.

Berne, Eric, M.D. (1964). *Games people play: The psychology of human relationships.* NY: Ballantine Books.

Bodenhamer, Bobby G.; Hall, L. Michael. (1997). *Time-Lining: Patterns for adventuring in time.* Wales, United Kingdom: Anglo-American Books.

Bodenhamer, Bobby G.; Hall. L. Michael. (1999). *The user's manual for the brain: A comprehensive manual for neuro-linguistic programming practitioner certification.* United Kingdom: Crown House Publishers.

Conlan, Roberta. (Ed., 1999). *States of mind: New discoveries about how our brains make us who we are.* NY: John Wiley & Sons, Inc.

Csikszentmihalyi, Mihaly. (1990). *Flow: The psychology of optimal experience.* NY: HarperCollins.

Diagnostic and Statistical Manual of mental disorders (DSM- IV™). (1994). Wash. D.C.: American Psychiatric Association.

Hall, L. Michael. (1987). *Speak up, speak clear, speak kind.* Grand Jct. CO: Empowerment Technologies.

Hall, L. Michael. (1995, 2000). *Meta-states: Managing the higher levels of your mind.* Grand Jct., CO: Neuro-Semantics Publications.

Hall, L. Michael; Bodenhamer, Bob. (1997). *Figuring out people: Design engineering using meta-programs.* Wales, UK: Anglo-American Books.

Hall, L. Michael; Bodenhamer, Bob. (1997, 2000). *Mind-lines: Lines for changing minds.* Grand Jct. CO: Neuro-Semantics Publications.

Hall, L. Michael. (1998). *The secrets of magic: Communicational excellence for the 21st century.* Carmarthen, Wales: Anglo-American Book Company Ltd.

Hall, Michael; Belnap, Barbara. (1999). *The sourcebook of magic: A comprehensive guide to the technology of NLP.* UK: Crown House Publishers.

Hall, L. Michael; Bodenhamer, Bob. (1999). *The structure of excellence: Unmasking the meta-levels of submodalities.* Grand Jct. CO: Empowerment Technologies.

Hall, L. Michael. (2000). *Frame games: Persuasion elegance.* Grand Jct. CO: Neuro-Semantics Publications.

Isaacs, Jerry D. (1994). Dealing With Fear Using Neuro-Linguistics. *Anchor Point, 1994,* pp. 4-21.

James, Tad; Woodsmall, Wyatt (1987). *Time Line Therapy.* CA: Meta Publications.

Lederer, Debra; Hall, Michael. (1999). *Instant relaxation: How to reduce stress at work, at home, and in your daily life.* Wales, UK: Crown House Publications.

Pliskin, Zelig. (2000). *Courage: Formulas, stories and insights.* NY: Shaar Press.

Rossi, Ernest L.; Cheek, David B. (1987).*Mind-body therapy: Methods of ideodynamic healing in hypnosis.* New York: W.W. Norton & Co.

Schmidt, Brad. (1997). Psychology Today "Panicked Is As Panicked Does" (July/August 1997).

Seligman, Martin, E.P. (1975). *Helplessness: On depression, development, and death.* San Francisco: Freeman.

Seligman, Martin P. (1990). *Learned optimism.* New York: Alfred A. Knopf.

Selye, Hans, (1976). *The stress of life.* NY: McGraw-Hill Book Co.

GLOSSARY OF TERMS

Anchoring: Linking a stimulus to a response, a "user-friendly" version of Pavlovian or classical conditioning.

Beliefs: A thought *confirmed* at a meta-level, a conscious or unconscious generalization about an idea.

Calibration: Tuning in to a person's state via reading non-verbal signals.

Content: The specific details of an event; content answers *"what?"* in contrast with process or structure.

Context: The setting, frame, or process in which events occur and provide meaning for content.

Dissociation: Stepping back from an experience and representing it from an *outside* position, seeing and/or hearing it as if being a spectator.

Ecology: Examining the relationship between idea, skill, response and larger environment or system; the dynamic balance of a system.

Frame or frame of reference. We put people, ideas, events, experiences, etc. into contexts or frames; a mental, cognitive, or linguistic context.

Frame Analysis: Analyzing frames, detecting them, identifying leverage points for shifting them, the processes for transforming them, the games that they engender, etc. *Frame Analysis* provides a way to articulate the levels of mind and the influence they exert over life's experiences.

Frame Argumentation: Frames argue for themselves when they are threatened. Cognitive psychology calls this state or mood dependency.

Frame Clearing: We clear a frame when we deframe, dissolve a frame, or bust up a frame. This creates mental and emotional room in a person's model of the world for new Games.

Frame Cues: The signals, indicators, clues, linguistic markers of a frame.

Frame-of-Reference: The *reference* that we use to understand something else. The reference can be an actual experience (an event), a person, idea, etc. A referent can be something real and actual or imaginary and vicarious.

Frame of Mind: Created by repeating and habituating a frame of reference. Over time this leads to making the represented referent something always on our mind, our frame of mind or attitude.

Frameworks: When a particular frame of mind becomes so solidified in our orientation, it becomes our characteristic mind-set or attitude. This transforms it into one of the very basic frameworks of our mind and personality, thereby giving it even more power and influence over us.

Frame Terms: Using the metaphor and structuring device of "frames" we can now "think in terms of and work with" something.

Frame Wars: The conflict of ideas, beliefs, and mental frames within ourselves and with others.

Future Pacing: Mentally practicing or rehearsing an event as we imagine it in our future, a process for installing a new way of operating to make it permanent.

Game: A set of actions that play out some concept, idea, etc. for some purpose, i.e., to "win" something, another emotion, stroke, transaction.

Game Consciousness: Awareness of a game, who it works, who sets it, how it invites people into it, the states it elicits, etc.

Generalization: Process of representing a whole class of experiences based on one or a few specific experience/s.

Gestalt: The overall configuration, impression or feel of thoughts & feelings, the whole of an experience that is more than the sum of the parts.

Kinesthetic: Sensations, feelings, tactile sensations on surface of skin, proprioceptive sensations inside the body, includes vestibular system or sense of balance.

Matrix: A metaphorical way to think about the "world" or universe of discourse that we create perceptually, mentally, and emotionally via our frames. As we build meta-levels of the mind, we tend to become "paradigm blind" and to see the world "in terms of our ideas and concepts."

Meta: Anything "above or beyond" something else and therefore "about" it. A relationship of levels, as when a thought is *about* another thought, a feeling *about* a feeling, a thought *about* a feeling, etc.

Meta-Awareness: The ability to *step aside* from our thinking and feeling and to recognize our thoughts and feelings, their layers, etc.

Meta-State (M-S): A meta-state arises as we T-F about (@↓) our T-F. Our conscious awareness *reflects back* onto itself (self-reflexive consciousness) to create T-F at a higher logical level. This generates a state-about-a-state. Meta-states relate to, or reference, a previous state rather than something about the world, they have to do with something *about* some previous "thought," "emotion," concept, or understanding. Meta-states are higher level states of mind and emotion.

Meta-Stating: A verb, bringing one mind-body state to bear upon another state accessing a higher logical level to organize, drive, and modulate a lower state.

Meta-Model: A model of linguistic distinctions that identifies language patterns that obscure meaning via distortion, deletion and generalization. Questions that clarify imprecision to enrich a person's model of the world.

Meta-Programs: The mental and perceptual programs for sorting and paying attention to things; perceptual filters governing attention.

Modal Operators: A linguistic distinction in the Meta-Model indicating a person's "mode" for operating (i.e. mode of necessity, impossibility, desire, possibility, etc.).

Model: A pattern, example, or description of how something works.

Modeling: The process of observing and replicating the actions, skills, knowledge, and states of someone (typically an expert). Modeling discerns the sequence of internal representations and behaviors that comprise the structure of a skill.

Nominalization: A linguistic distinction in the Meta-Model involving a process (or verb) turned into an noun; a process frozen in time.

Out-of-Frame: Activities, thoughts, scripts that do not fit a given frame. This creates a loosening of the frame, a threat to the frame. When we step out of a frame of reference, we "break frame" or "lose frame" and so become *out of frame.*

Outframing: Going above all frames to create new frames-of-reference.

Reframing: Altering a frame-of-reference by presenting an event or idea from a different point of view or with a different meaning ascribed to it.

References: The idea, person, event, belief, etc. that we have in mind and use in our thinking. **Reference Point:** identifies a singular idea, person, or event. **Reference Frame:** involves understandings of how the points are related.

Representation Systems: Sights, sounds, sensations, smells & tastes make up the basic primary RS. Language makes up the meta-RS. **1) VAK:** Visual, Auditory, Kinesthetic; the three primary modalities. **2) A_d:** Auditory digital, digital representations, i.e. words, language, symbols.

Sensory-Based Description: Directly observable and verifiable information; see-hear-feel language one can test empirically.

State: A state of mind- body, which never occurs in isolation, hence *a mind-body state* driven by ideas and meanings (conceptions and the significance we attach to things, a neuro-linguistic or *neuro-semantic state*). Our states generate an overall *feel* or gestalt—thus we refer to our states as *emotional states*. We notate thoughts-feelings as T-F, and the state as a circle. A *primary* state relates to or references some object (person, event, thing) out in the world ($\rightarrow$).

Unsanity: Stage of poor adjustment between sanity (well adjusted) and insanity (totally maladjusted to reality); the "lack of consciousness of abstracting, confusion of orders of abstractions resulting from identification practically universally operating in every one of us" (Korzybski, 1933: 105).

VAK: A short-hand for the sensory representation systems of Visual, Auditory, and Kinesthetic. **K** also including smells (Olfactory) and tastes (Gustatory).

Value/ Valuing: The process of deeming something important; a meta-level phenomena.

TRAININGS AVAILABLE
The Institutes of Neuro-Semantics

Meta-NLP Practitioner: An intensive 7-day training in the Essential NLP Skills. This training introduces NLP as a model for discovering the structure of human functioning with a focus on *how to run your own brain* and to manage your own states. Learn the basic rapport-building, listening, and influence skills of NLP, as well as how to access and manage states through anchoring, reframing, and using dozens of NLP patterns. Discover how to use language both for precision and hypnotic influence. Required reading, *User's Manual for the Brain* and *The Sourcebook of Magic.*

Meta-Masters NLP Practitioner: An intensive 13-Day Training in mastering all three of the meta-domains of NLP: Language (Meta-Model), Perception (Meta-Programs) and States and Levels (Meta-States). This training focuses on the pathway to mastery and how to develop the very spirit of NLP—curiosity, accelerated learning, flexibility, confidence, passion, playfulness, etc.

Accessing Personal Genius: Introduction to Meta-States as an advanced NLP model (3 days). This training introduces and teaches the *Meta-States Model* and is ideal for NLP Practitioners. It presupposes knowledge of the NLP Model and builds the training around accessing the kinds of states that will access and support "personal genius."

Advanced Modeling Using Meta-Levels: Advanced use of Meta-States by focusing on the domain of modeling excellence. This training typically occurs as the last 4 days of the 7 day Meta-States Certification. Based upon the modeling experiences of Dr. Hall and his book, *NLP: Going Meta— Advanced Modeling Using Meta-Levels,* this training looks at the formatting and structuring of the meta-levels in Resilience, Un-Insultability, and Seeing Opportunities. The training touches on modeling of Wealth Building, Fitness, Women in Leadership, Persuasion, etc.

Secrets of Personal Mastery: Awakening Your Inner Executive. This training presents the power of Meta-States *without* directly teaching the model as such. The focus instead shifts to *Personal Mastery* and the *Executive Powers* of the participants. Formatted so that it can take the form of 1, 2 or 3 days, this training presents a simpler form of Meta-States, especially good for those without NLP background or those who are more focused on Meta-States

Applications than the model.

Frame Games: Persuasion Elegance. The first truly *User Friendly* version of Meta-States. Frame Games provides practice and use of Meta-States in terms of frame detecting, setting, and changing. As a model of frames, Frame Games focuses on the power of persuasion via frames and so presents how to influence or persuade yourself and others using the Levels of Thought or Mind that lies at the heart of Meta-States. Designed as a 3 day program, the first two days presents the model of Frame Games and lots of exercises. Day three is for becoming a true Frame Game Master and working with frames conversationally and covertly.

Wealth Building Excellence (Meta-Wealth). The focus of this training is on learning how to think like a millionaire, to develop the mind and meta-mind of someone who is structured and programmed to create wealth economically, personally, mentally, emotionally, relationally, etc. As a Meta-States Application Training, Wealth Building Excellence began as a modeling project and seeks to facilitate the replication of that excellence in participants.

Selling & Persuasion Excellence (Meta-Selling). Another Meta-States Application Training, modeled after experts in the fields of selling and persuasion and designed to replicate in participants. An excellent follow-up training to Wealth Building since most people who build wealth have to sell their ideas and dreams to others. This training goes way beyond mere Persuasion Engineering as it uses the Strategic Selling model of Heiman also known as Relational Selling, Facilitation Selling, etc.

Mind-Lines: Lines for Changing Minds. Based upon the book by Drs. Hall and Bodenhamer (1997), now in its third edition, Mind-Line Training is a training about Conversational Reframing and Persuasion. The Mind-Lines model began as a rigorous update of the old NLP "Sleight of Mouth" Patterns and has grown to become the persuasion language of the Meta-State moves. This advanced training is highly and mainly a linguistic model, excellent as a follow-up training for Wealth Building and Selling Excellence. Generally a two day format, although sometimes 3 and 4 days.

Accelerated Learning Using NLP & Meta-States (Meta-Learning). A Meta-State Application training based upon the NLP model for "running your own brain" and the Neuro-Semantic (Meta-States) model of managing your higher executive states of consciousness. Modeled after leading experts in the fields of education, cognitive psychologies, this training provides extensive insight into the Learning States and how to access your personal learning genius. It provides specific strategies for various learning tasks as well as processes for research and writing.

Defusing Hotheads: A Meta-States and NLP Application training for handling hot, stressed-out, and irrational people in Fight/Flight states. Designed to "talk someone down from a hot angry state," this training provides training in state management, first for the skilled negotiator or manager, and then for eliciting another into a more resourceful state. Based upon the book by Dr. Hall, *Defusing Strategies (1987),* this training has been presented to managers and supervisors for greater skill in conflict management, and to police departments for coping with domestic violence.

Advanced NLP Flexibility Training Using General Semantics. An advanced Neuro-Semantics training that explores the riches and treasures in Alfred Korzybski's work, *Science and Sanity*. Originally presented in London (1998, 1999) as "The Merging of the Models: NLP and General Semantics," this training now focuses almost exclusively on *developing Advanced Flexibility* using tools, patterns, and models in General Semantics. Recommend for the advanced student of NLP and Meta-States.

Neuro-Semantics Trainers Training. An advanced training for those who have been certified in Meta-States and Neuro-Semantics (the seven day program). This application training focuses the power and magic of Meta-States on the training experience itself—both public and individual training. It focuses first on the trainer, to access one's own Top Training States and then on how to meta-state or set the frames when working with others in coaching or facilitating greater resourcefulness.

Instant Relaxation. Another practical NLP and Meta-States Application Training designed to facilitate the advanced ability to quickly "fly into a calm." Based in part upon the book by Lederer and Hall (Instant Relaxation, 1999), this training does not teach NLP or Meta-States, but coaches the relaxation skills for greater "presence of mind," control over mind and neurology, and empowerment in handling stressful situations. An excellent training in conjunction with Defusing Hotheads.

About the Authors

L. Michael Hall, Ph.D.
P.O. Box 9231
Grand Jct. Co. 81501

Michael@neurosemantics.com
NLPMetaStates@OnLineCol.com
(970) 523-7877

Dr. Michael Hall, psychologist and entrepreneur, lives in the Colorado Rocky Mountains. For twenty years he had a private psychotherapeutic practice and then began teaching and training— first in Communication Training (Assertiveness, Negotiations) then in NLP.

He studied NLP with co-founder, Richard Bandler in the late 1980s when he became a Master Practitioner and Trainer. From that came *The Spirit of NLP* and *Becoming more Ferocious as a Presenter,* he also edited *Time For a Change.* As a prolific author, he has written and published more than two dozen books including *The Spirit of NLP* (1996), *Dragon Slaying, Meta-States, Mind-Lines, Figuring Out People, The Structure of Excellence, Frame Games,* etc.

Michael's earned doctorate is in Cognitive-Behavioral Psychology with an emphasis in psycho-linguistics. His doctoral dissertation dealt with the *languaging* of four psychotherapies (NLP, RET, Reality Therapy, Logotherapy) using the formulations of General Semantics. He addressed the Interdisciplinary International Conference (1995) presenting an integration of NLP and General Semantics.

In 1994, Michael developed *the Meta-States Model* while modeling *resilience* and presenting the findings at the International NLP Conference in Denver. He has hundreds of articles published in *NLP World, Anchor Point, Rapport, Connection, Meta-States Journal.*

Michael is the co-developer, along with Dr. Bob Bodenhamer, of Neuro-Semantics having co-authored a unified field model using the 3 Meta-Domains of NLP. They initiated *The Society of Neuro-Semantics,* and have begun to establish *Institutes* of Neuro-Semantics in the USA and around the world. Elvis Keith Lester joined the team in 1998, and then established the *LEARN Institute of Neuro-Semantics* in Tampa, Fl.

Today Michael spends his time researching and modeling, training internationally, and writing. Recent modeling projects have included modeling excellence in sales, persuasion, accelerated learning, state management, wealth building, women in leadership, fitness and health, etc. These are now Meta-State Gateway Trainings.

Books:

Meta-States: Managing the higher states of your mind (Self-Reflexiveness) (2000 2nd edition)

Dragon Slaying: Dragons to Princes (2000, 2nd edition)

The Spirit of NLP: The Process, Meaning & Criteria for Mastering NLP (1996)

Languaging: The Linguistics of Psychotherapy (1996)

Patterns For "Renewing the Mind" (w. Dr. Bodenhamer) (1997)

Time-Lining: Advance Time-Line Processes (w. Dr. Bodenhamer) (1997)

NLP: Going Meta—Advanced Modeling Using Meta-Levels (1997)

Figuring Out People: Design Engineering With Meta-Programs (w. Dr. Bodenhamer) (1997)

A Sourcebook of Magic (formerly, How to Do What When (w. B. Belnap) (1999)

Mind Lines: Lines For Changing Minds (w. Dr. Bodenhamer) (1997, 2000 3rd edition)

The Secrets of Magic: Communicational Magic for the 21st. Century (1998)

Meta-States Journal, Patterns, Volume I, II, III (97, 98, 99)

The Structure of Excellence: Unmasking the Meta-Levels of Submodalities (Hall and Bodenhamer, 1999)

Instant Relaxation (1999, Lederer & Hall)

The User's Manual of the Brain (1999, w. Bodenhamer)

Secrets of Personal Mastery (2000)

Frame Games: Persuasion Elegance (2000)

The Structure of Personality: Modeling "Personality" Using NLP and Neuro-Semantics. (Hall , Bodenhamer, Bolstad, Harmblett, 2001)

Games Slim People Play (2001)

Books in Development

Games Business Experts Play (2001)

Persuasion Games (2001)

Accelerated Motivation: Human Propulsion Systems (2002)

Neuro-Semantics (2002)

Bobby G. Bodenhamer, D.Min.
1516 Cecelia Dr.   Bob@neurosemantics.com
Gastonia, NC 28054   www.neurosemantics.com
(704) 864-3585
Fax: (704) 8641545

Dr. Bodenhamer first trained for the ministry, earned a doctorate in Ministry, and served several churches as pastor. He began NLP training in 1990, studying with Dr. Tad James and receiving Master Practitioner and Trainer Certifications. Since then, he has taught and certified NLP trainings at Gastona College.

Beginning in 1996, Dr. Bodenhamer began studying the Meta-States model and then teamed up with Michael to begin co-authoring several books. Since that he has turned out many works as he and Michael have applied the NLP and Meta-States Models to various facets of human experience.

In 1996 also, Dr. Bodenhamer with Michael co-founded the Society of Neuro-Semantics. This has taken his work to a new level, taken him into International Trainings, and set in motion many Institutes of Neuro-Semantics around the world.

Books:

> *Patterns For "Renewing the Mind"* (w. Hall, 1997)
> *Time-Lining: Advance Time-Line Processes* (w. Hall, 1997)
> *Figuring Out People: Design Engineering With Meta-Programs* (w. Hall, 1997)
> *Mind Lines: Lines For Changing Minds* (w. Hall, 1997, 2000 3rd edition)
> *The Structure of Excellence:* Unmasking the Meta-Levels of Submodalities (w. Hall, 1999)
> *The User's Manual of the Brain* (1999, w. Hall)
> *Hypnotic Language* (2000, w. Burton)
> *The Structure of Personality: Modeling "Personality" Using NLP and Neuro-Semantics.* (Hall , Bodenhamer, Bolstad, Harmblett, 2001)
> *Games for Mastering Fears* (2001, with Hall)